Polyphonic Federalism

Polyphonic Federalism

Toward the Protection of
Fundamental Rights

ROBERT A. SCHAPIRO

The University of Chicago Press
Chicago and London

Robert A. Schapiro is professor at the Emory University
School of Law.

The University of Chicago Press, Chicago 60637
The University of Chicago Press, Ltd., London
© 2009 by The University of Chicago
All rights reserved. Published 2009
Printed in the United States of America

18 17 16 15 14 13 12 11 10 09   1 2 3 4 5

ISBN-13: 978-0-226-73662-4 (cloth)
ISBN-10: 0-226-73662-8 (cloth)

Library of Congress Cataloging-in-Publication Data

Schapiro, Robert A.
   Polyphonic federalism : toward the protection of fundamental
rights / Robert A. Schapiro.
        p. cm.
   Includes bibliographical references and index.
   ISBN-13: 978-0-226-73662-4 (cloth : alk. paper)
   ISBN-10: 0-226-73662-8 (cloth : alk. paper)
   1. Federal government—United States. 2. Civil rights—United States.
I. Title.
   KF4600.S32 2009
   342.73'042—dc22   2008026888

♾ The paper used in this publication meets the minimum requirements of the
American National Standard for Information Sciences—Permanence of Paper
for Printed Library Materials, ANSI Z39.48-1992.

To my family

CONTENTS

This book represents the culmination of a long process of thinking about the relationships of state governments and the federal government in the United States. I attended law school at a time when a nationalist vision of the United States was well established in the legal academy and in the courts. For my teachers, the civil rights movement of the 1960s had proved the value of a strong central government and had established the need for careful federal supervision of the states. Federalism, it seemed, belonged to a course on legal history.

Like my teachers, I appreciated the essential role of the federal government in promoting equality and individual rights, yet I wondered whether federalism could have a positive role in promoting these aims. After all, the great champion of federal power on the United States Supreme Court, Justice William J. Brennan, Jr., had written a landmark article in the *Harvard Law Review* in 1977 urging greater attention to state constitutions. In 1977, it had been clear to Justice Brennan that state constitutions could have a valuable role in supplementing the federal Constitution. All states in the United States have their own constitutions, and states can interpret their charters independently of the federal Constitution. By the mid-1990s, when I entered the legal academy, some state courts had indeed turned to their own constitutions as sources of fundamental rights. I wanted to learn more about this state constitutional practice.

I soon discovered that when it came to grand principles of equality and human rights, few state courts actually accepted the invitation to develop a distinctive state approach. In interpreting state constitutions, state courts generally hewed closely to the federal path. Most scholars of state constitutional law decried this reliance on federal models; some praised it. However, I became fascinated by the interaction of state and federal constitutions as a particular focus of inquiry. It was by examining the relationship between the state and federal constitutions, I came to believe, that one could understand the true significance of state constitutions in the United States.

Attention to the interplay of state and national constitutions led me to this broader study of federalism. To appreciate the relationship of state and national constitutions, I decided, required a more general conception of the role of states in the federal system of the United States. The concept of "polyphony," which first struck me as an apt metaphor for the interrelationship of state constitutions and the federal government, turned out to be a useful way to describe the larger framework of federalism. Similarly, although my work had initially focused on judicial decisions, I became convinced that the executive and legislative branches of government represented crucial sites for the development of principles of federalism. Courts presented only part of the picture. So a study of the judicial interpretation of state constitutions grew into an exploration of the overall relationship of states and the national government.

Along the way, I have benefited greatly from the foundations laid by my teachers and mentors, the support of family, colleagues, and institutions, and the aid of talented research assistants. At each stage of my education, I was especially fortunate to have the guidance and insight of a pair of skilled scholars and teachers. At Phillips Academy, Thomas T. Lyons and Edwin G. Quattlebaum III opened my mind to the excitement of history and inspired an abiding interest in American government. As an undergraduate at Yale, I was introduced to the complex webs of Western intellectual history by Louis Dupré and the late Franklin L. Baumer, two men who radiated a deep respect for the power of ideas. In the course of graduate history work at Stanford, Paul Robinson and James J. Sheehan showed me the joys and rigors of the scholarly profession. When I arrived at Yale Law School, Owen Fiss demonstrated how the precise study of procedure could provide insights about justice, and Akhil Amar proved that the debates about the jurisdiction of federal courts could illuminate critical issues of politics and governance. I am deeply grateful that Professors Lyons, Quattlebaum, Dupré, Baumer, Robinson, Sheehan, Fiss, Amar, and so many other teachers took the time to share with me their love of teaching and learning. Judge Pierre N. Leval and Justice John Paul Stevens continued my education in the course of my clerkships. With their deep commitment to the legal craft, they showed me how law could follow a path that was both rigorous and humane. Their examples remain an inspiration.

Various institutions have proved vitally important in providing fertile incubators for ideas. It was as a graduate fellow at the Stanford Humanities

Center that I encountered the concept of "polyphony," which serves as the master trope of this volume. I am grateful to the staff and fellows of the Center and especially its then director, W. Bliss Carnochan, for fostering such a rich intellectual environment. My study at Stanford was supported by a Mellon Fellowship in the Humanities, for which I am also deeply grateful. Emory Law School has provided a wonderfully dynamic and supportive environment for my work. I have benefited greatly from the unwavering support of all who have served as dean during my time at Emory, Howard O. Hunter, Peter Hay, Thomas C. Arthur, Frank S. Alexander, and David F. Partlett. My colleagues on the faculty provided extraordinary friendship and assistance in working through my ideas on federalism. I am especially grateful for the intellectual engagement and warm collegiality of Robert B. Ahdieh and William W. Buzbee, my fellow directors of Emory Law School's Center on Federalism and Intersystemic Governance. My former colleague and associate dean, Marc L. Miller, has always been a great mentor and a great friend. The extraordinary students at Emory have provided a constant source of stimulation. This book has benefited from the superb research assistance of many students, including Priya Bhoplay, Justin Critz, Michael Eber, Andrew Fedder, Jack Figura, Myles Levelle, Robert McKeehan, Noah Robbins, Gregory Sicilian, Matthew Spivey, and Cullen Stafford. Terry Gordon, Will Haines, and their colleagues at the Emory University School of Law Library provided invaluable aid. Whatever sources I sought, they managed to locate with great speed and never-failing good humor.

Scholars at other institutions have been extremely supportive as well. For me, as for so many others interested in state constitutional law, Robert F. Williams has been a magnificent mentor. The dean of state constitutional studies, Bob has gone out of his way to welcome new scholars and new approaches to the field. All who study state constitutional law owe a great debt to Bob and his colleague G. Alan Tarr. Bob and Alan provide the intellectual infrastructure for the field. James A. Gardner also has been a wonderful colleague and friend as we have explored our shared interest in state constitutions. In the great tradition of scholarship, Jim never seemed to mind that some of my work has diverged in its conclusions from some of his.

I am grateful, as well, for the longstanding encouragement of my editors at the University of Chicago Press, J. Alex Schwartz and David J. Pervin. They patiently guided me through the challenging process of turning ideas into a book.

Through it all, my family has been a constant source of support. My mother, Ruth Goldman Schapiro, died before I entered the legal academy, but her strength, intellect, and deep respect for the law continue to inspire me. My father, Donald Schapiro, and my sister, Jane Schapiro, always have provided love and encouragement and a great sounding board for ideas. My wife, Lillian Goldstein Schapiro, and my children, Rebecca, Ruth, and Sarah, fill my life with joy and excitement. This book would not have been possible without their support and forbearance.

In writing this book, I have drawn in several places on previously published work. I sketched the overall themes of this book in "Toward a Theory of Interactive Federalism," 91 *Iowa Law Review* 243 (2005), and some of the material in chapters 3 through 6 first appeared in that article. Parts of chapter 4 first appeared in "Monophonic Preemption," 102 *Northwestern Law Review* 811 (2008). Portions of chapter 5 first appeared in "Polyphonic Federalism: State Constitutions in the Federal Courts," 87 *California Law Review* 1409 (1999), and in "Interjurisdictional Enforcement of Rights in a Post-*Erie* World," 46 *William & Mary Law Review* 1399 (2005). Portions of chapter 7 first appeared in "Monophonic Preemption," 102 *Northwestern Law Review* 811 (2008), and in "Federalism as Intersystemic Governance: Legitimacy in a Post-Westphalian World," 57 *Emory Law Journal* 115 (2007). I thank the publishers of all of these works for permission to use this material.

INTRODUCTION

Sometimes, as ocean waves crash in against a beach, you can feel the undertow pulling out to sea. Even before the wave has fully expended its force,
while it still pushes strongly upon the shore, the power of the countercur-
rent is unmistakable. So it was with federalism in the 1980s. That period
corresponded to the most nationalistic period in the rulings of the United
States Supreme Court. In a series of decisions the Supreme Court disavowed
judicial review of congressional encroachment on state prerogatives[1] and
upheld Congress's authority to legislate away any immunity that the states
might enjoy in federal court.[2] Not since 1937 had the Supreme Court held
that Congress exceeded its broad authority to regulate interstate commerce,
a power that was sufficiently capacious to support a ban on racial discrimination in restaurants and a limit on growing wheat on a farm for home
consumption. National power seemed unbounded.

Yet even as the waves of nationalism crashed higher up on the beach,
the strength of the federalism undertow was manifest. Strong voices on the
Supreme Court and in national politics decried the centralization of power
and vowed to return authority to the states. Politicians of all stripes praised
federalism. Soon, the undertow became stronger, as the Supreme Court—
with new members—began relying on federalism as a basis for imposing
limits on the national government. The champions of the states claimed
the mantle of history. Theirs was a project of constitutional restoration, to
reinstitute the just division of authority decreed by the Framers, to retrieve
power wrongly arrogated by nationalist forces. But could the clock really be
turned back? Could the nationalist tide be turned?

Federalism, the idea of dividing power between a national government and constituent states, has been central to the political identity of the
United States since its creation. The founding symbols embody the concept

of a nation formed from preexisting states. The motto *e pluribus unum*, or "out of many, one," expresses that notion, as does the national flag, which consists of representations of the states. The very name of the polity, itself, emphasizes the importance of the states. Nevertheless, the story of the United States since the framing has been a thoroughly nationalist tale, including the Civil War, the New Deal, the civil rights movement, and other triumphs of nationalism over regional variation. Recent advances in technology, transportation, and communication ensure the continuation of that narrative. The States are ever more United. How can the revival of federalism fit within that story of unification?

This book began as an attempt to solve that puzzle. How could federalism and nationalism both be such strong forces in law and society in the contemporary United States? The political power of federalism is undeniable. Its impact on legal doctrine is significant. The rhetoric of federalism, however, appears to have little connection to the social reality of the United States in the early twenty-first century.

Judicial opinions and scholarly articles wax rhapsodically about the importance of local communities. Judges and commentators stress the need to preserve states as distinctive entities with their own values and culture. Centralized policies, it is asserted, cannot respond to the differing needs and interests of the people living throughout the United States. When Warren Burger was chief justice of the United States, he described federalism in these terms, as driven by the fundamental differences among the states. In explaining why the federal Age Discrimination in Employment Act should not apply to state employees, he appealed to natural features of geography:

> The Framers did not give Congress the power to decide local employment standards because they wisely realized that as a body, Congress lacked the means to analyze the factors that bear on this decision, such as the diversity of occupational risks, climate, geography, and demography. . . . And even if Congress had infinite fact-finding means at its disposal, conditions in various parts of the country are too diverse to be susceptible to a uniformly applicable solution. Wyoming is a state with large sparsely populated areas, where law enforcement often requires substantial physical stamina; the same conditions are not always encountered by law enforcement officers in Rhode Island, which has far less land area, no mountains, and no wilderness. Problems confronting law enforcement officers in Alaska or Maine may be unlike those encountered in Hawaii and Florida. Barring states from making employment decisions tailored to meet specific local needs undermines the

flexibility that has long allowed industrial states to live under the same flag as
rural states, and small, densely populated states to coexist with large, sparsely
populated ones.[3]

When Chief Justice Burger wrote this opinion in 1983, his was a dissenting
voice, but with a succession of Republican presidents, that view of the states
achieved majority status.

The newer language of federalism is less poetic than Chief Justice Burger's, but similar in conception. Can Congress allow a victim of rape to sue
in federal court when she finds the state system unresponsive? Writing for
a majority, a new chief justice, William Rehnquist, said no, intoning, "The
Constitution requires a distinction between what is truly national and
what is truly local."[4] Federalism protects the "truly local" from the "truly
national." This terminology hearkens back to an earlier period in which the
Supreme Court enforced a regime of "dual federalism," setting firm boundaries around areas of state and federal power. The goal of dual federalism
is to protect the states, as authentic, self-governing communities, from the
intervention of an alien and remote federal government.[5] Some matters are
"truly national," and the states are barred from meddling with them, but
the range of the national is limited and well defined. In this dualist conception, the imposition of a federal age discrimination law on state employees
represents the attempt of a national bureaucracy to undermine the diverse,
local, democratic communities in each state. Making a federal case out of
an instance of local, interpersonal violence similarly threatens the vitality
of integral state communities. Dual federalism safeguards states from a national government that might destroy state communities by imposing uniform rules, formulated in a distant national capital, that cannot possibly
take account of the diverse, vibrant states, with their own distinctive values
and traditions.

The critics of federalism meet the Supreme Court on this field of battle.
They accept the premise that federalism serves as a political accommoda-
tion for a nation constituted by fundamentally diverse states. The critics,
however, insist that the United States does not fit this description. Accordingly, they contend that federalism is an anachronism. Dean Edward Rubin, one of the most vigorous academic opponents of federalism, argues as
follows:

Federalism is a political expedient to achieve partial unity when people are
divided into territorial groups, with identifiable differences between them
and a sense of loyalty to their particular group. In the United States, there are

no longer any such territorial groupings; everyone lives in the same place, and that place is a vast, interacting, homogenized national culture. Thus, no compromise is required and no expedient is necessary.[6]

In Dean Rubin's account, no "truly local" exists. We all live in the same, homogenized national place. In these circumstances, how can a court claim to separate the "truly local" from the "truly national"? That which does not exist is certainly not worth protecting.

The battle lines are drawn. Chief Justice Burger says that the states are very different, and Dean Rubin says that they are basically the same. If one wants to, it is easy enough to line up on one side or the other of this debate. Two faculty members at the University of Texas, for example, insisted that Dean Rubin, who had been a professor at the University of California, Berkeley, and the University of Pennsylvania, was suffering from a coastal misperception of the United States. As a rejoinder to Dean Rubin's claims, they suggested geographical reeducation: "[W]e simply would invite him to come live in Texas for six months."[7]

When law professor James Gardner questioned regional distinctiveness, he received a similar "Don't mess with Texas" kind of reply. Then a member of the faculty at Western New England College School of Law, Professor Gardner wrote, "Americans are now a people who are so alike from state to state, and whose identity is so much associated with national values and institutions, that the notion of significant local variations in character and identity is just too implausible to take seriously as the basis for a distinct constitutional discourse."[8] This assertion of a nationalized culture elicited a stinging rejoinder from the justices of the Texas Supreme Court. In a majority opinion, they stated:

> When contrasted with the just pride that our citizens feel in being Texans, perhaps this very writing by an Associate Professor at the Western New England College School of Law demonstrates how truly diverse this nation remains. Texans value our institutions and heritage, and our citizens would certainly dispute that their concerns are identical to those of the people of Rhode Island or North Dakota.[9]

Though not often expressed so directly, my sense is that the Rubin/Gardner critique of regionalism is widely shared, certainly in the legal academy. The triumph of the civil rights movement remains the great morality tale of legal culture. The legal fight against racial segregation served as a defining monument for a generation of lawyers. To the extent federalism meant a celebration of distinctive state cultures and institutions, these lawyers had fought hard against it. Concern for preserving the "Southern way of life" had functioned as a code for racist practices that had to be eradicated. The end of regional variance was the goal to be accomplished, and many in the legal academy believed that this laudable end had been achieved.

All of this discussion of federalism and distinctive states left me dissatisfied. Perhaps reflecting my northeastern biases, I tended to agree with Rubin and Gardner on the growing cultural integration of the United States. The United States remains wonderfully diverse. Abundant variations persist in food, music, art, recreation, work styles, and other social patterns. The growing international influence in the United States has enriched the potpourri. *Regional* variation, however, appears to have declined. The cultural medley occurs within, rather than between, states. In most metropolitan areas, an appetite for southwestern cuisine can be satisfied locally; no trip to Arizona is required. But did that really mean the demise of federalism? Did federalism have to be understood in Chief Justice Burger's conception of allowing Rhode Island to be Rhode Island and Wyoming to be Wyoming and Mississippi to be Mississippi? It seemed to me that Dean Rubin conceded too much in accepting Chief Justice Burger's conception of federalism. Does the significance of federalism really turn on the distinctiveness of Texas? Could not federalism maintain a place in our governmental structure, even as the inhabitants of Texas and Rhode Island drew closer together?

I came to the conclusion that the equation of federalism and romantic regionalism was misguided. Picturing federalism as a return to local communities, as a restoration of Norman Rockwell's America, misunderstands its power. This romantic federalism is easy to caricature and dismiss. The force of federalism, it seems to me, lies elsewhere than in myths about the American past. At the same time that federalism was gaining strength, so were other concepts of decentralization. In a variety of areas, appreciation grew of the power of individual, autonomous units, linked by a network, rather than a hierarchical structure. The triumphs of the personal computer and, more abstractly, of markets generally told that story. The existence of multiple, independent components appeared to make all systems stronger, be they social, mechanical, or biological. This story of decentralization seemed to provide a much more compelling context for federalism than did a romantic tale about the lost cause of state identity. The resurgence of federalism fit comfortably within the growing appreciation of networks.[10] In this sense, the exemplar of federalism is not the Confederate States of America, but Wikipedia.

But what does this have to do with constitutional governance? Dean

Rubin has insisted that federalism should not be equated with decentralization, that federalism has to be understood as a constitutional concept, not
merely as an organizational principle.[11] As Dean Rubin has pointed out,
a centralized government can choose to devolve power onto administrative regions. France does not have a federal system of government. French
provinces enjoy no constitutionally protected autonomy. Nevertheless, not
all decisions are made in Paris. Dean Rubin's point was that the benefits of
decentralization do not require constitutional federalism.

Dean Rubin's argument is correct as far as it goes. Not all issues of governmental organization need to be constitutionalized. However, federalism is the constitutional system of government in the United States. To
some extent, then, the relevant question is not "why federalism," but how
federalism should best operate. I believe that the legal and organizational
components of federalism must be understood together. The appeal of federalism, reflected in its support in the executive, legislative, and judicial
branches of government, builds on the power of decentralization. Rather
than insist that federalism, as traditionally understood, has no relevance to
contemporary society, it seems to me that the central task is to reconceive
federalism. The problem is not federalism, but the widespread misconcep-
tion of federalism as the protection of divergent state communities from
the evils of nationalization.

The stakes involved are substantial. The supporters of federalism, on the
courts and elsewhere, build on the romantic rhetoric of state distinctiveness
and allied notions of localism. They paint a dualist picture in which courts
must protect the local from the national, must safeguard state autonomy
from the threats of national incursion. That language, and the conceptions that follow, lead to mistaken rulings and bad policy. Federalism is
often lauded as a way to protect individual rights, yet that function seems
ill served by current federalism doctrine. In the name of federalism, the
Supreme Court has struck down statutes keeping guns out of schools,[12] protecting women from violence,[13] preserving intellectual property from state
infringement,[14] and requiring compensation for state employees for workplace wrongs ranging from age[15] and disability[16] discrimination to failure to
honor minimum wage and overtime requirements.[17] At the same time, the
Court has invalidated important state health and safety laws on the theory
that they encroach on protected preserves of federal power.[18] The harms
wrought by the Supreme Court's conception of federalism are significant.

Federalism indeed can be central to protecting fundamental rights in the
United States, but to achieve that goal a new conception of federalism is
required. What is needed is a way of understanding the meaning of federal-

ism given the realities of the contemporary United States. The solution, I argue, lies not in denying the power of federalist impulses, but in constructing a model of federalism that replaces an outdated focus on local variation with an emphasis on the organizational benefits of multiple agents of power. The goal of this book is to offer such a reconceptualization. I seek to provide an account of contemporary federalism that accords with its real power, with its organizational ingenuity rather than its nostalgia for lost community. Having developed that conception of federalism, I then explore its implications for legal and policy debates.

The plan of the book follows that pattern. The first two chapters discuss in more detail the puzzle of how federalism can gain strength at the same time that forces of nationalization remain ascendant in politics, culture, and society. Chapter 3 explores the failure of the dualist conception of federalism still dominant on the United States Supreme Court and in the halls of the academy. Chapter 4 develops an alternative model of federalism, which I term "polyphonic." This conception emphasizes the value of multiple independent voices of governance. In this way, polyphonic federalism seeks to save federalism by freeing it from outmoded concepts of state distinctiveness. The remainder of the book applies the polyphonic conception of federalism to a variety of political and legal debates. Chapters 5 and 6 focus on domestic settings, especially the complex structure of judicial federalism in the United States. Chapter 7 considers the implications of polyphonic federalism for incorporating foreign law into state and federal legal systems.

To what end? I have mentioned the harms of the Supreme Court's current view of federalism. What are the benefits of the polyphonic conception? Throughout this book, I discuss two kinds of advantages that polyphony brings. First, polyphonic systems, by which I mean systems that involve the interaction of multiple sources of power, are more innovative and resilient than systems, such as dualist federalism, that compartmentalize different kinds of power. When faced with new challenges, polyphonic systems are better able to find novel responses that allow the systems to adapt, rather than atrophy. Second, in the contemporary United States, a polyphonic conception of federalism does a better job than dualism in advancing the goals traditionally associated with federalism, including responsive and efficient policymaking, participatory self-governance, and prevention of tyranny. In sum, polyphonic federalism yields multiple rewards.

One kind of benefit deserves special emphasis. The protection of fundamental rights has attained global recognition as a value of universal concern. In the United States, the safeguarding of rights is sometimes associated with the restriction of governmental action. In this view, governments must be limited so as to create a space for people to enjoy their fundamental rights. However, the vindication of rights may instead require affirmative governmental conduct. Laws may be necessary to protect against discrimination, to guarantee education, to preserve the environment. This book argues that in the contemporary United States, rights are often best protected not through confining state and federal power in different areas, but by promoting the dynamic interaction of state and federal governments. It is through the overlap and concurrence of state and federal authority that human rights are vindicated. The subtitle of this volume emphasizes that crucial role of federalism.

Is a polyphonic reconceptualization of federalism a genuine possibility in the contemporary United States? I believe so. In some ways, polyphony already has triumphed. My conception of polyphonic federalism has both a descriptive and a normative aspect. It is a theory of what is, as well as what should be. In the United States today, the domains of state and federal power are thoroughly intermixed. Despite the hopes and fears of the advocates of dual federalism, the states and the federal government both address all major areas of importance to the citizens of the country. From crime, to schools, to securities law, neither the states nor the federal government has a regulatory monopoly. In this sense, polyphonic federalism is an account of the status quo. As the following chapters explain, it is useful to recognize and to acknowledge the system we have so as best to promote its benefits and to mitigate its risks. This book also presents a defense of polyphonic federalism. I argue that polyphony has many advantages when compared to the alternatives, such as dualist federalism. Without a theory of polyphonic federalism, certain contemporary regulatory schemes and judicial doctrines appear deviant, as aberrations that should be erased, or at most tolerated, but never celebrated. To provide a firm theoretical foundation for the polyphonic practices that abound serves as one important goal of this book. At the same time, certain pockets of dualist federalism persist. Some legal doctrines remain mired in a dualist past. The United States Supreme Court deploys a dualist conception of federalism with unfortunate consequences. Freeing the law from such dualist remnants is another aim of this work. Thus unshackled from its dualist history, federalism can serve a crucial role in protecting fundamental rights.

A note of clarification is in order. Federalism is a widespread form of government throughout the world. Depending on the definition one employs, somewhere between 40 percent and 80 percent of the world's population lives in a federal system.[19] The conception of federalism I develop in this book is not intended as a universal formula for the functioning of every federal polity. Similar institutions may have different functions in different contexts. By emphasizing an organizational understanding of federalism, this book I hope will prove useful in efforts to analyze other federal systems. The values of polyphonic federalism that I explore—plurality, dialogue, and redundancy—have broad application across many different settings. The implementation of polyphonic federalism, however, is inextricably linked with the society of the United States in the early twenty-first century. In different nations with divergent challenges, other conceptions might better realize the promise of federalism in protecting individual rights and human dignity. This book presents a theory of federalism for the United States today.

CHAPTER ONE

The Paradox:
The Revival of Federalism
in a Nationalizing Society

Federalism certainly has its enemies, past and present. In 1964, a noted political scientist wrote that, "if in the United States one disapproves of racism, one should disapprove of federalism."[1] In August 2005, two thousand people in Kirkuk, Iraq, participated in a protest rally, chanting "No to Federalism."[2]

In the contemporary United States, however, federalism has few open opponents. Perhaps the clearest sign of the unquestioned status of federalism appears in the remarks of a Democratic president. From Franklin Roosevelt's New Deal to Lyndon Johnson's Great Society, Democratic presidents had championed the important role of the national government in addressing the nation's challenges. By 1996, however, it was a Democratic president, Bill Clinton, who declared, "The era of big government is over."[3] President Clinton intended to signal his understanding of the limits of the appropriate role of the national government. In the new era President Clinton presaged, private parties would play a strong role, but states ("small government") would as well.

This resurgent interest in federalism in the United States presents something of a puzzle. Federalism often is linked with localism, with a respect and affection for local institutions and local culture. Federalism generally exists in opposition to nationalism. The nationalizing trends in the United States, though, seem to be increasing. Technology has rendered state boundaries less significant. Ease of communication and transportation has decreased the importance of geography. Indeed, some innovations, such as the Internet, operate largely without reference to traditional political borders. How can one account for the simultaneous revival of federalism and the continuing nationalization of society? That is the puzzle that this book seeks to address and that this chapter seeks to frame.

Resurgence of Federalism in Politics

Much of this book is devoted to analyzing different conceptions of federalism. For the purposes of this chapter, though, I am interested in exploring attitudes about the general idea of federalism. Most broadly, federalism tends to mean the affirmation of a significant role for states in the political system of the United States. In this sense, the signs of the federalism revival are pervasive. All branches of the federal government have professed increased deference to state prerogatives. At the same time, the states have taken more active roles in formulating and implementing policy in a variety of areas. As I will argue later, some aspects of this federalism revival are purely symbolic, while others are deeply misguided. Nevertheless, the resurgence of interest in federalism is clear.

FEDERALISM IN NATIONAL POLITICS

Federalism has strong support in national politics. In professing allegiance to federalism, President Clinton was following the lead of other branches of the national government. In the wake of the Republican takeover in the 1994 elections, Congress sought to institutionalize certain protections for states. In 1995, the new Republican Congress adopted the Unfunded Mandates Reform Act (UMRA).[4] Under UMRA, the Congressional Budget Office generally must assess the costs of new legislative mandates on state, local, and tribal governments, as well as on the private sector. Special procedures apply if the mandates exceed $50 million for governmental entities or $100 million for the private sector. Federal agencies also must assess the impact of proposed regulations when the effect exceeds $100 million.[5] In addition, Congress gave the states more flexibility in administering welfare and other joint federal-state programs.

The year 1995 also proved to be a banner year for federalism in the courts. In *United States v. Lopez*,[6] the United States Supreme Court imposed limits on the national government's power to adopt wide-ranging laws pursuant to Congress's constitutional authority to regulate interstate commerce. The particular statute at issue in *Lopez*, a prohibition on carrying guns within a thousand feet of a school, did not constitute part of a major federal program. Nevertheless, *Lopez* provided a significant marker for the resurgence of constitutional federalism. Not since 1937 had the United States Supreme Court struck down a federal statute as exceeding Congress's Commerce Clause power. In 1996, the Court held that states enjoyed a constitutionally based sovereign immunity that Congress could not displace.[7]

Accordingly, while general federal laws, such as minimum wage require-ments, applied to states, if the states violated these laws, private individu-als could not sue the states for back pay or other monetary compensation. The Court asserted that such private raids on state treasuries interfered with state autonomy and insulted state "dignity."[8]

In each of these areas, the events of 1995–96 represented the culmina-tion of much longer trends. President Clinton's federalist rhetoric followed the path successfully trod by Ronald Reagan. In his first inaugural, Presi-dent Reagan declared, "Government is not the solution to our problem. Government is the problem." Drawing on the deep political tradition of federalism, President Reagan cast his antigovernmental rhetoric under the rubric of New Federalism. He thus helped to restore federalism to its central place in American political discourse. His political success inspired many imitators, including President Clinton.

In keeping with his focus on federalism, President Reagan issued Ex-ecutive Order 12,612, entitled "Federalism," on October 26, 1987.[9] The order was designed "to restore the division of governmental responsibili-ties between the national government and the States that was intended by the Framers of the Constitution and to ensure that the principles of fed-eralism established by the Framers guide the Executive departments and agencies in the formulation and implementation of policies." Executive Order 12,612 created nine "Fundamental Federalism Principles" to guide the formulation and implementation of policies having federalism impli-cations. Among these principles was a statement concerning the wisdom of a smaller national government: "Federalism is rooted in the knowledge that our political liberties are best assured by limiting the size and scope of the national government." Several principles referenced the Tenth Amend-ment[10] and emphasized that unenumerated governmental powers should be reserved to the states unless expressly prohibited by the Constitution. A strong presumption in favor of state authority was established.

In addition to these general principles, Executive Order 12,612 required federal departments and agencies to use "Federalism Policymaking Crite-ria." When proposed federal actions could limit state discretion, federal de-partments and agencies were required to examine closely the specific con-stitutional and statutory authority behind the action and to consult with states, "to the extent practicable," before any implementation of the action. Federal actions limiting the policymaking discretion of states could be taken only if "the national activity is necessitated by the presence of a problem of national scope." President George H. W. Bush affirmed his commitment to

Executive Order 12,612 in a 1990 memorandum to the heads of executive departments and agencies.[11]

In October 1993, President Clinton issued Executive Order 12,875, entitled "Enhancing the Intergovernmental Partnership."[12] The order sought to restrict the imposition of unfunded federal mandates on the states. President Clinton did not issue an executive order specifically on federalism until 1998, and when he did, it proved very controversial. Executive Order 13,083[13] superseded the provisions of the Reagan order and weakened substantially the language purporting to limit national authority so as to empower the states. The substance of the order, along with the failure to consult with state and local governments, ignited a firestorm of controversy.[14] President Clinton quickly suspended the order, and a year later he issued a new order, Executive Order 13,132,[15] which largely restated the principles of the Reagan order.[16]

These executive orders functioned largely as symbols. They did not constitute law that could be used in litigation against the United States. Commentators have questioned whether the orders actually limited the imposition of federal regulations on states.[17] The orders did, however, demonstrate the continuing significance of federalism. After some initial disastrous efforts to tinker with the prior federalism order, President Clinton embraced it. Affirmation of support for federalism had become a necessity of executive governance. President Clinton recognized that he, too, had best get on the federalism train, rather than attempt to stand in front of it.

On the Supreme Court, the *Lopez* case represented the culmination of a quarter-century crusade by William Rehnquist. From his initial appointment in 1972, Rehnquist attempted to move the Supreme Court to recognize more limits on the scope of national authority. In a lone dissenting opinion penned in 1975, then-Justice Rehnquist sketched the outlines of his program to reinvigorate constitutional limitations on the national government.[18] This project of restricting the federal government achieved its goal twenty years later, but it won several notable victories in the intervening years. The federalism assault began in the field of criminal law and targeted the role of federal courts in supervising criminal prosecutions in state courts. In several areas, the Court limited the ability of state court criminal defendants to seek a federal forum to press their federal constitutional claims. Most notably, the Court cut back on the availability of the writ of habeas corpus, a legal procedure that had allowed lower federal courts to review the legality of state criminal proceedings. The Court erected several procedural hurdles, reducing the frequency of such federal reexamination of state trials.[19] In the habeas area, the Court blazed a trail later followed by Congress. The federal Antiterrorism and Effective Death Penalty Act of 1996[20] codified and strengthened the Supreme Court's restrictions on federal habeas corpus.

FEDERALISM IN STATE POLITICS

States, as well, are flocking to the banner of federalism, developing judicial theories and administrative policies in areas once dominated by the federal courts and the federal government. State officials have interpreted the federalism message in Washington as a new empowerment of states to address a broad range of concerns. State courts no longer passively follow the federal lead in elaborating constitutional rights. In many areas, state courts have advanced where federal courts have not dared to tread. State politicians also have pursued national issues, finding political benefit in addressing prominent problems in which the federal response is perceived to be inadequate.

In a movement called the "New Judicial Federalism," state courts are interpreting their constitutions independently of the federal Constitution, thus protecting rights that federal courts have refused to vindicate. Equity in public school financing has served as one notable example of the New Judicial Federalism in action. Public schools traditionally have been funded from local tax revenues. For this reason, schools in wealthier areas, with higher tax bases, have received more money to spend on each pupil than schools in poorer areas. In 1973 in *San Antonio Independent School District v. Rodriguez*,[21] the United States Supreme Court upheld the constitutionality of this financing method. In the wake of *Rodriguez*, advocates of educational equality brought state constitutional challenges to the district-based funding system. Suits attacking school financing inequities now have been filed in nearly all states, with about half succeeding on the merits.[22] Litigation related to sexual orientation provides another example of the New Judicial Federalism. In the *Goodridge* decision in 2003, the Supreme Judicial Court of Massachusetts found the right to same-sex marriage protected by the Massachusetts Constitution.[23] The California Supreme Court followed suit in 2008, holding that the California Constitution guaranteed the right to same-sex marriage.[24]

Other state officials also have found inspiration in federalism to develop independent regulatory agendas. When he was New York's attorney general, Eliot Spitzer took an active role in investigating securities fraud and other types of corporate misconduct usually targeted by federal regulators.[25] His successor, Andrew Cuomo, followed a similar path. Cuomo pursued an aggressive program of investigating potential abuses in student loans, which implicate issues of federal banking law and bankruptcy law and are subject to a range of federal regulations. According to Cuomo, federal agencies with oversight responsibilities, including the Office of the Comptroller of the Currency, the Federal Deposit Insurance Corporation, and the Federal Trade Commission, had not been doing their jobs.[26] Cuomo articulated a concept of the benefits of overlapping state and federal jurisdiction. If the federal regulators failed to protect consumers, then the states remained available to offer the needed safeguards. He remarked, "I believe in the pendulum swing of federalism. When you have a federal government that is not fulfilling its role, then let the states step in. . . . I will use the state consumer protection laws to protect consumers at a time . . . when the federal government isn't acting."[27] Cuomo spearheaded a group of state attorneys general who pressed Congress to enact new laws in the area. The attorneys general envisioned a concurrent state-federal effort. A group of thirty-two attorneys general wrote to congressional leaders promoting this kind of partnership: "This problem cries out for a federal solution that supplements the work of state-attorney-general offices across the country."[28] For the attorneys general, the question was not whether the federal government or the states should be policing student loans. The question was how the overlapping state and federal efforts could bring the best results.

Addressing another area typically regulated by the federal government, some states have sought to develop their own environmental policies, targeting auto emissions and greenhouse gases.[29] California has taken the lead in many of these areas. Governor Arnold Schwarzenegger has made clear his sense of his state's independent authority, describing California as "the modern equivalent of the ancient city-states of Athens and Sparta."[30]

From the perspective of both the national government and the states themselves, states are being recognized as important, independent sources of authority. Federalism, though, traditionally has been conceived as resting on more than just statutes, judicial decisions, or broad presidential pronouncements. Federalism typically has involved real commitment to, and affection for, local decision making. People must feel some attachment to the states. Do the Unfunded Mandate Reform Act and the Supreme Court's sovereign immunity cases sufficiently warm the hearths of independent state identity? It seems unlikely. Legal doctrines provide the prose of federalism, but where is the poetry? John McGinnis, a leading scholar of federalism, put the problem this way: "A successful constitutional federalism must be a federalism of the heart rather than of the intellect."[31] Is the state where the heart lies today?

The answer appears to be no, and therein lies the puzzle. Nationalizing forces have been breaking down local and regional barriers since the nation's founding. As the next section discusses, those nationalizing trends have continued unabated. The growing interest in federalism has done nothing to diminish political and social nationalization.

Nationalizing Trends in Politics and Culture

ALL POLITICS IS LOCAL NO LONGER

"All politics is local" famously declared Thomas P. "Tip" O'Neill Jr., who rose to become Speaker of the United States House of Representatives. That phrase may remain accurate, but it seems that "all politics is national" has a good claim to truth as well. Political figures have national constituencies, traveling around the country, raising money from like-minded individuals in each region. Hillary Clinton can move to New York and run for Senate. William Weld, the former governor of Massachusetts, can move to New York to try a gubernatorial campaign there. Clearly, as William Weld discovered, outsider status remains a problem. Nevertheless, political imports are becoming increasingly possible. When Illinois Republicans sought a candidate for the United States Senate, they looked to Alan Keyes, a resident of Maryland. Keyes had little success in that race, winning less than 30 percent of the votes, though the popularity of Barack Obama probably played a larger role than Keyes's outsider status.

The political parties have become more nationalized as well. Whereas state and local parties exercised a great deal of influence in the past, the national party structures have now become dominant.[32] The Internet has allowed national parties to reach directly to individual donors and volunteers. "Grassroots" efforts now can be organized centrally from Washington, without the need for organization from state and local parties. In 2004, the Bush-Cheney campaign deliberately bypassed state and local party organizations and relied instead on its own recruits, who it viewed as loyal to the national party organization. Grassroots organizing no longer involved localized coordination. The roots ran directly to the national party headquarters.[33]

Money, the life-blood of modern politics, reflects and fuels this nationalizing trend. Federal candidates depend less on state party organizations to supply the needed funds. Candidates for federal office increasingly raise money from out-of-state sources.[34] Those national funds may exceed the amount raised locally. In 2004, the incumbent Democratic senator from South Dakota, Tom Daschle, raised more than 90 percent of his money from out-of-state contributors. His successful opponent, John Thune, raised nearly 80 percent of his contributions from out of state.[35] Daschle's status as minority leader of the Senate gave that election a particularly national cast, but other races also attract significant funds from nonconstituents. In 2006, senatorial candidates Conrad Burns (Montana), Maria Cantwell (Washington), Lincoln Chafee (Rhode Island), Harold Ford (Tennessee), and Sheldon Whitehouse (Rhode Island) all raised more than 60 percent of their money from contributors outside their home states.[36] That level of support from outside the state is unusual, but significant cross-border donations are not. Overall, in the 1996, 1998, and 2000 election cycles, thirty-five out of one hundred senators raised more money from out-of-state donors than from in-state ones.[37] The nationalizing trends apply even for primary elections. In 2004, 26 percent of individual donations to congressional primary candidates came from out-of-state donors.[38] Federal candidates look to national constituencies and national interest groups for their support. State elections too are becoming nationalized.[39] Representative Tom DeLay's success in Texas, which I discuss in more detail below, provides a prime example of the national focus of local politics.

Local politics, of course, remains crucial. Not only state officials, but also national representatives are elected in each state. Senators and members of the House of Representatives must remain attuned to local concerns. Alfonse D'Amato, the former senator from New York, proudly carried the sobriquet of "Senator Pothole."[40] If constituents needed help with local problems, they could call on Senator D'Amato for assistance. Senator Strom Thurmond also was renowned for great attention to constituent services. Thurmond decreed that no telephone in his office should ring more than twice, lest a citizen-caller be left waiting too long, and he insisted that all constituent requests receive a response within twenty-four hours.[41]

The constitutional system for legislative districts provides another example of the power of local politics. The state legislatures draw the districts for elections to the United States House of Representatives. Thus, the state legislators play a major role in choosing the national representatives from the state. Modern redistricting technology has enabled state politicians to wield their districting power with great skill. Legal analyst Jeffrey Toobin has observed that the current redistricting power has produced a kind of historical irony.[42] Under the Constitution as originally conceived, state legislatures would choose the senators from each state, but the people would choose the members of the House of Representatives. After the Seventeenth Amendment, senators are now elected directly by the people. Because United States senators are elected statewide, no district manipulation is possible. With regard to election of members of the United States House of Representatives, by contrast, the state legislatures play a major part. The districts drawn by the state legislatures play a critical role in determining the election of representatives. In this sense, because of the power of districting, the state legislatures choose the members, or at least the political affiliations, of the members of the House. Thus the reversal from the original design is complete. The state legislatures now do not choose the senators, but they have a major role in choosing the members of the House of Representatives.

At the same time, however, local politics has become increasingly nationalized. The ties between national political parties and local political parties have increased. One of the reasons for the victory of the Republican Party in 1994 was its success in nationalizing local elections. The Contract with America, prepared by the Republican leadership of the House of Representatives, provided a visible symbol of this nationalizing effort. The contract set forth a core program of governmental reform that the Republican Party pledged to undertake if voted into the majority. All but two of the Republican members of the House and all nonincumbent Republican candidates signed the contract. It is not clear that the contract itself proved to be a factor in local elections, but Bill Clinton did. The Republicans succeeded in translating unhappiness with Bill Clinton into success in congressional districts all across the United States. The year 1994 was thus a year freighted with symbolism. Tip O'Neill died, and so did his mantra. As political scientist Gary Jacobson noted, "All politics was not local in 1994."[43]

President George W. Bush furthered this nationalizing trend in his aggressive leadership of the Republican Party. He campaigned energetically on behalf of Republican candidates throughout the nation. During the 2002 midterm election campaign, President Bush made 108 campaign stops on behalf of twenty-six House candidates and twenty candidates for the Senate. Moreover, he campaigned on the national issue of his leadership in the War on Terror. Not only his personal appearances, but his rhetoric as well cast the election in national terms.[44]

President Bush's success in 2002 contrasts with the failures of previous presidents to nationalize elections. Seeking to strengthen support for his New Deal programs in the 1938 elections, President Franklin D. Roosevelt tried to unseat his legislative opponents. President Roosevelt came to

Georgia to campaign in the Democratic primary against incumbent senator Walter George, who had begun resisting some of Roosevelt's New Deal
plans. Roosevelt was a popular president, and he sought to use his influence in this state race. Georgia apparently did not appreciate the president's
attempt to meddle in its electoral process. Senator George defeated two
opponents to win the primary and went on to win the general election.[45]
President Roosevelt's efforts to unseat Senator Ellison "Cotton Ed" Smith of
South Carolina and Senator Millard Tydings of Maryland proved similarly
unsuccessful.[46]

When President George W. Bush came to Georgia in 2002 to campaign
against incumbent senator Max Cleland, Cleland sought to take heart in
the experience of President Roosevelt and Senator George. President Bush,
however, proved more successful than President Roosevelt in unseating a
troublesome incumbent. Cleland lost his reelection bid. Georgia's voters
apparently did not resent the president's participating in a local political
campaign. Of course, many factors explain Cleland's loss, but the factors
tend to relate to national trends.[47] The year 2002 proved to be a good year
for Republicans throughout the country. President Bush's popularity trans-
lated into support for Republican candidates all along the ticket. Southern
Democrats failed in their generation-long project of encouraging voters who
leaned Republican in national elections to continue to vote Democratic in
state and local elections. Local politics had become nationalized.

The success of the Democratic Party in 2006 reflected a similar nationalization of the election. With an unpopular president conducting an unpopular war, the Democratic Party managed to turn opposition to President
Bush into a winning formula throughout the United States. As political
scientists Sidney Milkis and Jesse Rhodes put it, "by the 2006 election, the
subordination of state and local issues to executive administration had become a severe liability to Republican candidates whose political fortunes
suffered dearly as a result of the nationalization of the congressional elections."[48] The plight of Republican senator Lincoln Chafee of Rhode Island
illustrated the power of nationalized politics. Senator Chafee opposed
President Bush's policies in Iraq, and he enjoyed an approval rating of 62
percent among Rhode Island voters. Nevertheless, he was defeated in his
reelection bid in 2006. The national Democratic trend was too strong.[49]

Perhaps a more accurate assessment would be that all politics is both
local and national. National politics is local, and local politics is national. Little in politics is exclusively local or national. Tom DeLay provides a prime example. A Republican congressman from Texas who served
as majority whip and then majority leader in the United States House of

Representatives, DeLay wished to buttress the Republican majority in the House. To support the Republican cause in Washington, DeLay sought to have more Republicans elected from Texas. He accomplished that goal by working from the bottom up. First, he worked to elect more Republicans to the Texas state legislature with the aim of controlling that body. In 2003, he achieved his goal when Republicans attained a majority in both houses of the state legislature.[50] DeLay then forcefully urged the state legislature to redraw the congressional districts. Traditionally, the legislature had revised the districts only once after each decennial census, but DeLay did not want to wait until 2010.

With DeLay's encouragement, the Texas legislature did redraw the districts, and Texas sent six more Republican congressman to Washington. The overlap of national and local politics became patent when Democrats in the Texas legislature fled to neighboring states in an ultimately futile effort to prevent legislative action on the redistricting by depriving the legislative chambers of a quorum. As the Democrats flew out of Texas, DeLay asked the Federal Aviation Administration and the Federal Bureau of Investigation to try to hunt down the airplanes containing the fleeing legislators.[51] So the majority leader of the United States House of Representatives asked federal agencies to intercede in a state redistricting dispute, a dispute that arose because of national political issues.[52] Is politics local or national? Yes.

One of the most striking recent demonstrations of the nationalization of politics was the controversy surrounding the death of Terri Schiavo. In 1990, Terri Schiavo, then twenty-six years old, suffered a cardiac arrest. The cause of the cardiac arrest has never been decisively determined. Because her brain was deprived of oxygen, Schiavo lapsed into a coma, and she was diagnosed as being in a persistent vegetative state. Eventually, her husband, Michael Schiavo, and her parents became embroiled in a nasty legal battle. Terri Schiavo left no living will, but her husband asserted that she had made clear her desire not to be kept alive in such a debilitated state. When Michael Schiavo attempted to have his wife's feeding tube removed, her parents protested, and a protracted legal dispute ensued. The Florida courts had to sort out a variety of claims about Terri Schiavo's actual medical condition, the wishes she had expressed if such circumstances arose, and the fitness of her husband to serve as her legal guardian. The Florida courts eventually sided with Michael Schiavo, finding that he had legal authority over Terri's care. The Florida courts even rebuffed state legislation attempting to order the maintenance of the feeding tube.

Up to this point, the Schiavo dispute had been largely a local affair. Decisions about end-of-life care are made routinely throughout the United

States every day, following the laws in each state. In the *Cruzan* case in 1990,[53] the United States Supreme Court had suggested that patients had a federal constitutional right to refuse unwanted medical treatment, even if it would lead to their death. However, *Cruzan* also allowed the states broad latitude in assessing the wishes of the patients. In the *Cruzan* case itself, the Supreme Court rejected a challenge to the rigorous procedures adopted by Missouri for ascertaining the patient's choice.

The Schiavo case, though, clearly touched a national nerve and became a major national political issue. The Republican leadership in Congress rushed through legislation seeking to give the federal courts jurisdiction to hear the claims of Terri Schiavo's parents. President Bush made a much-publicized midnight flight from Texas to Washington, D.C., to sign the bill immediately upon its passage. In the end, all federal courts, including the United States Supreme Court, refused to overturn the order of the Florida courts allowing the removal of Terri Schiavo's feeding tube. Without her feeding tube, Terri Schiavo finally died on March 31, 2005. The imbroglio surrounding her death became a national symbol. To some, her death embodied the undervaluing of life in American culture. For others, the controversy revealed the power of religious fundamentalists and provided further evidence of the hypocrisy of Republicans who praise federalism in some matters, while enacting special legislation inviting federal courts to overturn state judicial decisions with which they disagree. To those who saw hypocrisy, their anger was magnified by the Republicans returning to the scene of their last major effort—that one successful—to have the federal courts overturn the Florida state courts: the *Bush v. Gore* controversy of 2000.[54]

However one interpreted the Schiavo story, the overall tale clearly had a national dimension. Cable networks and Internet sites with insatiable appetites for content to fill their around-the-clock coverage feast on dramatic human interest stories, providing continuous updates to a nationwide audience. These media frenzies naturally attract publicity-seeking politicians. In this way, compelling personal dramas easily become national political issues. It is not uncommon for personal and natural tragedies to take on a political character. In the contemporary United States, that political character has broad national resonance.

ALL POLICY IS NATIONAL

Just as all politics is national, all policy is national as well. In the United States, certain areas traditionally have been the province of state, rather than national, control. Heading the list of domains generally conceived of as reserved for state, or local, supervision are crime, education, land use, and family relations. It was not lack of importance that led these areas to be understood as preserves of local control. Quite the contrary. These realms were understood as having special significance for each community. What are the issues that matter in local elections? Crime, education, and land use often top the list. Recently, family law has joined the roster. Issues of marriage, and particularly same-sex marriage, have become staples of state electoral politics.[55]

Keeping people safe stands as the most basic function of government. Thomas Hobbes, among other political philosophers, understood protecting people from the state of nature as the core justification for government. In Hobbes's famous phrase, without government, life would be "nasty, brutish, and short." Policing and crime control in the United States have traditionally been handled at the state and local levels, not by the national government. Typically, each city, county, and town has its own law enforcement personnel. State police tend to have more specialized functions. National law enforcement agencies, such as the Federal Bureau of Investigation, have had an even more specialized portfolio.

Education also is a prototypically local affair. School boards are locally elected. School budgets tend to come from local revenue sources.[56] The United States Supreme Court, along with many state courts, has understood local control of education to be a value of constitutional significance.[57] As with law enforcement, the emphasis on state and local, rather than national control, did not reflect a perception of the lack of importance of the topic. Education has come to symbolize the promise of the United States. Public schools are the great engines of social progress, allowing people from all backgrounds to advance in society. The public school teacher is probably the government employee with whom citizens have the most regular contact. It is no accident that schools became the focus of the civil rights movement. Unequal schools at once symbolized and perpetuated the state-sponsored racism that belied the ideals of equality set forth in the Declaration of Independence and reaffirmed in the Civil War and the Reconstruction-era amendments to the United States Constitution.

Geared to the particular conditions of each locality, land use and zoning regulations have been determined at the local level. These laws enable a community to define itself, to determine its own character. Land use law also helps to protect, or jeopardize, the value of a home, the most significant asset that most people own.

By longstanding custom, family law has been determined at the state level. Each state defines the terms of marriage and of divorce. Child custody, child support, and alimony are all determined at the state level according to state standards. Indeed, while state law disputes generally may end up in federal courts if the litigants are citizens of different states, family law matters may not. Courts have created a "domestic relations" exception to federal jurisdiction, keeping such matters out of federal court, even if they otherwise appear to come within the terms of the congressional statute governing federal court jurisdiction.[58]

These important local issues defined a realm beyond national control. But no longer. The importance of each issue has led citizens to demand action from all levels of government. Drug trafficking constitutes the most notable example of federal law enforcement, but federal laws reach many crimes of violence (such as carjacking) and almost all white collar crime (including any act that involves use of the mails or telephones).[59] Federal lawmakers have tried as well to reform state criminal justice policies. Unhappy with state parole programs, Congress has sought to impose "truth-in-sentencing" rules on the state system.[60]

Education remains an issue of importance at all levels of government, but the federal government continues to increase its involvement. Enacted in 2001, the No Child Left Behind Act[61] (NCLB) institutes massive federal regulation of the administration of elementary and secondary education in the United States. In return for receiving federal education funds, states must accept provisions that regulate the qualifications of teachers, establish student performance goals, and impose detailed reporting requirements.[62] NCLB requires states to establish proficiency goals for the performance of students. Yearly testing monitors the progress in achieving these benchmarks. Under the act, schools that fail to make adequate yearly progress toward the proficiency goals are subject to an escalating series of sanctions. For example, if schools fall below the standards for two consecutive years, students are allowed to choose a different school in the same district. After five years of failed performance, the school must surrender control to the state.[63] NCLB passed with overwhelming bipartisan support,[64] indicative of the broad consensus that education should be a central concern of the national government.[65]

The Supreme Court has imposed new restrictions on local autonomy in the land use area as well. The vehicle for greater national control has been the Takings Clause of the United States Constitution, which states "nor shall private property be taken for public use, without just compensation."[66] The

Takings Clause clearly requires the government to compensate the owner when the government takes physical possession of private property, as it sometimes does when it builds roads or schools. Recently, however, the Court has used the Takings Clause aggressively to restrict not only the actual appropriation of private property, but also regulations that diminish the value of property. The Court, for example, has found that various restrictions on development implicate the Takings Clause.[67]

Where the Court has feared to tread, Congress may well rush in. *Kelo v. City of New London* in 2005 presented the question whether a court should assess if the government's use of its takings power actually furthered a "public" purpose.[68] The City of New London sought to force property owners to sell their land to make way for private retail development. Refusing to countenance robust judicial review of this issue, the Supreme Court held that the courts must defer to the democratically elected officials' determination of public purpose. That decision sparked widespread controversy. For many, "protect private property" provides a more compelling slogan than "local control of land use." Following the public outcry, Congress has shown signs of exerting federal control in this area. Recently introduced legislation threatens states with funding reductions if they use their eminent domain powers to promote "private" development.[69]

Family law remains predominantly subject to state control, but in this area too, the changed attitude is apparent. Congress has federalized certain interstate aspects of family disputes, particularly those pertaining to interstate child support and custody issues. The federal Child Support Recovery Act[70] and the federal Parental Kidnapping Prevention Act[71] attempt to deal with interstate enforcement issues. More directly, legislators have been considering the Federal Marriage Amendment designed to create and enforce a national definition of heterosexual marriage. Though many advocate state-by-state resolution of the gay-marriage issue,[72] opinions vary. Some argue that the right to same-sex marriage deserves constitutional protection. Others seek a constitutional amendment banning the practice. Partisans on the two sides of the issue may agree on little else, aside from the need for a national resolution of this family law issue.[73]

All of these subjects remain local, but they have become nationalized as well. It is not just that national movements seek to have impacts on the laws of each state, though that is surely true. Rather, the federal government has acted to impose certain uniform national rules. Policies, like politics, have become nationalized. All important issues now end up in Washington, D.C.

NATIONALIZATION OF CULTURE

Along with the nationalization of politics, the contemporary United States has witnessed the nationalization of culture. These two trends are of course related, with the growth of national media and the ease of transportation overcoming former geographical hurdles. Before the rise of national news organizations, people received their information from newspapers. Newspapers can better focus on local events and can print local sections targeted to different localities.[74] Roper surveys show that in the early 1960s, Americans began to rely on television rather than newspapers as their primary media source of news. By 1994 the disparity had grown such that 72 percent of people received their news primarily from television, as opposed to 38 percent who read it in a newspaper.[75] Local newspapers, moreover, often publish the same news drawn from the same national outlets. With the ownership of newspapers increasingly concentrated in large chains, less regional and local variation in coverage occurs.[76]

Today, people often get their news from national and international outlets such as Fox News, CNN, and all manner of Internet sources. Local television stations may offer little in the way of local news. A 1998 survey found that 35 percent of these stations provided no local news coverage, and 25 percent provided neither local news nor local public affairs programming.[77] The variety that does exist does not track geographical boundaries. Cable television, satellite radio, and the Internet have enabled national niche programming. People with particular tastes in music or politics can find appealing programming, which can be enjoyed by those with similar preferences throughout the United States or the world. Tastes always will vary, and diverse media will target diverse audiences, but geography does not define the relevant audience.

The national market has reduced local commercial variation. Go shopping anywhere in the United States, and you will often end up in a mall filled with national chains. Political scientist Samuel Krislov described the phenomenon as follows: "Modern merchandising has proved the ultimate homogenizer. McDonald's, Wal-Mart, Home Depot and their peers continuously make most American communities and their main street indistinguishable at first sight."[78] Check out the clothing at The Gap, The Limited, or Victoria's Secret and then grab a latte at Starbucks. You could be anywhere.

At one time, culture had strong regional identification. The entertainment and leisure options varied greatly from state to state. Music or sports of a certain kind might be unavailable or even unknown on the other side of the country. Today, though, cultural phenomena with strong regional roots are expanding throughout the nation. Country star Garth Brooks played in Manhattan's Central Park. After thirty-eight years in Nashville, the Country Music Awards show moved to New York for 2005.[79] Formerly regional sports, such as auto racing, have attracted a national audience. At one time, the NASCAR fan base consisted of the rural South and Midwest. Now NASCAR has proven popular with people throughout the United States.[80] Fueled by increased national television exposure, interest in NASCAR has expanded both numerically and geographically.

The balance of trade is not one-sided. Thanksgiving shed its northeastern origins several generations ago.[81] Even ice hockey is spreading to the South and West, with the necessary adaptations to its new settings.[82] Thus, the Minnesota North Stars can live on happily as the Dallas Stars. Rap music, too, has spread well beyond its urban roots.[83] Moreover, when regional phenomena become national, they inevitably change. The process of nationalization transforms the product itself. NASCAR fans complain that the sport has lost its soul as it has moved beyond its region of birth. Drivers from all over the United States compete on large tracks in big cities, with popular music figures providing entertainment. The sport has moved from regional grit to national glitz. The change has been a self-conscious response by the organizers of NASCAR, who have been driven in part by their perception of the waning of certain distinctive regional cultural patterns. The president of NASCAR declared, "We believe strongly that the old Southeastern redneck heritage that we had is no longer in existence."[84]

The point is not that everyone listens to the Jay-Z (or Confederate Railroad), while waiting in the drive-through lane to pick up a Venti Cappuccino, before heading home to watch Dale Earnhardt Jr. take the checkered flag (though it sometimes seems that way). Of course, tastes differ widely. The growth of cable television, the Internet, and other specialized media outlets allows the culture industry to target these varying preferences. Narrowcasting is replacing broadcasting as the paradigmatic means of cultural dissemination.[85] Given the proliferation of television channels and other methods of providing entertainment, national programming is giving way to programming targeted as specific cultural niches.[86] The niches, though, are defined by taste and demographic factors that have little relationship to region. To be sure, regional variation certainly remains. Cultural patterns may exhibit some regional variations, but it is increasingly difficult to identify people's home state based on their cultural preferences.

THE RED AND THE BLUE

But what about the much-touted "culture war" between the "blue" (Democratic) and "red" (Republican) states? Does this "color war" suggest that regional variance is growing, that the increased interest in federalism does indeed reflect an increase in identification with the state rather than the nation? To the extent that states do reflect integral communities of value, with moral and cultural views different from those of other states, then allocating certain kinds of power to the states makes sense. A traditional argument for federalism is that it permits states to coexist within a larger polity, the nation, while maintaining their distinctive local practices. In circumstances of deep disagreement on important issues, federalism allows states to agree to disagree, while remaining part of a political whole. This account of federalism depends on the presence of two factors: deep moral disagreement in the nation and relative homogeneity within the state. Without division on key principles, federalism is not necessary. If those divisions do not track geographical boundaries, then allocating power to the states will not help. On one view, the culture war between blue and red states seems to satisfy those two conditions. People in the United States seem to be divided about a variety of important moral issues, and they seem to be grouped into homogenous blue or red states. On closer examination, however, the purported color war does not support this understanding of federalism.

In the wake of the 2000 presidential election, some news accounts did indeed trumpet the divide between blue and red states. Maps that coded states by the presidential candidate receiving the most votes appeared to demonstrate a blue/red divide, with blue states clustered on the coasts and in the Northeast and northern Midwest, and red states spreading across the South, the central Midwest, and the northern Plains. Closer analysis, though, showed that this dichotomous color-coding vastly overstated regional differences. Rather than a sharp divide between blue and red states, scholars have argued that the United States is fundamentally purple.[87] Democratic and Republican leaning voters live in close proximity. State borders do not define deep ideological divisions.

Historical comparison serves to illuminate the relative decline in regional variation. One of the striking features of the blue/red map in 2000 was its similarity to the electoral map of 1860. The main difference was the reversal in the Democratic and Republican affiliations. The South was solidly Democratic in 1860. Given the bloody Civil War that followed, it would be difficult to argue that the map of 1860 did not reflect a country

deeply divided. Professor Douglas Laycock, however, has emphasized a crucial distinction between 1860 and 2000. The depth of regional variation
differed markedly. In 1860, Republicans received essentially no votes in
the southern states. Indeed, Lincoln's name did not appear on the ballot in
most of the South. By contrast, in 2000, in thirty-four of fifty states, both
major presidential candidates received more than 40 percent of the popular
vote. Even when analyzed at the county level, little geographical polarization appeared. In both the 2000 and the 2004 presidential elections, in the
majority of counties no candidate received 60 percent or more of the vote.[88]
By historical standards, this level of polarization is low. Political scientist
Philip Klinkner measured several indicators of geographical polarization
following the 2000 and 2004 elections. He found some increase in the
last few elections. However, the various measures all recorded much lower
levels of polarization than in the mid-twentieth century and the hundred
years before that.[89] Contrary to news reports of a growing blue-state/red-
state divide, the historical trajectory shows a general decline in geographical
polarization. Part of the confusion stems from the insistence on using only
two colors. If a state is defined by the majority preference in an election,
it will appear blue or red, but that coloration reflects the imposition of a
dichotomous framework. If maps showed the full range of preferences in a
state, then most states would have a purple hue. Region no longer provides
such a strong indicator of electoral preference.[90]

The view of the country as divided into a blue nation and a red nation
is misleading for another reason as well. Not only are the states purple, but
people are purple. Again, if color coded by whether they voted for George
W. Bush in 2000 or 2004, people appear blue or red. However, when ana-
lysts examine citizens' views on a broad range of issues, they find a large
common ground, with few people occupying the ideological extremes.
Contrasting streams of traditionalist and individualist morality run strongly
in the United States, but they both appear within the same people. Most
Americans feel some attraction to both principles. Discussing this moral
division, political scientist Alan Wolfe summarized the point this way: "it
is not a division between red state and blue state America; it's a division
inside every person."[91]

In an influential study, political scientist Morris Fiorina, along with co-
authors Samuel Abrams and Jeremy Pope, sought to debunk the myth of
a polarized nation.[92] In both 2000 and 2004, voters in blue and red states
showed a remarkable level of agreement on a range of issues, including im-
migration, environmental protection, school vouchers, the death penalty,
racial preferences in employment, gender equality, and the need to tolerate

others' moral views.[93] Even on the hot-button issue of abortion, a considerable degree of consensus emerged. The majority of Americans believe that abortion should be legal in some circumstances. In its 1992 decision in *Planned Parenthood v. Casey*,[94] the United States Supreme Court reaffirmed the constitutional right to an abortion before fetal viability, while allowing greater state regulation of abortion. A survey found that 58 percent of Republicans and 58 percent of Democrats approved of the decision.[95] On some issues, such as those relating to sexual identity, including gay marriage and gays in the military, the ideological divide is much greater. Even with these issues, though, the story of a deeply divided nation needs substantial qualification. Most Americans do not rank gay marriage as a particularly important issue. Further, the overall greater acceptance of homosexual rights among younger citizens suggests that over time the ideological cleavage will diminish.[96]

These studies do not dispute that some polarization exists. Overall, however, the studies conclude that it is the political elites, rather than the people, who exhibit the polarizing tendencies. The positions of Republican elected officials and party activists increasingly diverge from those of their Democratic counterparts. However, underneath that thin stratum, much less polarization occurs.[97] Nor does the public polarization track the traditional narrative of the "culture war." A recent study by political scientists Shawn Treier and Sunshine Hillygus concluded that the public was less polarized than commonly portrayed and that to the extent significant ideological differences between Democrats and Republicans did occur, they tended to track economic and not social concerns.[98]

In sum, the idea of a culture war between blue and red states is misleading. Most states are not really blue or red, but somewhere in between. Moreover, with regard to many important moral and policy questions, Republican and Democratic voters do not exhibit widely varying views. Even if we divide the country into blue states and red states, the blue and red states are not that different. Some scholars disagree,[99] and the conclusions about polarization vary with the indicators chosen and one's assessment of the significance of the differences that do appear. No one, though, argues that 2000 is the same as 1860. The overall trajectory does not suggest increasing regional variance. Mississippi is not moving farther away from Connecticut. Despite the increased emphasis on federalism, the tectonic plates of culture are shifting in the opposite direction, bringing the states closer together.

The focus on federalism has increased over the past twenty years, but politics has an increasingly national flavor. The renewed interest in federalism does not correspond to a growing differentiation among the states. In some nations, federalism provides a power-sharing arrangement that allows clashing ethnic groups to coexist within one state. That is not the story in the contemporary United States. Federalism is not an answer to the problem of how a blue nation and a red nation can inhabit the same country in peace. That problem does not exist because a blue nation and a red nation do not exist.

Neither politics nor culture has become homogenous. Political views vary sharply on some issues. Culture flowers with great diversity. States, however, no longer provide the primary identifiers in politics or culture. The diversity occurs throughout the nation rather than between different states. These nationalizing trends make the resurgence of federalism all the more puzzling. If federalism is about creating fifty areas of local control with the freedom to vary radically from each other, federalism would be quite out of step with life in the contemporary United States. It would seem odd to confer so much constitutional significance on states and interstate variation at a time when interstate variety appears to be diminishing.

Odd indeed. As I will suggest in the next chapter, to look for the revival of state particularism is to misunderstand the fundamental character of contemporary federalism in the United States. That mistake is quite understandable because of the diverse functions federalism has performed in the past in the United States and in the present across the world. This chapter began with reference to federalism and Iraq. In Iraq, federalism offers the chance for fundamentally diverse groups to coexist within a single polity. Other countries, such as Ethiopia, have looked similarly to ethnic federalism as a way to incorporate divergent communities into a modern state.[100] As I will explain, the rise of contemporary federalism in the United States has followed exactly the opposite pattern. The increasing cultural integration of the United States throughout the 1960s, 1970s, and 1980s provided the very precondition for the flowering of modern federalism. In the United States today, federalism is not the solution to ethnic strife. Rather, federalism is a powerful organizational system made possible by the relative lack of internal division.

CHAPTER TWO

Federalism Old and New

The central paradox of federalism in the United States is how a concept that emphasizes the significance of states can be gaining strength at the same time that nationalizing forces seem dominant in culture, politics, and society. How can one account for this tension? The resolution, this book argues, comes from an appreciation of the character of contemporary federalism. It is useful to think of federalism as a linked set of social theories and legal doctrines. On one account, federalism entails dividing power between the states and the national government in recognition of the profound, underlying differences among states. This book rejects that conception. As discussed in chapter 1, such fundamental divergence does not exist. So what is federalism today? To answer that question requires a brief exploration of what federalism used to be and is no longer. An account of the historical trajectory of federalism in the United States helps to explain its current character.

Federalism in the Early Republic

THE ARTICLES OF CONFEDERATION

The American Revolution left the United States an independent nation. Figuring out the best way to govern that polity proved quite difficult. The first charter of the new nation, the Articles of Confederation, adopted in 1781, reflected the concerns of those who had just endured a long struggle with a distant monarchy. The citizens of the United States feared centralized power. They had little tolerance for strong central rulers, be they in London, Philadelphia, or New York. Accordingly, the Articles left most of the governing powers with the states, providing little authority for the new national government. In view of the concern about monarchy, the new national government had no executive. Nor did it have any national courts. The citizens did not want to cede the authority exercised by their local tribunals. The national legislature had authority over foreign policy, but little domestic influence. Each state enjoyed one vote in this Congress, and the representatives functioned as delegates of their states. Some decisions required a unanimous vote of the states; other required a supermajority. The national institutions were weak and unwieldy, and intentionally so.[1] The Articles of Confederation provided little unifying structure to the new nation. In many ways, the Articles read like, and functioned like, a treaty among sovereign states.

The lack of interstate coordination provided the motivating force for the calling of a Constitutional Convention. The delegates to the Convention attempted to solve the problems of the Articles by providing a more powerful unifying force. Allocating authority between the states and the national government was the key issue facing the Framers of the United States Constitution. The Framers sought to establish a unified nation, a government emanating from We the People of the United States, while recognizing the continued preeminence of the states.[2]

THE CONSTITUTIONAL DESIGN

The story of the framing of the Constitution during that hot summer in Philadelphia in 1787 has been told often enough.[3] Many leading citizens had the view that the Articles did not provide an adequate system of governance. The problems were legion. The states erected barriers to interstate trade, stunting the national economy. The national government had no authority to address these commercial issues. Local courts sometimes favored local interests over out-of-state creditors. Without a mechanism for enforcing contracts, the interstate credit market could not function. With little authority to raise money, the national government lacked the resources to fund the military. The United States could do little to defend its citizens on the high seas. The continuing conflicts among European powers created military threats that the national government was too weak to address.[4]

The problem facing the Framers was how to create a more robust national government, while recognizing the continuing strong role of the states. The Framers sought to overcome the deficiencies of the system created by the Articles, without rekindling the fear of centralized oppression. The theory of federalism provided an important component of the solution. (Other checks on the national government, including the separation of powers and, slightly later, the Bill of Rights, provided additional safe-guards.) Federalism established a constitutional role for the states and the national government. By recognizing the constitutional status of the states, federalism appeared to foster a national government without the despotic authority of European monarchs. Indeed, given the long separate political identity of the states, only a political organization that gave a strong role to states was politically viable. Virginia had existed for over 150 years before the Declaration of Independence; Massachusetts was only slightly younger. The Constitution had to recognize that organizational reality.[5]

Power was divided between the national government and states largely along lines of subject matter. The national government addressed foreign policy, commerce among the states and with Indian tribes, and certain other defined topics. The states had primary authority in other areas. This arrangement came to be known as "dual federalism."[6] In this conception of dual federalism, the states and the national government each enjoyed exclusive authority over defined and nonoverlapping realms. Because of the mutually exclusive nature of state and national power, conflicts between the two appeared unlikely. During the debates over the ratification of the Constitution, Edmund Pendleton, a leading public figure in Virginia, em-phasized the distinction between the state and federal spheres, as follows:

> The two governments act in different manners, and for different purposes—the general government in great national concerns, in which we are interested in common with other members of the Union; the state legislature in our mere local concerns. . . . Being for two different purposes, as long as they are limited to the different objects, they can no more clash than two parallel lines can meet.[7]

The conflicts that did occur resulted from the need to work out immunities for governmental entities, to carve out special protections for state and fed-eral governments when they operated in areas generally within the jurisdic-tion of the other government.

The dispute in *McCulloch v. Maryland*[8] in 1819, for example, resulted from Maryland's attempt to subject the Bank of the United States to its state taxation authority. The United States Supreme Court held that the federal entity enjoyed immunity from such taxation. In the 1793 case of *Chisholm v. Georgia*,[9] the United States Supreme Court sought to assert its constitu-tionally authorized judicial jurisdiction over a commercial dispute with a state. This assertion of federal jurisdiction over a state aroused fears that culminated in the adoption of the Eleventh Amendment in 1795.[10]

Some areas of regulatory overlap inevitably occurred, but the courts worked to minimize the significance of this concurrence. *Gibbons v. Ogden*,[11] decided in 1824, concerned a steamboat attempting to ply its trade between New York and New Jersey. The owner had obtained a federal maritime license, but New York had granted a statutory monopoly to Robert Livingston and Robert Fulton for all steamboats in New York waters. The United States Supreme Court faced the issue of how to understand this potential overlap of state and federal regulatory authority. Justice Johnson urged a strong dual federalist approach. He argued that once it was determined that running a boat between New York and New Jersey constituted interstate commerce, the area became an exclusive federal preserve. Even if no federal license had been at issue, the states simply had no power to regulate in this area. Chief Justice John Marshall stated that this argument had "great force."[12] However, Chief Justice Marshall followed a more cautious path, asserting that the existence of a valid federal license negated any possible state regulatory authority. He declined to address whether New York might otherwise be able to regulate in this area. He thus showed some reluctance to accept or reject the possibility of overlapping state and federal power.

The existence of some kind of concurrent authority was difficult to deny. State inspection laws, for example, had effects on interstate commerce. Chief Justice Marshall insisted, however, that the purpose of the state inspection laws differentiated them from regulations of commerce. Inspection laws concerned health, not commerce. By this reliance on purpose, Chief Justice Marshall sought to preserve the regulation of commerce as a potentially exclusive federal domain.[13] States laws could reach the same targets as congressional regulations of commerce, but that concurrence did not mean that states were necessarily regulating "commerce." Rather the state regulation could be understood as reflecting the historical police power of the state. In *Gibbons*, then, Chief Justice Marshall managed to acknowledge the reality of overlapping state and federal regulation, without conceding state authority over commerce.

Nineteenth-Century Federalism

FEDERALISM AT MIDCENTURY

In 1851, in *Cooley v. Board of Wardens*,[14] the Supreme Court suggested a more receptive attitude toward concurrent federal and state regulation of commerce. The case concerned a Pennsylvania law that required vessels entering or leaving the port of Philadelphia to hire a local pilot to guide them through the harbor. Rather than attempting to fashion an argument that the Philadelphia law did not actually regulate commerce, the Court took a different tack. The Court distinguished between different kinds of commercial subjects, some requiring uniform regulation, others appropriate for local diversity. Upholding the Pennsylvania law, the Court found the regulation of pilotage to be a local topic, subject to local rules.

The *Cooley* opinion, however, did not exert much influence in its day.[15] More typical of the period were strong declarations of dual federalism, affirming the separateness of state and federal authority. Writing in 1859, Chief Justice Roger Taney described the system as follows: "The powers of the General Government, and of the State, although both exist and are exercised within the same territorial limits, are yet separate and distinct sovereignties, acting separately and independently of each other within their respective spheres."[16] The main theme of the Court's jurisprudence in this era was that the states and the national government each enjoyed largely exclusive areas of power. Even the protections of the Bill of Rights did not apply to the states. The Supreme Court held the states subject only to the much more modest protections of individual rights imposed on states in the body of the original Constitution.[17]

The actual operation of governmental affairs gave practical realization to the Court's theory of dual federalism. States enjoyed largely exclusive control over vast areas of policy, including elections, civil rights, family law, criminal law, business organization, property, and perhaps most significantly, slavery.[18] Indeed, the imperative to avoid federal regulation of slavery lent considerable support to the idea of limiting federal power. Social and economic policies differed among states. Political parties, too, had a decidedly local cast. Parties tended to organize on a state-by-state basis, and the party ideologies differed among the states.[19]

Some scholars have claimed that a more cooperative model of federalism always flourished in the United States.[20] These scholars, such as Daniel Elazar, however, tend to focus on state and federal cooperation in undertaking particular tasks, such as building roads and bridges, more generally "internal improvements" as they were then styled. Such joint projects certainly existed. Even different nations, though, can cooperate on specific tasks. The existence of joint efforts does not undermine the theoretical and practical dominance of the dual federalism paradigm.[21] In the final analysis, however, this historical debate about the relative strength of dual federalism and cooperative federalism is not central to the project of this book. No one doubts that, overall, states and the federal government have engaged in increasing cooperation over time. As discussed below, federalism has become less dual and more cooperative. More tasks fall within the shared jurisdiction of the state and national governments, and fewer come within the exclusive domain of either.

THE CIVIL WAR AND RECONSTRUCTION

The relationship of states and the national government remained a subject of controversy. The most significant debate about federalism began at Fort Sumter, ended at Appomattox Courthouse, and consumed the lives of more than half a million Americans. In some ways, the Civil War changed everything. In other ways, it changed very little.

After 1865, the possibility of secession as the ultimate expression of resistance to central authority disappeared. The Civil War established that whatever other powers states might possess, they did not have the power to exit the Union. The Thirteenth, Fourteenth, and Fifteenth Amendments to the United States Constitution provided a constitutional basis for much greater national control over the states. The Thirteenth Amendment abolished slavery, which had served as a defining prerogative of states since the founding. The first sentence of the Fourteenth Amendment nationalized the definition of state citizenship, removing from states the right to define the domain of their polities.[22] The second sentence of the Fourteenth Amendment prohibited states from interfering with due process of law, equal protection of law, and national privileges and immunities of citizenship.[23] The Fifteenth Amendment forbade states from denying the right to vote based on race. These Reconstruction Amendments removed significant areas from the exclusive domain of state control. Civil rights, election law, and certain criminal processes became matters of shared state and federal concern.[24]

Or such was the theory of the Reconstruction Amendments. In fact, the federal government retreated from its obligations to supervise the areas of joint authority. After the Compromise of 1877, national troops withdrew from the former Confederate states, and national attention largely turned elsewhere.[25] In the ironically named *Civil Rights Cases*[26] in 1883, the Supreme Court restricted the authority of Congress to guarantee equal rights. In the infamous case of *Plessy v. Ferguson*[27] in 1896, the Court held that the system of pervasive, legally enforced racial segregation in the South did not violate the constitutional command of equal protection of law.

Civil rights presented the most salient example of the continued regime of dual federalism, but other instances abounded. The federal government remained relatively weak, leaving most governing authority with the states. As one leading historian has summarized the situation, "In its quantitative dimension, the federal system of the 1880's was much closer to the government as it had been in the 1790's than it was to the post–New Deal system."[28]

Federalism in the Twentieth Century

DUAL FEDERALISM AND THE *LOCHNER* ERA

The character of federalism in the United States began to change in the 1890s. In statutes such as the Interstate Commerce Act of 1887[29] and the Sherman Antitrust Act of 1890,[30] Congress began to assert much broader authority over the national transportation system and the economy more generally. Federal regulation intruded into domains in which states had formerly enjoyed exclusive control, such as corporate law, safety regulations, and workplace rules. The overlap of state and federal power grew. The dual federalist ideal of distinct and nonoverlapping realms of state and federal authority no longer accurately described the governmental structure in the United States.[31] The United States Supreme Court, however, engaged in a kind of rearguard action, attempting to separate state and federal domains.

The Court imposed various restrictions on federal authority. The Court's response was not monolithic. It did not constrict federal authority in all areas. With respect to some topics, such as the regulation of railroads, the Court generally accepted broad federal power. In other realms as well, with proper proof of connection to interstate commerce, the Court acquiesced in new federal regulations. Thus, after initially rejecting the Grain Futures Trading Act of 1921[32] as beyond congressional authority,[33] the Court eventually upheld the law after Congress enacted a new statute with extensive findings about the need to regulate grain futures as a means of facilitating interstate commerce.[34] With regard to many subjects, however, the Court struck down federal enactments as exceeding Congress's Commerce Clause authority.[35] Sugar manufacturing, agricultural production, and industrial relations all turned out to be beyond the reach of the federal government.[36]

In keeping with its commitment to dual federalism, the Court also attempted to limit state regulation of interstate commerce. The Court used its formalistic notions of intrastate and interstate commerce to restrict both state and federal governments from overstepping their assigned domains.[37] During this period, roughly from 1890–1936, the Court applied its dormant Commerce Clause and preemption doctrines so as to curtail the exercise of concurrent state and federal authority.

Under the dormant Commerce Clause doctrine, the constitutional grant of authority to Congress to regulate interstate commerce embodies a prohibition on state regulation of interstate commerce. This prohibition flows not from the constitutional text, but from the negative implications of the affirmative grant of power to the national government. The dormant Commerce Clause limits state activity even when Congress has not regulated a particular area. With respect to activities imposing burdens on interstate commerce, the states may not act even in the face of congressional silence.

In the pre-1937 era, the Court broadly deployed the Commerce Clause to limit state regulatory activities. In *Leisy v. Hardin*,[38] for example, the Supreme Court struck down an Iowa statute that banned the sale of all intoxicating liquor. *Leisy* purported to apply the *Cooley* framework, asserting that states enjoyed concurrent authority except when national uniformity was required.[39] However, *Leisy* insisted that any matter concerning interstate commerce required national uniformity and broadly construed the content of interstate commerce. Thus, even though the statute at issue applied a neutral scheme of regulation, banning domestically produced spirits as well as imports, the Court held that the regulation constituted an impermissible burden on interstate commerce. In a characteristically formalist turn, the Court also embraced the "original package doctrine," deeming imported goods to be part of interstate commerce as long as they remained in their original package.[40] This broad construction of the state conduct that interfered with interstate commerce constricted the ability of states to regulate in important areas of local concern, if those areas also could be regulated by Congress. The dormant Commerce Clause thus minimized the overlap of state and federal authority.

Moreover, even in the areas in which concurrent state and federal jurisdiction was permitted, the Court developed a preemption doctrine to limit state power. In this period, the Court fashioned a theory of "latent exclusivity." Under this conception, states could regulate a variety of areas, but only if Congress did not enact legislation in these domains. Once Congress did act, the Court held that congressional authority was exclusive. In effect, the Court developed an expansive doctrine of field preemption, broadly interpreting congressional action as prohibiting any state regulation, even if the state rules did not conflict with the federal.[41]

Stephen Gardbaum has identified *Southern Railway Co. v Reid*[42] as a key case in the development of the doctrine. *Southern Railway* concerned a North Carolina statute that regulated the rate practices of railroads in the state. In striking down this act, the Court used language that appeared to accept the potential exercise of concurrent state and federal power, while rejecting actual instances of overlap. In certain areas, either the states or the federal government could regulate. However, if the federal government did step in, then states lost all authority. The Court stated, "It is well settled that if the state and Congress have a concurrent power, that of the state is superseded when the power of Congress is exercised."[43] Even if an area could be regulated by the state or the federal government, state and federal power could not overlap. The dual federalist framework could accept some ambiguity about where the line between state and federal authority stood, but a border was necessary. Congressional action provided the bright line that then formed a boundary dividing state from federal prerogatives.

During this period, the United States Supreme Court also vigorously applied its substantive due process doctrine to strike down state, as well as federal, laws that regulated contractual relations. In *Lochner v. New York*,[44] the Court invalidated a New York statute setting maximum hours for bakery workers. *Lochner* became a symbol of intrusive judicial review of social and economic legislation.[45] It may seem ironic that a Court committed to restricting the power of the federal legislature would take such an expansive view of the role of the national judiciary. As Robert Post has explained, the Supreme Court during this time did not view the exercise of federal judicial power as itself implicating issues of federalism. In the Court's self-conception, the judiciary protected the division of authority between states and the national government. In this view, the federal courts did not serve as agents of the national government. The courts stood above this state-federal divide. In striking down state legislation infringing on rights of property or contract, the courts did not trump state authority with federal authority. Rather, the courts enforced traditional common law concepts, emanating from the people, not identified as essentially state or federal.[46]

The Court's jurisprudence in this period illustrates an important point about dual federalism. Dual federalism does not guarantee the states any particular amount of power. Dividing state and federal authority into exclusive and nonoverlapping realms limits both state and federal governments. Depending on where the boundary between state and federal is constructed, the scope of state and federal power will vary. At some point, the subject matter limits on state and federal authority will restrict state prerogative. Further, issues aside from the scope of federal power will have significant influence on the amount of state discretion. After the adoption of the Fourteenth Amendment, the rights portions of the Constitution constrain states as well. In the *Lochner* era, it was the notion of the right to property and the right to contract, as understood by the Supreme Court, that hampered state regulatory efforts. Today, different individual rights have come to the fore.

Clearly, though, the dual federalist notion of defining realms of state and federal authority concerns only one aspect of overall state-federal relations. Dual federalism affords an incomplete account of the larger interaction of state and federal governments. The scope of individual rights and the institutional role of federal courts and other branches of the federal government exercise important influences over the relationship between state and federal governance.

THE NEW DEAL

The New Deal initiatives of President Franklin Roosevelt provided another important chapter in the history of federalism in the United States. In response to the national catastrophe of the Great Depression, President Roosevelt proposed an array of new national programs. Subsidizing farmers, protecting workers, and providing pensions for retirees became federal responsibilities. Following on the heels of the Great Depression, World War II furthered the centralizing trend. A national war effort required a strong national government.

The Court's striking down federal laws as exceeding the Commerce Clause and invalidating both state and federal statutes under the doctrine of substantive due process led to a collision between the Court and President Roosevelt. President Roosevelt attacked the Court as impeding the recovery of the nation from the ravages of the Great Depression. By 1936, the worldwide economic recession had helped to bring fascists to power in Germany and Italy. In the United States, radical movements of all kinds grew, fertilized by the disastrous economic circumstances of people throughout the country. President Roosevelt was reelected in 1936, along with tremendous Democratic majorities in Congress. The Democratic Party picked up 12 seats in the House of Representatives, bringing its total to 334, as opposed to 88 Republican members. In the Senate, the Democrats gained 5 seats, resulting in a total of 76 Democratic senators and 16 Republicans, with 4 senators from minor parties. In the wake of his electoral triumph, President Roosevelt proposed a plan to increase the size of the Supreme Court based on the number of justices exceeding seventy years of age. This "court packing" plan, as its enemies dubbed it, would immediately have given President Roosevelt six appointments. The plan eventually failed in Congress. Even with the huge Democratic majorities, President Roosevelt could not muster sufficient legislative support. The Court, however, began to change its approach to federalism. A series of retirements accelerated the transformation of the Court's doctrine.[47]

Beginning in 1937, the Court started to enlarge its conception of activity that could be regulated under the Commerce Clause. The Court did more than simply expand the subject matters on which Congress could legislate. The Court moved from a formalistic, categorical framework to a more pragmatic and instrumental approach. Whereas the Court previously had defined specific subjects on which Congress could act, the Court began to focus on the practical implications of the activity at issue, rather than on its formal characterization. Along with this change in perspective, from the formal to the functional, came a change in the conception of the judicial role. One of the key benefits of the formalistic approach of drawing lines between state and federal domains was that it was a job the courts could do. Courts had the institutional capacity to engage in such boundary maintenance activities. Once the Court adopted a more pragmatic approach, emphasizing the practical impact of an activity, judicial review inevitably became much more deferential. The justices understood that they lacked the competence to assess practical effects on commerce or to second-guess legislative determinations. The primary responsibility for evaluating effects on commerce had to lie with Congress. As the understanding of federalism changed, so too did the role of courts.

The 1942 case of *Wickard v. Filburn*[48] embodied this new approach. *Wickard* concerned the constitutionality of the federal Agricultural Adjustment Act (AAA).[49] In enacting the AAA, Congress sought to stabilize the wheat market and assist farmers by raising the prices at which they could sell their crops. The plan restricted wheat production, assigning a certain allotment to each farmer. Farmer Roscoe Filburn exceeded his quota of wheat. He claimed that the excess production was meant for consumption on his farm, not for sale on the market. Recent scholarship has cast some doubt on the notion that Filburn just wanted to set aside a few loaves for his family.[50] The Supreme Court, however, addressed the question whether Congress could regulate wheat destined for home consumption on the farm where grown.

Filburn argued that growing wheat for home use did not constitute "commerce," much less "commerce among the several states." Writing for the Court, Justice Robert Jackson upheld the AAA. Justice Jackson had no trouble rejecting a categorical focus on whether certain activity had a direct or indirect effect on commerce. In a thorough repudiation of that kind of formalistic approach, he wrote that even if Filburn's "activity be local and though it may not be regarded as commerce, it may still, whatever its nature, be reached by Congress if it exerts a substantial economic effect on interstate commerce and this irrespective of whether such effect is what might at some earlier time have been defined as 'direct' or 'indirect.'"[51] Practical considerations, "substantial economic effects," had become the key.

More difficult, however, was the question whether, as a practical matter, Filburn's homegrown wheat did affect interstate commerce. Justice Jackson began by reframing the issue. The proper focus, he asserted, was not the effect of Filburn's wheat, but rather the aggregate effect of all homegrown wheat. Justice Jackson asserted that the mere fact that Filburn's "own contribution to the demand for wheat may be trivial by itself is not enough to remove him from the scope of federal regulation where, as here, his contribution, taken together with that of many others similarly situated, is far from trivial."[52] This conceptual move gave great power to the "substantial effects" test. Without this aggregative perspective, many activities could be subdivided and fail to reach the "substantial effects" threshold. Any individual action, considered in isolation, might well have a "trivial" effect on the national market, but it was the cumulation of those "trivial" activities that constituted the market. To regulate the national market, Congress had to be able to reach the myriad small, decentralized actions that formed the market system. The power of the market came from its ability to coordinate countless individual decisions about planting, growing, reaping, buying, selling, letting lie fallow, and the like. The decentralized character of the market would not exempt it from national regulation.

Still, the question remained whether all homegrown wheat, taken together, had a substantial effect on interstate commerce. After the initial argument of the case, Justice Jackson believed that neither the materials compiled by Congress nor the trial court record established the necessary factual connection.[53] The evidence before the Court did not prove the role of homegrown wheat on the national market. Accordingly, Justice Jackson prepared two draft opinions, remanding the case for additional factual findings. This approach garnered the support of a majority of the justices.[54] Before these drafts were issued, though, Justice Jackson came to believe that it was not possible for the courts to develop adequate standards to review such factual questions. Instead, Justice Jackson concluded that it was up to Congress to assess the effects on interstate commerce.[55]

The opinion that Justice Jackson eventually prepared for a unanimous Court reflected this deference to congressional judgment. In its opinion, the Court refused to provide an independent analysis of whether the regulated activity—the production of wheat for home consumption—had a substantial effect on interstate commerce. The Court noted that the parties had "stipulated a summary of the economics of the wheat industry,"[56] and the

Court ventured a brief discussion of the volatility of the world wheat market. The Court did not, though, offer an independent judicial assessment of whether the home production of wheat had a substantial effect on interstate commerce. Instead, it deferred to the congressional resolution of that question. The Court stated: "This record leaves us in no doubt that Congress *may properly have considered* that wheat consumed on the farm where grown if wholly outside the scheme of regulation would have a substantial effect in defeating and obstructing its purpose to stimulate trade therein at increased prices."[57] The question for judicial review was not whether the activity substantially affected interstate commerce, but whether Congress could rationally so conclude. The Court no longer sought to draw formal boundaries around federal power. Given the economic realities of the complex national economy, the prior formal categories of dual federalism made little sense. State and federal power had to be understood functionally, and Congress had much greater institutional competence to make such functional assessments.

With its broad functional view of federal power, the Court had to acknowledge the overlap of state and federal authority. The acceptance of concurrent authority appeared in other aspects of the Court's evolving jurisprudence as well. Under its dormant Commerce Clause doctrine, the Court struck down state regulations that interfered with the congressional prerogative to regulate interstate commerce. In a dual federalist scheme, the dormant Commerce Clause doctrine provided a symmetrical counterpoint to the limits of congressional power under the Commerce Clause. If Congress regulated matters without a sufficient connection to interstate commerce, it would be crossing the boundary of state power and thus exceeding its Commerce Clause authority. If states regulated interstate commerce, they would be trespassing on federal turf and thus violating the dormant Commerce Clause. In this way, the Commerce Clause and the dormant Commerce Clause policed the line between state and federal domains (although, as discussed above, the *Cooley* doctrine accepted some overlap).

This notion of the dormant Commerce Clause could not survive the expansion of federal power in the post-1936 period. As with the scope of congressional power under the Commerce Clause, the restrictions on state power had to be understood functionally, not formally. Given the breadth of federal authority, the ability of Congress to regulate an area could not automatically immunize it from state supervision. With regard to the dormant Commerce Clause, the question could no longer focus on whether the challenged state law reached an activity that lay within Congress's authority to regulate. That test would now negate almost all state power. The dual federalist notion of distinct state and federal enclaves had given way to an acceptance of pervasive overlap.

The Court stopped speaking as if the states and the federal government inhabited discrete and separate realms. Justice Wiley Rutledge gave voice to this appreciation of concurrent authority in his opinion for the Court in 1946 in *Prudential Insurance Co. v. Benjamin.*[58] He wrote, "It would be a shocking thing, if state and federal governments acting together were prevented from achieving the end desired by both, simply because of the division of power between them."[59] From the perspective of dual federalism, there would be nothing shocking in understanding the important boundary between state and federal domains as inhibiting joint action. That view, though, accorded neither with the evolving character of intergovernmental relations nor with the Court's functional approach to federalism. One commentator has summarized this interactive vision as follows: "Instead of employing a 'two-value' (either/or) logic of exclusion, Justice Rutledge introduced another category of Commerce Clause thinking, based on the principle of synthesis. . . . [H]is primary emphasis was upon coordination as against separation of authority in the federal scheme."[60]

The Court transformed its dormant Commerce Clause and preemption doctrines to permit more concurrent state authority. In this new framework, only state regulations that discriminated against interstate commerce automatically violated the dormant Commerce Clause. States could burden interstate commerce, as long as the burden was not excessive in comparison with the local benefit. With regard to preemption, congressional intent became the key. Federal legislation preempted state law only if Congress intended that result. No longer did congressional action automatically occupy the field to the exclusion of the states. In both doctrinal areas, states gained significant opportunities to regulate concurrently with Congress.[61]

The themes of cases like *Wickard* and *Prudential Insurance*—concurrent authority, functionalism, and deference to Congress—persisted over the following fifty years. The Court repeatedly rejected the notion that the states exercised exclusive authority over some realm defined by a broad category, such as "local." The question of congressional authority turned on practical considerations of effects on commerce, not on categorical distinctions. The Court also followed *Wickard's* lead in understanding Congress, rather than the Court, as the body best able to assess effects on commerce. *Hodel v. Virginia Surface Mining & Reclamation Ass'n*[62] provides but one example. *Hodel* concerned the constitutionality of congressional regulation of strip mining. The plaintiffs objected that strip mining was a local activity, thus beyond the power of Congress to regulate pursuant to its authority over interstate commerce. Rejecting this argument, the Court reiterated its repudiation of the idea of categorical distinctions marking the bounds of national authority. The Court stated, "The denomination of an activity as a 'local' or 'intrastate' activity does not resolve the question whether Congress may regulate it under the Commerce Clause."[63] Rather, congressional power depended on the practical effects of the activity, which in turn was a matter for congressional decision, subject to very limited judicial oversight. As the Court explained, "Here, Congress rationally determined that regulation of surface coal mining is necessary to protect interstate commerce from adverse effects that may result from that activity. This congressional finding is sufficient to sustain the Act as a valid exercise of Congress' power under the Commerce Clause."[64] The congressional determination of the effects of strip mining on interstate commerce served to validate the legislation. In this reasoning, *Hodel* recapitulated the central message of the New Deal. Given the complexities of modern society, the national government needed to reach a vast array of activity. The judicial attempt to erect constitutional barriers to this felt necessity represented a ticket to disaster. This approach acquiesced in a vast overlap of state and federal regulatory authority.

THE CIVIL RIGHTS MOVEMENT

Along with the New Deal, the civil rights movement also dealt a strong blow to dual federalism. In striking down state-sponsored segregation, the Court's 1954 decision in *Brown v. Board of Education*[65] imposed new federal limits on state activity. The fiction of separate but equal facilities no longer sufficed to satisfy the constitutional command of equal protection. The *Brown* decision concerned the conduct of local schools, an area that traditionally lay at the heart of state prerogative. In declaring racial segregation in public schools to be unconstitutional, *Brown* federalized an important aspect of school administration. The judicial implementation of *Brown* proved largely ineffectual.[66] However, the Civil Rights Act of 1964[67] mandated school desegregation as a condition of receiving federal funds. That incentive, along with continued judicial prodding,[68] proved much more effective. In demanding that schools desegregate, the Civil Rights Act continued to undermine principles of dual federalism. The Civil Rights Act made meaningful *Brown*'s assertion of federal authority over schools.

The civil rights movement presented yet another struggle about the meaning of federalism, and once again the forces of nationalization triumphed. Claims of states' rights could not withstand the powerful moral and practical arguments favoring equal rights for African Americans. Through judicial decisions, military action, and legislative initiatives, the national government federalized the issue of racial discrimination. States lost their abilities to follow distinctive paths, marked by deep historical commitments to racial subordination. Scholars may debate whether *Brown v. Board of Education*, sending the United States Army into Little Rock, or the Civil Rights Act of 1964 succeeded in providing racial equality. The triumph of centralization, however, cannot be doubted. Indeed, the concept of federalism, with its redolence of arguments for states' rights, became tarred for a generation by its association with racism. The civil rights era represented a defeat not only for particular claims of state autonomy, but also for the very idea of decentralization. Federalism became linked to atrocities, such as the murder of three young civil rights workers in Philadelphia, Mississippi, in 1964. This kind of state-sanctioned racist violence provided the background for the comment on federalism that I mentioned at the beginning of chapter 1. It was in 1964 that a noted political scientist pronounced what appeared to be the epitaph for federalism: "if in the United States one disapproves of racism, one should disapprove of federalism."[69] Federalism, it seemed, stood firmly on the wrong side of history.

More generally, the civil rights struggle in the South focused national attention on the persistence of state-sponsored racial injustice. Aided by the relatively new medium of television, citizens throughout the United States could see government officials in the South using claims of local self-determination to justify brutal, oppressive racial practices. Federalism gained a face, or rather, a grotesque mask, in the form of segregationist officials such as Birmingham Commissioner Bull Connor, Governor Ross Barnett of Mississippi, and Governor Orville Faubus of Arkansas. The news was full of images of state and local officials claiming the right to resist federal authority. The concept of creating a sphere of protected state activity appeared dangerous, and the notion of a federalism that built on distinctive state traditions seemed pernicious. Federalism had long been associated with the concept of states as laboratories. Supporters lauded the benefits of state experimentation. The civil rights movement, though, pointed out that laboratories could produce deadly viruses as well as noble cures. The idea of federalism no longer seemed appropriate in polite society. The taint of racism was too strong. Federalism, like racism, seemed to be in decline, and as with racism, that decline seemed a cause for celebration. In the end, federalism survived, but only through a fundamental transformation.

FEDERALISM TRANSFORMED

The success of the civil rights movement both reflected and helped to create a growing national consensus on a variety of important issues. Racism came to be perceived as wrong all over the country. Sexism did as well. Racism and sexism still persist, but only as aberrant positions that may not be publicly endorsed in most circles. In every state, racism and sexism are terms of criticism. With regard to other issues as well, a national acceptance of certain fundamental principles has emerged. Illustrating the broad support for guaranteeing the rights of people with disabilities and of older Americans, Congress enacted the Americans with Disabilities Act[70] and the Age Discrimination in Employment Act[71] by huge bipartisan majorities.[72] Protecting the environment also has achieved strong popular support.[73]

Given the national consensus on many important values, the role of federalism stands ready for reevaluation. Part of the functional justification for dual federalism lay in the assumption that states formed distinctive communities of value. States differed from each other, and federalism allowed those distinctive cultural identities to flourish. Dual federalism sought to create well-defined areas in which states could develop their own cultures and societies free from national interference. The New Deal and the civil rights movement undermined this form of federalism. Effective regulation of all aspects of the economy came to be seen as the duty of the national government. The judicial effort to protect spheres of state autonomy seemed wrongheaded and delusive. The civil rights movement showed the pathologies of local control.

Yet the idea of local rule has a deep place in the culture of the United States. Suspicion of government in general, and the national government in particular, runs like a river through American history. The resistance to the large national social programs identified with President Johnson's Great Society initiative further fueled the movement for a devolution of political power. Resistance to national programs reflected a variety of different concerns. Some found the programs inefficient and patronizing. Others resisted the overall project of modest wealth redistribution.[74] Surveys showed that citizens' dissatisfaction with the federal government, in particular, increased throughout the late 1960s and 1970s.[75] These attitudes provided fertile ground for Ronald Reagan in 1980. He wanted to run against the national government, and federalism provided a traditional idiom in which to express his ideas. In accepting his party's nomination at the Republican National Convention, Reagan called for "a rebirth of the American tradition of leadership at every level of government."[76] He stated his policy that "everything that can be run more effectively by state and local governments, we shall turn over to state and local governments."[77]

In his first major rally after receiving the Republican nomination for president, Reagan traveled to Philadelphia, Mississippi, in August 1980. As the site of the murder of three civil rights workers in 1964, Philadelphia was hallowed ground for the civil rights movement. There, at the Neshoba County Fair, Reagan declared, "I believe in states' rights." He added that if elected, he would "restore to states and local governments the power that properly belongs to them."[78] In giving that speech in that place, candidate Reagan spoke to federalism's past. The continuing controversy surrounding the speech demonstrates its symbolic importance. As recently as November 2007, a dispute played out in the op-ed pages of the *New York Times* over the meaning and significance of Reagan's appearance in Neshoba County and what it reveals about the contemporary Republican Party.[79] Some commentators defended Reagan and his legacy, while others attacked him. But what is most revealing is that no one defended the speech itself. All acknowledged that an appeal to "states' rights" in Philadelphia, Mississippi, in 1980 was an unfortunate embrace of the ghost of federalism past. The disagreement concerned the larger significance of the address to the legacy of President Reagan. For present purposes, it is important to separate debates about the political strategy of the Republican Party from the analysis of federalism. In retrospect, the Neshoba speech appears as the last gasp of Old Federalism. The use of federalism as an appeal to racism is no longer politically acceptable.

Once in office, Reagan emphasized his understanding of federalism in less racially charged terms. He evoked the constitutional principle of federalism to support his decentralizing policies. The Tenth Amendment, the main textual marker of federalism in the United States Constitution, states, "The powers not delegated to the United States by the Constitution, nor prohibited by it to the States, are reserved to the States respectively, or to the people."[80] In his inaugural address, Reagan echoed that language and invoked the historical primacy of the states:

> It is my intention to curb the size and influence of the Federal establishment and to demand recognition of the distinction between the powers granted to the federal government and those reserved to the states or to the people.

All of us need to be reminded that the federal government did not create the states; the states created the federal government.[81]

In July of his first year in office, Reagan declared that his administration was "committed—heart and soul—to the broad principles of American federalism."[82] Reagan sought to implement his New Federalism philosophy through a number of decentralizing budgetary initiatives.[83]

The contemporary federalism movement differs in important ways from its predecessor. One way to note the change in federalism is by observing those who did not understand the difference. Senator Trent Lott of Mississippi became the majority leader of the United States Senate through the success of the Republican Party in capturing hostility to the national government. The Republicans found that the language of federalism struck a responsive chord with the electorate. Senator Lott, however, became the victim of this rhetoric, mistaking contemporary federalism for its predecessor. He had what might be termed a "Neshoba moment," and he did not survive it. On December 5, 2002, only a few weeks after their triumphs in the midterm elections restored Republicans to majority status in the Senate, Lott spoke at a party honoring Senator Strom Thurmond's one-hundredth birthday. Senator Lott praised Thurmond's 1948 campaign for president as the candidate of the States' Rights Democratic Party, commonly known as the "Dixiecrats."[84] The campaign had an explicit segregationist message. The party manifesto declared, "We stand for the segregation of the races and the racial integrity of each race."[85] At the celebration for Thurmond in 2002, Lott stated: "I want to say this about my state: When Strom Thurmond ran for President, we voted for him. We're proud of it. And if the rest of the country had followed our lead, we wouldn't have had all these problems over all these years either."[86] In explaining similar remarks that Lott had made in 1980, Lott's spokesman claimed that Lott meant to praise Thurmond's support for a smaller federal government.[87]

Lott, it appears, sought to salute Thurmond's embrace of federalism, of preserving a realm of state authority free from federal intrusion. The problem is that the state autonomy that Thurmond advocated in 1948 was inextricably linked to white supremacy. In 1948, that is what states wanted to do with their autonomy. The states wished to resist the encroachment of potential federal civil rights measures on the southern way of life. In accepting the nomination for president in 1948, Thurmond declared, "There's not enough troops in the Army to force the Southern people to break down segregation and admit the Negro into our theaters, into our swimming pools, into our schools and into our homes."[88] In other words, in 1948 Thurmond ran as an Old Federalist. In this conception, federalism created enclaves of state authority in which distinctive social practices could flourish.

Contemporary federalism, however, can exist only by disavowing the old. By praising Thurmond's 1948 campaign, and the Old Federalism it represented, Lott threatened to undermine modern federalism, which served as a principal campaign theme of his Republican Party. Lott's 2002 remarks eventually provoked a firestorm of controversy. Once the public debate began, Lott's leadership role in the Republican Party was doomed. Many opponents of Lott outside of the Republican Party expressed hope that he would retain his prominent office, thus tainting the party. The comments of *New York Times* columnist Bob Herbert, a critic of Lott's, were illustrative: "There are calls now for the ouster of Trent Lott as the Senate Republican leader. I say let him stay. He's a direct descendant of the Dixie-crats and a first-rate example of what much of his party has become."[89] With "supporters" like Herbert, it was not surprising that the Republican Party had to repudiate Lott. In the end, members of his own party dealt the decisive blow, with President Bush and his aides orchestrating the attack.[90] On December 20, 2002, with his support within the Republican Party eroded, Lott was forced to resign his leadership position. For federalism to remain a powerful issue for Republicans, its connection to its past had to be severed. Lott came to represent a link between contemporary federalism and its racist predecessor. That link had to be broken.

After the Republican debacle in the midterm elections of 2006, Lott managed a comeback, narrowly winning election to the post of minority whip, the number two spot in the party Senate leadership. His victory elicited much talk of "redemption." His return reflected several factors, including the party's need for his deal-making skills and the Republican senators' dissatisfaction with the Bush administration in the wake of the election defeat. Lott's work in the aftermath of Hurricane Katrina proved especially significant. He became a leader in seeking aid for the Gulf region and its inhabitants, many of whom are African American. Press reports after Lott's election noted that he had received a congratulatory call from Donna Brazile, a Democratic strategist and Louisiana native, who happens to be African American. Brazile reported that in the wake of Katrina she had asked Lott's help for her relatives in Mississippi. Brazile was quoted as saying that with regard to Katrina, Lott had been "a champion." Lott thus earned his power back in part by proving that he was not the ghost of federalism past, that he was not just a slick new version of the old Dixiecrats.[91]

The saga of the Confederate flag tells a similar tale. Georgia incorporated the Confederate battle flag into its state flag in 1956. The decision to change the flag came in the wake of southern resistance to the United States Supreme Court's 1954 decision in *Brown v. Board of Education*. Similarly, the Confederate battle flag was raised over the state capitols in Alabama and South Carolina in the early 1960s.

To many people, the battle flag appeared to glorify a regime defined by human bondage. The battle flag's embrace by the Ku Klux Klan rendered it an especially notorious symbol of racism. The battle flag also had served as a banner for the young Strom Thurmond in his Dixiecrat campaign. The leadership of the campaign actually shunned the flag because its regional associations threatened to undermine the national aspirations of the party. However, the local campaign activists used the Confederate battle flag as a campaign emblem.[92] Both the association with the Dixiecrats and the flag's display in reaction to the civil rights era marked the banner as a symbol of the bad Old Federalism. Like the Dixiecrat campaign of 1948, the battle flag tarred contemporary federalism with its racist heritage.

The flag proved somewhat more resistant to change than majority leaders, but the flag too had to give way to prove the disconnect between the Old Federalism and the New. In Alabama and South Carolina, difficult compromises were reached to move the flag from the Capitol domes to new positions, adjacent to Confederate war memorials on the grounds of the Capitols. In Georgia, the controversy had more intermediate steps with a higher political cost for the players.

In 2001, Georgia's Democratic governor Roy Barnes rammed a bill through the Democratic legislature changing the state flag. The legislation established a new flag with a state seal on a blue background and small replicas of previous flags that had flown over Georgia. This quick flag switch, along with a general surge in Republican voting and other controversial Barnes initiatives, led to Barnes's surprise defeat in his race for reelection in 2002. Although he had benefited greatly from the flag flap, the new Republican governor, "Sonny" Perdue, showed no urgency in returning to the pre-2001 flag. Instead a third, compromise flag was adopted, which did not include the offending Confederate battle flag. Luring international and out-of-state businesses to the New South proved more important than reinstating the controversial symbol of the opposition to civil rights. Governor Perdue wanted to tout Georgia as distinctive, but he also wanted to emphasize its "business-friendly" environment, which meant low wages, little union penetration, and limited regulation. Governor Perdue wished to stress the "New" in the New South, rather than its "Old South" heritage.[93]

The New Southern politicians understood the deal. It was the acceptance of civil rights, and the concomitant death of the Old Federalism, that provided the precondition for the new. The flags sometimes provided a useful political tool for mobilizing Republicans. However, in general, the flags changed as they became recognized as confusing the Old and the New Federalisms. Sonny Perdue did not want to suffer the same fate as Trent Lott.

Popular culture followed a similar path. As NASCAR sought to capitalize on its national appeal and move beyond its regional roots, it quietly ended the official use of Confederate symbols. In 1993, the organization banned a car sponsored by the Sons of Confederate Veterans, which displayed a Confederate battle flag.[94]

The Old Federalism had emphasized regional differences. Strom Thurmond and the Confederate battle flag symbolized that kind of distinctive heritage. The emergence of the New Federalism presupposed a broad national consensus on certain fundamental issues, such as civil rights. The national market and national media also served to undermine regional distinctions. This nationalization presented great opportunities. NASCAR and country music could be exported, with great profit, to the rest of the country. National and international companies could locate throughout the United States, confident that local customs would not offend their employees or their customers. Regional practices that did not travel well, particularly those that carried the baggage of prior invidious practices, had to disappear. To reap the political and economic benefits of the New Federalism, southerners had to give up their Confederate flags. The process of dispatching that powerful symbol was difficult and contested. However, the New Federalism proved to be too powerful a force. Sentimental attachment could not withstand the logic and the promise of the New Federalism.

The Old Federalism collapsed under the weight of baneful state practices that offended the nation. If federalism was a license to Ross Barnett to resist integration, federalism must be rejected. The Old Federalism was justified in part by the existence of widely divergent state values. The New Federalism builds on a foundation of consensus. The national convergence of values serves as a precondition for the resurgence of federalism. The very reason that states can be trusted with authority is that they no longer differ so much from each other. The new generation of southern governors, such as Jimmy Carter and Bill Clinton, sought to make their states more like the rest of the country, indeed to be leaders in issues of racial justice. They did not seek licenses to engage in deviant practices. This convergence of values allowed for federalism to lose its taint of racism. By 1987, political scientist William Riker had changed his view of federalism. He no longer condemned it as the means for perpetuating injustice.[95] More precisely, what had changed was federalism itself. Federalism no longer involved a celebration of distinctive, local culture.

As I will discuss, federalism was no longer about limiting the power of the federal government to protect workers or about permitting the states to tyrannize over their inhabitants. Federalism had become more a technology of power, a way of achieving generally shared aims such as prosperity, security, and justice. The goals themselves did not vary widely among the states. Rather, federalism allowed states to experiment with different means for accomplishing common ends. In this way, federalism had more in common with the personal computer and the market than with Orville Faubus. Federalism served as an efficient means for achieving goals through decentralized activity, harnessing the energy of dispersed nodes of power.

The rest of the book attempts to construct a legal framework for comprehending the New Federalism. As I will explain, contemporary discussions of federalism in the Supreme Court and among legal scholars often fail to take account of the character of the New Federalism. Too often, the old dual federalism model persists as the organizing construct. Judges and commentators understand the project of federalism as dividing state from federal power so as to protect enclaves of state prerogative. They make the mistake of Trent Lott, confusing the New Federalism for the Old. If federalism is not about maintaining boundaries, not about building Maginot Lines to protect distinctive state practices, how is federalism to be conceived? What is needed is a new metaphor and new set of legal understandings.

CHAPTER THREE

The Return of Dualism

The previous chapters consider the decline and resurgence of federalism. In them, I argue that federalism has returned to prominence through a process of transformation. The dual federalist project of drawing lines between national and state authority lost credibility, and a new era dawned, characterized by the overlap of state and federal power. The decisions of the post–New Deal United States Supreme Court, such as *Wickard v. Filburn*,[1] spelled an end to the active judicial supervision of the boundary between state and federal power. These developments in legal doctrine followed long-term trends in politics and society. Fundamental values, including equality, assumed national scope, with their expression no longer varying dramatically among the states. Local deviance from general norms was no longer tolerated. The civil rights movement exposed the moral bankruptcy of older notions of federalism and helped to usher in an era in which local communities enjoyed lesser autonomy. The Civil Rights Act of 1964,[2] which prohibited discrimination in employment, restaurants, and hotels, represented a culmination of these nationalizing trends. With the emergence of a national policy against racial discrimination, the treatment of diners at a neighborhood restaurant became a matter of federal concern. The Supreme Court's validation of the act as a legitimate regulation of interstate commerce confirmed the judicial recognition of the New Federalism.[3] At an earlier time, such morals legislation was reserved for the states, but the Court ratified Congress's judgment on the need to give legal form to the national consensus on fundamental human rights.

When the Supreme Court returned its attention to federalism in the 1990s, however, it spoke in decidedly dualist accents. The federalism that the Court sought to recapture hearkened back to pre-1937 understandings of the roles of states and the national government and the place of courts in enforcing those roles. A majority of the justices appeared to understand federalism as an exercise in drawing lines between state and federal authority. That dualist conception manifested itself in various areas of the Court's doctrine. The Court did not fully return to the earlier dual federalist conception of independent and nonoverlapping spheres of state and federal authority. Given the pervasive concurrence of state and federal functions, that notion of dual federalism has passed irretrievably into history. Under the leadership of Chief Justice William Rehnquist, however, the Court did attempt to draw some boundary between state and federal authority. The Roberts Court shows no signs of deviating from this path.[4] Because of this commitment to line drawing while accepting some overlap, I term the current Supreme Court's conception of federalism to be "dualist" rather than "dual."

By "dualist," I mean the view that principal authority for regulating a subject must be allocated to either the national government or state governments. The federal government will control certain topics, and state governments will have power over others. Unlike true dual federalism, dualist federalism can accept a large realm of coextensive authority; many matters may be subject to concurrent regulation by the state and national governments. The subjects of regulation, however, remain quintessentially state or federal. Thus, in this view, family law remains a quintessentially state subject, even if a certain amount of federal intrusion is tolerated.[5] Conversely, international commerce remains a quintessentially federal subject, even if some state regulation is permitted.[6] Some subject areas lie so close to the heart of quintessentially state or federal power that no regulations by the other government are acceptable. Thus, possession of guns in schools or mere interpersonal violence are outside of the boundaries of federal authority,[7] while addressing the fate of European Holocaust-era insurance policies lies beyond the realm of state power.[8] As I will explain, beginning in the 1990s, the United States Supreme Court adopted this dualist approach.

Following the lead of the Court, contemporary legal scholars also generally debate federalism in dualist terms. Scholars often express disagreement with the federalism decisions of the Court, but they adopt the dualist premises of the Court's understanding of federalism. Whether scholars praise or decry federalism, they focus on the dualist conception of federalism by framing the issue as one concerning where to place the appropriate line between state and federal authority.

As the previous chapters explain, dualism is a Procrustean bed. The dualist mindset divides the social order into the "local" and the "national." These terms, however, no longer have substantial referents. The local and the national cannot be isolated. Society does not come packaged in those boxes. This chapter discusses the harms that come from trying to force the world into these outdated categories. Strange contortions result from attempts to shape the law to conform to nonexistent templates. Further, dualism offers no resources for addressing the central question of contemporary federalism, which is how to manage the interaction of state and federal power. In the real world, state and federal problems and programs overlap and intersect. In ignoring this reality, dualism provides no guidance on how best to use the interplay of state and federal authority to advance important goals.

This chapter first reviews the dualist underpinnings of the current Supreme Court doctrine and the unfortunate results of the Court's dualist approach. It then turn to an examination of the scholarly commentary. Working within a dualist framework, scholars have developed functional understandings of federalism. Various theories seek to explain the purposes that federalism serves and the benefits to be derived by dividing authority between the states and the national government. These functional accounts then attempt to advance the dualist project of drawing the proper lines between state and federal power. I argue that because they are mired in dualism, these theories are doomed to failure. They do, however, point the way to the necessary reconceptualization.

The Doctrinal Costs of Dualism

Many critics decry the United States Supreme Court for the supposed inconsistency of its federalism cases. In addressing the scope of federal power, the Court has limited the reach of the national government, professing concern for maintaining the autonomy of the states. On the other hand, in cases considering the limits of state authority, the Court often has invalidated state law as unduly interfering with federal prerogatives. So, critics ask, does the Court like states or not? Is the Court really concerned about preserving a realm for state power, or is the Court bent on some kind of libertarian project of striking down as much regulation as possible, be it federal or state?[9]

By focusing on the dualist underpinnings of the Court's doctrine, this chapter offers a partial defense of the Court. From a dualist perspective, the Court's cases limiting federal authority and limiting state authority can be harmonized. The Court is engaged in boundary maintenance, preserving enclaves of distinctively federal and distinctively state authority. Both state and federal laws can violate constitutional principles of federalism when they cross into the area exclusively allocated to the other government.

The problem with the Court's jurisprudence is not internal inconsistency, but external inconsistency. While internally coherent, the Court's view of federalism does not match the actual circumstances of federalism in the contemporary United States. The Court attempts to build a constitutional jurisprudence on the concepts of "truly local" and "truly national," but those categories do not align with social reality. The Court's federalism is the Old Federalism of distinctive state cultures, rather than the New Federalism of an integrated national community.

The Court's project of reconstructing a federalism that no longer exists has substantial policy costs. In the name of preserving state prerogative, the Court has threatened civil rights enforcement, environmental protection, and a host of other important initiatives. State employees subject to discrimination based on age and disability may have no remedy.[10] Congress has less authority to safeguard environmentally sensitive wetlands.[11] Federal laws may go unenforced.[12] At the same time, to protect an exclusive federal realm, the Court has struck down significant state regulations. The Court has applied its preemption doctrines to prevent states from providing common law remedies for harmful conduct.[13] Under the dormant Commerce Clause, the Court has invalidated state efforts to address local problems, such as waste disposal.[14] The Court's dualist approach has narrowed the scope of both federal and state authority in important areas.

UNDULY RESTRICTING THE FEDERAL GOVERNMENT

The New Federalism of the Supreme Court constrains the power of the federal government in three main areas. In each realm, the Court applies a dualist framework, seeking to separate state and federal authority. The Court's new cases deviate dramatically from its prior decisions, which had accepted a vast overlap of state and federal power.

The first line of current doctrine concerns the ability of the federal government to regulate activities conducted by state governments. Even while the Supreme Court had acquiesced in comprehensive national regulation of the economy after 1937, the Court had occasionally expressed concern over federal regulation of states. In 1976, for example, the Court had held in *National League of Cities v. Usery* that Congress could not constitutionally apply the federal Fair Labor Standards Act to state or city employees performing "traditional governmental functions,"[15] such as police officers and firefighters. In dualist fashion, the Court carved out an area of exclusive state control. The power to regulate the wages of state employees was denied to the federal government, and the courts would enforce a barrier against federal intrusion into this protected sphere.

In 1985, however, the Supreme Court shifted course and overruled *National League of Cities*. Indeed, in *Garcia v. San Antonio Metropolitan Transit Authority*,[16] the Court appeared to disclaim judicial supervision in this area. Instead, the Court relied on the political process in Congress to resolve federalism-based objections to the national government's regulation of states. In the Court's view, the states could protect themselves in Congress. Writing for the five-justice majority, Justice Blackmun stated, "The principal and basic limit on the federal ... power is that inherent in all congressional action—the built-in restraints that our system provides through state participation in federal government action."[17] The Court thus abandoned its dualist project in this realm. The regulation of state employees lay within the jurisdiction of both states and the national government.

In 1992, dualism reemerged. With Justice Clarence Thomas replacing Justice Thurgood Marshall, a new dualist majority gained ascendancy. In *New York v. United States*,[18] decided in Justice Thomas's first term, the Court returned to the idea of maintaining realms of exclusive state prerogative. *New York v. United States* presented the question of the scope of federal authority to require states to regulate in accordance with a federal plan. The case concerned the disposal of low-level radioactive waste, a classic Not In My Backyard (NIMBY) problem. Radioactive material exists in many useful products, such as smoke detectors, watch dials, medical equipment, and materials used at nuclear power plants. Disposing of the material is the problem. The radioactive waste must be isolated from humans for long periods of time, sometimes hundreds of years, and millions of cubic feet must be disposed of each year.[19] When states could not agree on how to store the waste, they asked the federal government to devise a solution. In collaboration with state governments, Congress designed a plan of incentives and penalties to induce each state to make provision for the waste produced in that state. New York initially supported the process leading to the federal regulations, but when it found compliance to be onerous, it filed suit, seeking to have the federal plan declared unconstitutional.[20]

The Court voided the plan as violating constitutional principles of federalism. While Congress could create incentives for state cooperation, the Court held, Congress could not "commandeer" the regulatory apparatus of a state, dictating regulations. The Court emphasized the importance of separating state from federal areas of control.[21] The state regulatory apparatus must remain a zone protected from federal interference. Based on this theory, the Court struck down the low-level radioactive waste guidelines as unduly intruding on the state's regulatory autonomy. In *Printz v. United States*,[22] the Court extended its anti-commandeering doctrine to prohibit the federal government from requiring states to enforce federal law. In *Printz*, the Court held that Congress could not require local law enforcement officers to enforce the background checks mandated by the federal Brady Handgun Violence Prevention Act.[23]

In these anti-commandeering cases, the Court did not reverse *Garcia*. The Court did not reclaim the full realm of exclusive state control recognized in *National League of Cities*. By the 1990s, the idea of exempting certain state and local employees from all federal regulation did not have many followers on the Court. Most workers, public and private, enjoyed a variety of workplace safeguards, including protection from discrimination based on race, gender, religion, disability, and age. To prohibit the federal government from extending these civil rights protections to state workers smacked too much of the bad Old Federalism of the pre–civil rights era. Nevertheless, in its anti-commandeering doctrine, the Court has tried to create some kind of state sphere protected from federal intrusion.

The second area in which dualism flourishes is sovereign immunity. In a series of decisions stretching over two hundred years, the Court had wrestled with the proper scope, if any, of the immunity of states in federal court. In certain instances, the Court found, federal courts could not exercise jurisdiction over states. By the 1970s, the doctrine that had evolved generally prohibited private individuals from bringing federal suits against states for money.[24] However, many exceptions existed, offering broad possibilities for individual redress. Injunctions were permitted,[25] and Congress had the ability to abrogate states' immunity when enforcing the Thirteenth, Fourteenth, and Fifteenth Amendments to the United States Constitution.[26] Adopted in the wake of the Civil War, these amendments prohibited slavery, imposed equal protection and due process constraints on states, and banned racial qualifications for voting. Each of these amendments contained a clause specifically granting to Congress the power to enforce the provisions of the amendment.[27]

In *Pennsylvania v. Union Gas*[28] in 1989, the Supreme Court took a further step in holding that Congress could abrogate states' sovereign immunity when legislating pursuant to the Interstate Commerce Clause. The Commerce Clause covered a much wider array of federal activity than did the enforcement clauses. Thus, *Union Gas* significantly increased the breadth of Congress's authority to eliminate states' immunity. In *Union Gas*, the Court effectively disclaimed a judicial line-drawing function. Given the broad abrogation power conferred on Congress, it would be primarily the job of the federal legislature, not the federal judiciary, to determine to scope of state sovereign immunity.

That rejection of dualism, though, did not endure. In 1996, in *Seminole Tribe v. Florida*,[29] the Court overruled *Union Gas* and created another realm into which federal authority could not reach. The zone protected by the sovereign immunity doctrine is especially strange. Under cases such as *Garcia*, Congress has the authority to require states to pay a minimum wage to their employees. However, if a state violates the federal law, the employees cannot sue for their illegally withheld wages. The state employees have a right without a remedy, a situation that contradicts the traditional legal maxim, often rendered in the Latin, *ubi jus ibi remedium*.

Such was the fate of Patricia Garrett. Garrett, a registered nurse, worked for the University of Alabama at Birmingham Hospital, as director of nursing for OB/gyn/neonatal services. She was diagnosed with breast cancer and underwent a lumpectomy, followed by radiation treatment and chemotherapy. She first worked during her treatment, but then took a leave of absence. When she came back to work, she was transferred and demoted.[30] The Americans with Disabilities Act (ADA) prohibits discrimination based on actual or perceived disability.[31] The ADA applies to the states. However, because her employer was the state, Garrett could receive no compensation for her employer's violation of the act. Whereas other employees in her situation would have received back pay, that monetary relief was not available to her. The state's sovereign immunity deprived her of a meaningful remedy. The Court's protection of state autonomy thwarted the national consensus against disability discrimination.

The anti-commandeering and sovereign immunity doctrines illustrate the difficulty in executing the dualist project. The Court seeks to create enclaves of exclusive state control, but these areas have an odd shape. Federal power cannot be constrained by means that would fundamentally undermine the national role in protecting basic rights. So, Congress can extend civil rights laws to all state and local employees, and the employees can use injunctions to enforce these laws, but the employees cannot bring damages actions against states to recover their lost wages. The Court thus fashions protected reservations of state power that have little theoretical coherence. The walls that the Court constructs do little to protect state prerogative, but they impose severe burdens on particular individuals who are unlucky enough to require full federal protection, including a monetary remedy, for the violation of their rights.

The Interstate Commerce Clause completes the dualist trifecta. Since the New Deal, the Interstate Commerce Clause has served as the principal constitutional authorization for congressional action. When the Court upheld Congress's authority to prohibit discrimination based on race and gender, for example, it was on the Interstate Commerce Clause that the Court relied.[32] Beginning in 1995, in its cases interpreting the Interstate Commerce Clause, the Court has attempted to distinguish the "truly local" from the "truly national."[33] The Court generally has invoked some concept of "commercial activity" to define that boundary. The national government may regulate commercial activity, but has much less ability to regulate noncommercial activity. The distinction between commercial and noncommercial activity, however, turns out to be difficult to define and employ.[34] Consider a law that prohibits construction in an environmentally sensitive area so as to protect migratory birds.[35] Is the relevant activity construction or birds? Does it matter if the goal of protecting the birds is to facilitate the commercial activities connected with bird watching and hunting? Since 1937, the Court had allowed Congress broad latitude in answering these questions. Starting in 1995, the Court attempted to apply the distinction itself, asserting that although the commercial/noncommercial distinction may not work well, any distinction is better than no distinction.

The Court spelled out this focus on the commercial/noncommercial divide over the course of two cases, *United States v. Lopez*[36] and *United States v. Morrison*.[37] Alfonso Lopez Jr., a twelfth-grade student at Edison High School in San Antonio, brought a .38 caliber handgun to school. When school officials discovered the gun, state charges were filed against Lopez. Subsequently, federal authorities prosecuted Lopez for violation of the federal Gun-Free School Zones Act, which prohibits possessing a gun within a thousand feet of a school.[38] When Lopez's case came to the Supreme Court in 1995, the Court struck down the Gun-Free School Zones Act as beyond Congress's power under the Commerce Clause. The Court emphasized that possessing a gun was not a commercial or economic activity.

United States v. Morrison concerned the civil enforcement provisions of the Violence against Women Act (VAWA). Christy Brzonkala was a student at Virginia Tech who was allegedly raped by two members of the Virginia Tech football team, Antonio Morrison and James Crawford. During a Virginia Tech disciplinary hearing, Morrison admitted having sexual contact with Brzonkala despite the fact that she had twice told him no. Morrison was convicted by school disciplinary panels on two occasions, but the school administration set aside the punishments. In the end, the school and the state decided to take no action against Morrison or Crawford.[39] Brzonkala filed suit against Morrison and Crawford under the VAWA, which provided a civil cause of action for violent crimes motivated by gender.

As in *Lopez*, the Court struck down the statute. Writing for the majority, Chief Justice Rehnquist held that the VAWA exceeded Congress's power under the Commerce Clause. The opinion reiterated *Lopez*'s concern with distinguishing between the "truly local" and the "truly national,"[40] and as in *Lopez* emphasized that in the majority's view, the statute purported to reach noncommercial conduct.

In *Lopez*, Chief Justice Rehnquist defended the commercial/noncommercial distinction in language that, on examination, is remarkably revealing:

> Admittedly, a determination whether an intrastate activity is commercial or noncommercial may in some cases result in legal uncertainty. But, so long as Congress' authority is limited to those powers enumerated in the Constitution, and so long as those enumerated powers are interpreted as having judicially enforceable outer limits, congressional legislation under the Commerce Clause always will engender "legal uncertainty."[41]

Chief Justice Rehnquist acknowledged the inevitable problems in trying to draw lines between state and federal authority. In his view, though, if the Court was going to try to enforce federalism, it would have to draw lines. Dualism appeared in this account both as a conception of constitutional federalism and as a concomitant theory of the judicial role. Federalism means some firm limitation on federal power, and the way courts enforce that kind of concept is by drawing lines such as commercial/noncommercial.

The chief justice's argument thus gestured toward a theory of institutional competence. Drawing lines is something that courts can do. Some judicially administrable approach must be adopted; so some line must be drawn. The commercial/noncommercial distinction functions as a (relatively) administrable standard for courts to apply. Commentators, too, have defended the commercial/noncommercial distinction on the basis that some judicially administrable standard is required and this standard functions reasonably well.[42]

These defenses of the commercial/noncommercial distinction beg the most important questions. The chief justice asserted the need to distinguish between the "truly local" and the "truly national." This dualist commitment requires some means of enforcement. The commercial/noncommercial dichotomy holds out the promise of providing some kind of judicially administrable way of advancing the dualist project. The commercial/noncommercial distinction may be unclear, but it is better than nothing. But why must there be a distinction between the "truly local" and the "truly national"? What if that distinction no longer has meaning in contemporary society? Further, why must the courts take the lead in enforcing some division? To defend a standard on the basis that it is judicially enforceable places the Court before the Constitution. The first issue should be determining the proper relationship of the state governments and the national government. Only after this inquiry has run its course can the appropriate role for a court be decided. The job of the courts is to give meaning to the Constitution. It is not the job of the Constitution to find a role for courts. The content of federalism cannot be determined on the basis of what would be easy for the courts to enforce.

Lopez and *Morrison* represented a kind of oedipal revolt. The dualist approach undertaken by Chief Justice Rehnquist implicitly rejected the reasoning of Justice Robert Jackson, the man for whom Chief Justice Rehnquist had clerked. As discussed in the last chapter, when Justice Jackson contemplated the reality of an integrated national economy and the obliteration of any practical distinction between the local and the national, he took a very different path. Rather than impose a judicially mandated dualism, Justice Jackson deferred to Congress. Recall that in the *Wickard* case, Justice Jackson dispatched the Court's prior dualism. He stated that even if the "activity be local and though it may not be regarded as commerce, it may still, whatever its nature, be reached by Congress if it exerts a substantial economic effect on interstate commerce."[43] Speaking for the Court a half century before *Lopez*, Justice Jackson disavowed the judicial effort to distinguish the "local" from the "national." But with *Lopez* and *Morrison*, dualism has returned to the Commerce Clause.

The influences of this dualist framework have been felt in other areas in addition to guns in schools and violence against women. The regulation of environmentally sensitive wetlands has been a particular focus of controversy. In two decisions, *Solid Waste Agency of Northern Cook County v. United States Army Corps of Engineers* (SWANCC)[44] and *Rapanos v. United States*,[45] the United States Supreme Court limited the ability of the federal government to protect wetlands. Though the cases turned on issues of statutory construction, the Court adopted a narrow reading of the Clean Water Act[46] out of concern that a broader interpretation would involve unconstitutional federal regulation of noncommercial activity.[47] The full effect of the decisions has not yet become clear. One study has estimated that under a broad interpretation of *SWANCC*, the federal government would lose the power to regulate 80 percent of wetlands.[48] Decided in 2006, *Rapanos* indicates that the Roberts Court will continue the dualist path of the Rehnquist Court. This conclusion comes as no surprise. As lower court judges, both Chief Justice Roberts and Justice Alito demonstrated their dualist sensibilities. In *Rancho Viejo, LLC v. Norton*,[49] for example, the United States Court of Appeals for the District of Columbia Circuit considered the application of the Endangered Species Act[50] to a commercial development. The development plan had run afoul of the act because it threatened the arroyo southwestern toad, an endangered species. The court held that the commercial nature of the development brought this application of the act safely within Congress's authority under the Commerce Clause. Then-Judge Roberts criticized his court's decision, suggesting that the court should have analyzed the commercial impact of killing the toads, rather than focusing on the larger development.[51] Similarly, then-Judge Alito dissented from a decision upholding the federal ban on the possession or transfer of a machinegun.[52] In these cases, both Roberts and Alito suggested a dualist approach under which courts should carefully scrutinize congressional action so as to protect some zone of local authority, as opposed to the *Wickard* Court's deference to congressional judgments about the need for national regulation.

In view of the Supreme Court's construction of the Commerce Clause in *Lopez* and *Morrison*, lower courts continue to debate the constitutionality of certain applications of the Endangered Species Act.[53] The Supreme Court's dualist approach also has led some lower court judges to question the constitutionality of the Freedom of Access to Clinic Entrances Act (FACE),[54] a law designed to protect abortion clinics.[55]

So far, while troubling theoretically, the practical effects of the Court's restriction of federal authority have been limited. Lower courts generally have upheld the constitutionality of federal statutes, and Congress can usually find some way to achieve its intended goals.[56] The malleability of the categorical distinctions that the Court employs, however, makes it difficult to predict exactly what limits the Court will impose.

UNDULY RESTRICTING STATE POWER

The most significant victims of the Court's dualist approach have been the states. The same dualist federalism that creates regions of exclusive state authority also protects enclaves of federal power. State laws that intrude into federal domains are struck down. Just as in the pre-1937 period, strict enforcement of the limits of the Commerce Clause accompanies a robust view of the breadth of preemption and the dormant Commerce Clause. Lines must be drawn by courts to protect areas of state and federal hegemony. The dualist perspective tolerates overlap, but seeks sovereign clarity.

The areas in which the Court most actively polices the intersection of state and federal affairs are federal preemption and the dormant Commerce Clause.[57] Both topics concern state activity that does relate to commerce and is concededly within the scope of federal power. The question for the Court is how broadly states may act in areas in which the federal government clearly has authority. These doctrines present the converse of Commerce Clause decisions such as *Lopez* and *Morrison*. The Commerce Clause cases address situations in which the federal government has expressed a clear desire to regulate an area, and the Court has intervened to protect interests that the states may or may not have.[58] In cases raising issues under federal preemption and under the dormant Commerce Clause, the states have expressed a clear desire to regulate, and the question is whether the courts should intervene to protect an interest that the federal government may or may not have.

In these areas, the focus on drawing lines between state and federal authority has restricted state power. The Court often has been hostile to state regulation of activities that are, or could be, subject to concurrent federal law. Here, too, the Court has sought to erect a barrier between state and federal realms, broadly construing the scope of state conduct that impermissibly infringes on federal prerogative. In both the preemption and dormant Commerce Clause contexts, the Court has struck down a considerable array of state regulations based on statutory or constitutional foundations that could most charitably be termed modest at best.[59]

The Dualism of Preemption

As discussed in chapter 2, the Court in earlier periods followed a doctrine of latent exclusivity.[60] In a variety of areas, states could regulate, unless the federal government entered the field. Once the national government acted, that realm became an exclusive federal enclave. Any state laws in the area became invalid, even if they did not conflict with the federal law. The very activity of federal regulation broadly preempted the field, ousting the state of any regulatory authority. Latent exclusivity constituted a dialectical perspective on dual federalism. The federal and state governments would operate in separate, nonoverlapping spheres, but their proper domains were not set in advance. Instead, their separate spheres were recognized on an ongoing basis depending on where the federal government chose to act.

The Court has not formally returned to an attitude of latent exclusivity. Nevertheless, the broad interpretation of the preemptive effect of federal statutes hearkens back to this earlier period. The Court creates a wide protective band, preempting state laws that might interfere with federal interests. As with limitations on congressional power, the Court's dualist approach to preemption entails its actively drawing lines delimiting the proper scope of governmental activity.[61]

Geier v. American Honda Motor Co.[62] exemplifies the Court's dualist framework. *Geier* concerned the ability of a state law tort system to hold a manufacturer liable for an allegedly unsafe automobile. The connection to commerce was clear, and no one doubted the constitutional power of Congress to regulate this area. Nor did anyone question the general authority of the state to impose liability for unsafe products. *Geier* stood in the vast area of concurrent state and federal jurisdiction. The Court's dualist understanding of federalism offered little guidance, and the state authority received no protection.

The specific question presented in *Geier* was whether federal automobile regulations preempted a state law tort action that sought to impose liability based on the manufacturer's failure to equip an automobile with an airbag.[63] The federal statute at issue contained both an express preemption provision and a savings clause, which stated that "[c]ompliance with" a federal safety standard "does not exempt any person from any liability under common law."[64] The Court held that neither the express preemption provision nor the savings clause applied. Falling back on "ordinary preemption principles," the Court concluded that the state tort suit was preempted because it "stood as an obstacle" to the accomplishment of a federal objective.[65]

Writing for a four-justice dissent, Justice Stevens declared, "This is a case about federalism."[66] The majority made no explicit reference to federalism, but its approach manifested its strong dualist presuppositions. In its invocation of "obstacle preemption," the Court showed no particular concern for accommodating the overlap of state and federal interest or power. Rather, in accord with dualist premises, the Court viewed concurrent regulation with suspicion. To the Court, the existence of a federal regulatory scheme suggested a congressional desire to prohibit concurrent state oversight.

Geier is just one of several decisions in which the Court has insisted on a wide sweep of federal preemptive authority.[67] As Caleb Nelson has demonstrated, the Court has developed a broad concept of conflict preemption under a theory of "obstacle preemption."[68] Under the "obstacle preemption" doctrine, a state law will be preempted if a court concludes that the state law will hinder the accomplishment of the purposes underlying the federal law. The Court has deployed this doctrine to strike down state regulations that it finds in tension with a federal statute, without regard to whether the state law actually conflicts with some textual provision of the federal enactment.[69] As evidenced by *Geier*, this approach narrows the scope of state authority in areas of concurrent state and federal regulation.

In areas relating to foreign affairs, the Court has demonstrated even greater reluctance to accept overlapping state and federal regulation. The Court has applied its dualist approach to strike down a variety of state programs intended to augment federal efforts. These kinds of state initiatives in the United States parallel the growth of local and regional authority throughout the world.[70]

The dispute over Holocaust-era insurance policies presents a notable example of the Court blocking state plans. Before World War II, insurance policies were common investment and savings vehicles for European Jews. The policies were especially popular in this turbulent period because they often designated payment in relatively secure currency, such as United States dollars. Estimates of the value of such insurance policies owned by Jewish families range from $17 billion to $200 billion in today's currency.[71] As part of its confiscation of Jewish assets, the Nazi government in Germany took a number of steps to obtain the value of the policies. One scheme occurred in November 1938 in the wake of *Kristallnacht*, a government-sponsored rampage of vandalism and looting of Jewish synagogues, businesses, and homes. Jews owned insurance policies that covered an estimated $270 million of the damage in today's dollars. However, the Nazi government ordered the insurance companies to pay the proceeds to the state, rather than to the policy holders. The government ended up settling the claims with the insurance companies for a fraction of their value.[72] Soon thereafter, the Nazi regime began outright confiscation of the insurance policies.[73]

After the war, even policies that escaped confiscation would likely not be paid. Beneficiaries had difficulty documenting the fate of the insureds, and insurance companies created obstacles to payment, including refusing to assist in locating policies and asserting that the policies had lapsed because of unpaid premiums. Claims for reparations for the insurance policies, along with other claims, became entangled in Cold War politics. After initially promoting restitution claims, the western Allies signed the London Debt Agreement in 1953, which effectively suspended all claims against Germany pending an ultimate postwar treaty. West Germany did enter into several compensation agreements and had paid more than $60 billion in compensation by 2000. However, many kinds of claims, including those against the insurance companies, remained unpaid. It was not until the re-unification of Germany in 1990 that litigation against German companies could proceed. In the *Krakauer* case, the German Federal Constitutional Court held that the reunification treaty satisfied the terms of the London Debt Agreement, thus lifting the moratorium on claims against German industry.[74]

Extensive litigation seeking compensation began in the 1990s. Prodded by class action suits to recover unpaid policies, the European insurance companies organized the International Commission on Holocaust-Era Insurance Claims (ICHEIC) in 1998. ICHEIC eventually included vari-ous European insurance companies, the National Association of Insurance Commissioners (consisting of state insurance commissioners), European governments, Holocaust survivor organizations, and the State of Israel. Chaired by former United States secretary of state Lawrence Eagleburger, ICHEIC's goal was to set up a process for resolving compensation claims relating to the insurance policies. The insurance claims constituted only one part of the overall compensation litigation. Other suits sought recovery from banks for Holocaust-era accounts and from companies that employed slave labor. The defendant companies came from several European coun-tries, including Austria, France, Germany, and Switzerland.

In an attempt to resolve the compensation litigation, President Bill Clin-ton and German Chancellor Gerhard Schroeder entered into an executive agreement in 2000 setting up the German Foundation to address Holo-caust-era compensation claims. Germany agreed to provide funding of 10 billion deutsche marks (approximately $5 billion) contributed equally by the government and German industry. Similar agreements followed with other countries. With regard to insurance claims, the United States and Ger-many agreed that the German Foundation would work with, and provide funding for, the ICHEIC process.[75]

Many claimants became frustrated by the ICHEIC procedures. They complained that the process was slow and imposed burdensome eviden-tiary requirements. Further, the insurance companies resisted publishing full lists of the unpaid policies, making it difficult for potential claimants to identify and document relevant policies. A report in *Forbes* magazine in May 2001 found that 70,000 claims had been filed, but that ICHEIC had offered compensation in only 496 cases. By November 2001, 797 claims had been resolved, with that number climbing only to 3,006 in April 2003. Payments averaged about $12,000 per claimant.[76]

California pursued its own efforts to promote the payment of insurance claims. The state legislature used its authority over insurance licensing to require the state Department of Insurance to investigate insurers' treatment of Holocaust-era claims. In 1999, the legislature enacted a statute requiring insurers doing business in California to disclose the details of insurance policies issued in Europe from 1920 to 1945. The duty extended to corporate affiliates.[77]

California thus sought to supplement the ongoing and only moderately successful efforts of the federal government. The insurance companies challenged the California statute, and in *American Insurance Ass'n v. Garamendi* in 2003, the United States Supreme Court invalidated the state law, holding it preempted. Normally, preemption cases involve finding a federal law that conflicts with state law. In this case, no such federal law existed. The Clinton-Schroeder executive agreement had the force of law, but it did not contain a provision preempting state remedies. Nevertheless, by a 5–4 vote, the Court held that the California law was invalid because it interfered with the national government's control of foreign relations.[78]

Garamendi reflects the power of a dualist approach to federalism. The California statute did not conflict with the ICHEIC process. Insurers could comply both with the ICHEIC procedures and the statute. Indeed, the disclosures required by California could enhance the ICHEIC process by assisting potential claimants in identifying relevant policies. However, a majority of the Supreme Court found it important to demarcate clear boundaries beyond which states could not venture. California had trespassed into the domain of foreign affairs, thus exceeding its realm of authority.

The majority justified its decision by asserting that California's chosen policy differed from that of the federal government. Writing for the Court, Justice Souter colorfully characterized the conflict as follows: "California seeks to use an iron fist where the President has consistently chosen kid gloves."[79] Of course, whenever a regulator acts in a particular area, one could argue that the regulator has chosen not to do anything else. By relying on the ICHEIC process, the federal government in some sense "chose" not to require disclosure on pain of losing one's business license. This kind of reasoning, however, replicates the classic dualist approach of latent exclusivity. Once the federal government acts, the states are prohibited from intervening, for the federal government has implicitly chosen not to do whatever it did not do. Concurrent regulation becomes impossible. This approach refuses to contemplate the possibility that regulatory activity may be partial or incomplete. A regulator may not attempt to cover the field with comprehensive regulations. A regulator may impose one set of rules and not another not because it rejects the second course of action but because it is taking one step at a time. Additional regulations need not contradict, but rather may advance, the regulator's goals. But in *Garamendi* and other preemption cases, the Court opted for a presumption of exclusivity, not inclusivity. Indeed, the language of the Court's opinion in *Garamendi* suggests potential exclusivity even in the absence of federal action. The states, it seems, have no business meddling in matters involving foreign governments. Lines must exist between state and federal authority, and California crossed the line.

The ICHEIC process concluded in March 2007. The organization reported receiving 91,558 eligible claims and reported that 48,263 offers of compensation resulted, totaling $300,090,000.[80] Of these amounts, 31,284 claims were considered "humanitarian" claims, meaning that ICHEIC considered the claim to be based on merely anecdotal information. These "humanitarian" claims received $1,000 each as a symbolic payment. It is difficult to gauge the overall success of the process. Some, however, believe the process clearly remains inadequate. In the same month that the ICHEIC process ended, the federal Holocaust Insurance Accountability Act[81] was introduced in Congress. Among other provisions, the bill requires insurance companies to reveal their Holocaust-era insurance policies, exactly the regulation that California attempted to impose in 1999 and that was invalidated in *Garamendi*. The proposed legislation represents a kind of federal learning from a state experiment. It is notable that the drafters seek to avoid the exclusivist conclusions of the Supreme Court's dualist federalism. This federal disclosure proposal contains a provision expressly disclaiming any preemptive effect on state law, and the bill purports to take advantage of concurrent state efforts. The delay caused by the *Garamendi* decision, however, may impose insuperable obstacles. The ICHEIC process has concluded, and the insurers will likely resist the prospect of any future payments.[82]

Dualism and the Dormant Commerce Clause

The Court has maintained a similarly broad understanding of the kind of state regulatory authority prohibited by the dormant Commerce Clause.[83] The Court's doctrine has occasioned widespread criticism. Both commentators[84] and justices[85] decry it as unprincipled and without foundation. As Dean Jim Chen has noted, the term "quagmire" has become commonplace in characterizing dormant Commerce Clause doctrine.[86] Maxwell Stearns recently captured the distinction of the dormant Commerce Clause as a much-maligned doctrine with a broad application:

Despite these general criticisms of the doctrine, in the name of the dormant Commerce Clause, the Court has significantly limited the power of states to regulate across a wide range of subject areas, including train and truck safety, imports and exports of myriad goods and services, the conditions for the intake and outflow of solid and liquid waste, and insurance and corporate law.[87]

The Court's renewed interest in limiting the Commerce Clause authority of Congress has not diminished the scope of the dormant Commerce Clause. The Court's professed solicitude for states in restricting the power of Congress has not corresponded to a greater solicitude for state regulations that affect interstate commerce.[88]

The Court's position on preemption and the dormant Commerce Clause corresponds to its general dualist framework. In this regard, the Court's approach represents a continuation of its pre-1937 Commerce Clause jurisprudence. Under the dual federalism theory that figured prominently in the Court's opinions in that era, state and federal authority generally did not overlap. Thus, a broad construction of congressional authority under the Commerce Clause would have entailed a constriction of state power under the dormant Commerce Clause.[89] If Congress had the power to regulate a certain area, then the states were not permitted to exercise authority in that domain, regardless of whether Congress actually implemented its power. The dormant Commerce Clause functioned as a broad principle of field preemption, blocking state action even in the absence of conflicting federal regulation.

The expansion of federal power after 1937 made any such strict division of authority impossible. Given the scope of federal authority, a refusal to tolerate concurrent state regulation would eviscerate state power. To return to concepts of exclusive state and federal jurisdiction is impossible. Nevertheless, the current Court appears to retain that concern with drawing lines. The same Court that has struck down federal laws in the name of preserving state autonomy has vigorously applied the dormant Commerce Clause to invalidate state laws.

One study found that the United States Supreme Court has decided thirteen major dormant Commerce Clause cases from 1992 to 2005.[90] Of these, the Court struck down the state law in ten of the thirteen.[91] Such raw figures can be misleading because the cases argued before the Court may not be a representative sample. Qualitative analyses, however, also conclude that the Court has broadened its understanding of situations that amount to prohibited state discrimination against interstate commerce and has strengthened the restraints on state regulation, even when doing so required overruling precedent.[92] In the dormant Commerce Clause area as well, then, dualism persists.

If the Court sees itself as marking boundaries between state and federal authority, then it can deploy the category of commercial activity to limit the scope of federal power in some areas and limit the scope of state power in others. Federal regulation of noncommercial activity is prohibited, while state regulation of commercial activity is subject to exacting review. This line drawing leads to strange results. Most notably, the Court disempowers the federal government in some areas and disempowers the states in others with little attention to the overall effects of its doctrine. By focusing on drawing lines, rather than on developing a working relationship between state and federal power, the Court fails to advance a coherent normative framework.

The Court's problem, in this area, is not doctrinal inconsistency. The limitations of federal power under the Commerce Clause cases and the limitations of state authority under the preemption and dormant Commerce Clause cases both correspond to a dualist emphasis on dividing state and federal power. However, this consistent dualism produces results that make little sense in terms of an overall theory of normative federalism. One can understand how *Lopez* and *Geier* can coexist within the Court's dualist perspective. The Court sees itself as protecting noncommercial activity as an enclave of state sovereignty and as protecting valid federal regulation of commerce from state interference. What is more difficult to understand is why it is desirable to adopt an approach to federalism that embraces both *Lopez* and *Geier*.

The Persistence of Dualist Theories of Federalism

The scholarly commentary largely mirrors the judicial approach. Like the Court's doctrine, federalism scholarship rests on dualist foundations. Commentators focus on the question: What is the value of dividing state and federal authority? A vast literature discusses the values of federalism,[93] but the writing analyzes the potential benefits (and sometimes costs) of separating state and federal power. Indeed, even the few scholars who directly attack federalism accept the underlying dualist premises. For example, Dean Rubin, whose work I mention in the introduction, has presented many cogent criticisms of contemporary theories of federalism.[94] His critique, though, focuses on the attempt to create enclaves of state power protected from

federal intrusion. In other words, the federalism that he so vigorously criticizes is not federalism generally, but dualist federalism. As Dean Rubin's
work illustrates, the federalism that federalism's supporters support and its
opponents oppose is fundamentally dualist.

This dualist orientation saddles the scholarly literature with several
problems. First, the dualist perspective fails to give fundamentally satisfying answers to the central question it purports to address: How should
power be divided between the states and the federal government? The dualist emphasis on line drawing leads to unresolvable disputes about the
proper allocation of state and federal power. Dividing state and federal authority generates potential benefits and potential harms. From within the
dualist framework, one can identify the conflicting normative implications,
but one cannot resolve them. For this reason, I use the term "antinomies"
to describe the account of federalism that emerges from the dualist perspective. As I will explain, the very structure of the dualist approach to federalism gives rise to these antinomies. Only by moving beyond dualism can the
antinomies be resolved.

Second, with regard to each benefit associated with federalism, the question remains whether constitutional federalism, as opposed to mere decentralization, is necessary to achieve the identified value. Dean Rubin, along
with Professor Malcolm Feeley, has emphasized that administrative decentralization can and does occur without constitutional federalism.[95] Even
in a unitary system, in which the central government retains absolute, plenary authority, the central government may well choose to delegate some
of its power to geographical subunits. Accordingly, an argument in favor
of decentralized authority does not necessarily support federalism. Only
if certain power must necessarily be granted to states and placed beyond
the control of the national government does the argument require constitutional federalism. Each of the three conceptual categories I discuss below
does generate a theory of why federalism must attain constitutional status
to realize the relevant values. However, with regard to each category, strong
counterarguments remain that a decentralized system could achieve similar
values with less danger of harmful consequences.

For these reasons, the dualist accounts of federalism fail on their own
terms. A further problem is that the dualist project simply does not address
the most common issue of state-federal relations, which is how to manage
the vast realms of concurrent state and federal authority. The categories of
analysis that dualist federalism employs do not shed light on these complex, and very common, situations.

THE ANTINOMIES OF DUALIST FEDERALISM

In discussions of federalism, commentators generally offer a variety of presumed benefits, clustering around five areas: responsive governance, governmental competition, innovation, participatory democracy, and resisting tyranny. I believe that the list can be grouped more usefully into three conceptual categories based on economic theory, republican political theory, and liberal political theory. Each category embodies a linked set of conceptions, including an implied political theory and an implied understanding of the states. Each category also constitutes an attempt to justify dividing state and federal authority.

Economic Argument

The economic argument focuses on choice, competition, and innovation. In this view, federalism serves a vital role in ensuring that states can offer differing baskets of services in accordance with the preferences of the citizens/consumers. States will compete so as to provide the best package of policies to attract the most people, and this competition will spur efficiency and innovation.[96]

STATE AS FIRM. This theory emphasizes that local decision making can allow government better to meet the preferences of the populace. People may have different views on important issues, and if these views correlate to some extent with geographic location, then more decentralized decisions will please more people. Federalism provides a way for groups that are local majorities, but national minorities, to have their views realized. Federalism thus ensures the greatest good for the greatest number.

Judge Michael McConnell has provided a classic statement of the utilitarian calculus underlying this view of federalism. Consider a nation consisting of two states, each with a population of 100 voters. In one state, 70 people wish to *ban* smoking in public places, and 30 wish to *allow* smoking. In the other state, only 40 people wish to *ban* smoking in public, while 60 wish to *allow* it. If a "national" (in this case, two-state) decision is made, then the smoking ban will be enacted with a vote of 110 to 90. Under this scenario, 90 people will be unhappy. If instead, local option is permitted, public smoking will be banned in the first state by a vote of 70 to 30, but allowed in the other state by a vote of 60 to 40. In this "federalist" world, 130 people will be in the smoking environment of their choice, and only 70 people will be unhappy. Federalism thereby makes 20 more people happy.

The ability for dissenters to move to a different state allows for even greater convergence between governmental policies and citizen preferences.[97]

Federalism allows each state to reach distinctive decisions on policy questions. States can adopt different baskets of taxes, services, regulations, and the like. The possibility of people and businesses moving into or out of the state provides an incentive for the states to design the best packages. States in this sense compete for populations and economic resources. This competition provides a kind of discipline that drives states to provide the basket of goods that best meets the needs of their citizens. Again, as with private firms, decentralized decision making can promote innovation and experimentation. States have the ability to test novel social policies, and interstate competition provides an incentive for states continuously to seek new and improved ways of operating. Supreme Court Justice Louis Brandeis memorably characterized the states as "laboratories," in which different social policies can be tested on a small scale, rather than at the national level.[98] One can think of a variety of contemporary policies, such as charter schools or community policing, which originated in one or a few states and are subject to borrowing, revision, or rejection in others. Successful experiments will reap rewards as people and businesses flock to the innovating state. Thus, optimal social policy can be determined scientifically, rather than by top-down bureaucratic speculation. In sum, in this conception, each state is a firm, and federalism ensures a well-functioning policy market, conferring maximum utility on each citizen/consumer.[99]

FEDERALISM AS ANTITRUST PRINCIPLE. This economic model also embodies a theory on why federalism must have constitutional foundations. Like firms in a marketplace, states may be tempted to conspire to avoid the discipline of competition. Rather than facing the relentless pressure to produce a better basket of services, states may seek to collude rather than compete. They may try to agree with each other on a standard set of policies so that citizens cannot shop around for a better policy deal. For example, states may feel pressure from a powerful and wealthy interest group to promulgate a certain kind of regulation. Adopting this regulation might yield rewards to state officials in the form of campaign contributions, favors, or other signs of gratitude. The regulation itself, though, might be economically inefficient. In such circumstances, state officials might wish to stifle interstate competition by agreeing with each other to adopt the regulation. The officials would all reap the benefits, without the danger of another state drawing away business or citizens by pursuing the more economically efficient path. Such a policy cartel would benefit state officials, while harming citizens, who have no choice but to bear the cost of the inefficient policy. With no possibility of interstate variation, citizens have no opportunity to "vote with their feet" by moving to another state.[100]

Of course, a cartel of fifty firms might be difficult to maintain. States would face temptations to defect and reap competitive advantages. That is where the federal government comes in. The federal government acts as a kind of super trade association. If the states can convince the federal government to mandate the regulation as national policy, then they have achieved a binding and legally enforceable agreement not to compete. National regulatory policy ensures that all states must stick with the policy, thus squelching choice, innovation, and competition. In this economic conception, if the federal government is free to decide on the proper amount of centralization, one can expect the federal government to enable the collusive state conduct.[101] Only constitutionally grounded federalism can ensure the proper functioning of the interstate policy market. Federalism acts as a constitutional antitrust principle, preventing the federal government from interfering with interstate competition. Federalism ensures that certain decisions must be made on a state-by-state basis, with the attendant benefits of choice, innovation, and competition. Further, on this account, it would not be surprising for the states to attempt to acquiesce in unconstitutional arrogations of power by the federal government. The states might well want the federal government to intervene to eliminate interstate competition. Properly understood, however, federalism protects citizens, not states.[102] Thus, constitutional federalism provides an important check on the states and the federal government colluding in promulgating national regulations.

LIMITATIONS OF THE MARKET MODEL. This economic model of federalism is subject to a variety of limitations, both from a market and a nonmarket perspective. First, market failure, particularly in the form of externalities, may occur.[103] The states' policy choices may have effects that extend beyond their borders. Pollution in one state may reach another state. If one state provides a vital habitat for migratory wildlife, that state's decision as to whether to protect the habitat will have cross-border effects. Treating each state as an autonomous firm obscures important and inevitable interconnections.

Second, the market model itself may fail to capture important aspects of policy debates. The market model generally assumes that preferences cannot be normatively evaluated.[104] A preference for or against a particular policy is entitled to equal consideration. Policy choices, however, may not be morally equivalent. The health claims of nonsmokers may deserve greater value than the pleasure claims of smokers. Changing the example to racial discrimination helps to illustrate the conceptual problem. What if the local majority favors discriminating based on race? Should the national majority allow local option on that issue? Is racial discrimination just another item in a basket of state policies that states may be free to offer or not?[105] Further, typically not all inhabitants of a particular area have the right to vote. Who is in the best position to represent the interests of those too young or otherwise unable to vote?[106]

Mobility provides a potential escape hatch. Those who do not like smoking or racial discrimination can move to other states. Assuming free movement and free competition among fifty states, surely some state will seek to offer a smoke-free, discrimination-free environment. Moving has its costs, however. The question remains whether those who disagree with policies endorsed by a local majority should bear the burden of exit. To put it slightly differently, although federalism allows states to be responsive to their citizens, certain principles may inhere in the concept of national citizenship. Being an American may give one the privilege of not being subject to racial discrimination anywhere in the nation. Federalism may impair the recognition of such privileges of national citizenship.[107]

To build on the scientific trope of states as laboratories, the subjects of these experiments are human beings. Humans may be able to exit, but they may have certain rights against experimentation that cannot be satisfied by an emigration strategy. Scientific research tends to have strict review procedures for experiments involving human subjects.[108] Even when participation is wholly voluntary, ethical principles provide important constraints on the permissible range of experimentation. In the policy context, who is to serve as the Human Subject Review Board? Should the federal government regulate policy experimentation with humans, or should each state be able to decide within the broad constraints of constitutional principles?[109]

The question between federalism and decentralization is who decides when externalities, arguments from justice, or other factors militate against localized decision making and in favor of empowering national majorities. The individual rights portions of the United States Constitution provide some answers. Intentional discrimination by the government is generally not within the power of any state or locality. The dormant Commerce Clause represents a check against states' imposing certain economic harms on other states. However, many important principles lack constitutional status. Guarantees against private discrimination rest on statutory, not constitutional foundations.[110] Federalism ensures some competition among states, free from interference by the federal government. The question remains who is to decide whether a federal law banning guns in schools[111] or violence against women[112] constitutes a pernicious federal cartel, a correction of a failure of the political market, or a guarantee of a right of national citizenship.

Republican Political Theory

Federalism also may promote the values of political participation often associated with the civic republican tradition.[113] Republicanism emphasizes the intrinsic value of citizens' participating in their self-government. In this view, merely registering preferences in the voting booth cannot substitute for direct participation in deliberative decision making. To enjoy political freedom, individuals must exercise the rights and duties of citizenship through active engagement in self-government.[114]

STATE AS REPUBLIC. If participating directly in the political process, rather than merely indirectly through elections, is valuable, local decision making would seem to be essential. To provide sufficient opportunities for citizen participation, there must be many fora of decision making. It is difficult for citizens in every state to participate in national decisions. However, citizens can participate in decisions at the local level. Federalism reserves certain decisions for local, or at least state-by-state, determination. In this regard, federalism guarantees that opportunities will exist for local decisions and thus citizen participation in this local decision making.[115]

FEDERALISM AS A GUARANTEE OF MEANINGFUL SELF-GOVERNMENT. This argument for federalism understands the state as a kind of self-governing republic. The republican conception could support a constitutional understanding of federalism as a way to guarantee meaningful local control. To be sure, local participatory politics does not require federalism. A centralized government may permit localities to decide issues.[116] Nonfederal polities do indeed allow local decision making, just as states, which are generally under no obligation to share power with their cities and counties, do so anyway. However, only constitutional protection for localized decision making ensures real self-government. Federalism guarantees that local political participation will translate into real control over certain policy areas.[117] Without such constitutional protection, local democratic deliberation might become merely a kind of model legislature, an academic enterprise, in which people go through the motions of participation without exercising any true self-government.[118]

LIMITATIONS OF THE REPUBLICAN MODEL. Because federalism reaches only to the state level, however, it cannot guarantee the opportunity to participate in republican self-government. At the framing of the Constitution, some feared that republican values could not thrive in such a large nation.[119] Today, about half the states have populations larger than that of the entire United States in 1787.[120] Meaningful direct participation is very difficult on that scale. Direct involvement in state governance may be easier than participation in national governance, but opportunities for active engagement remain attenuated. To ensure real opportunities for citizen participation, decisions must be made in counties, towns, or cities. The central government, just as well as the states, could allocate decisions to localities.[121] If the ultimate goal is meaningful local participation, then it would seem that constitutional protection of localism, rather than federalism, would be the most direct path. Federalism might be a second-best solution, not as good as localism, but preferred to a unitary nationalism—but only if states are more likely than the federal government to foster local decision making. Some scholars have questioned that proposition.[122]

Republican theory, moreover, presupposes certain basic prerequisites of participation. Citizens must have the legal right to participate in political decisions. Determining who is a citizen is a critical element in republican theory, and republics often have invoked exclusionary criteria in making that fundamental decision.[123] Citizens also must have the educational and material resources to make the promise of self-government real. Without an adequate education, including an introduction to civic values, a person cannot fully engage in the political interchange that republican theory posits as central to individual self-realization.[124] Full participation also requires a certain minimum level of fundamental resources, such as food, clothing, and housing.[125] Without basic material necessities, people cannot take the time to participate in public affairs. As with localized decision making, a state might provide such guarantees of social welfare to its citizens. However, the federal government might have a role in guaranteeing the existence of the conditions necessary to allow republican government.[126]

The question, once again, is who gets to decide. A choice has to be made as to what issues are appropriate for local resolution and at what level of local government the issue should be resolved. Perhaps the state would be more inclined than the federal government to devolve decisions to the local level, and the state level is closer to the people than the national government. Similarly, the state might be the best guarantor of the prerequisites for full participation. On the other hand, a strong national government might be necessary to ensure equal participation by all citizens. For these reasons, it is not clear that federalism necessarily advances participatory democracy.

Liberal Political Theory

One of the most common defenses of federalism rests on its supposed capacity to protect individual liberty from governmental oppression.[127] To the extent that it can check the abusive exercise of governmental authority, federalism promotes a central goal of liberal political theory.

STATE AS GUARDIAN. The division of governmental power between states and the national government may hinder tyranny. For a faction to dominate a society, it would need to gain power at both the national and the state levels. Like the "horizontal" separation of powers between the different branches of government, the "vertical" separation of powers embodied in federalism diffuses power so as to protect individuals from tyrannical exercises of government authority.[128] Moreover, states could act as loci of resistance to abuses of federal authority. In this conception, states serve as valuable guardians of the people's liberties. States protect citizens from the overwhelming power of the national government.[129]

FEDERALISM AS BULWARK OF LIBERTY. From this liberal perspective, the advantages of federalism over mere decentralization are apparent. If the desired goal is preventing the central government from exercising oppressive power, allowing the central government to make power allocation decisions would be counterproductive. The focus on preventing tyranny bespeaks a fundamental mistrust of the central government. Conferring plenary authority on the national government, in the manner contemplated by mere decentralization, conflicts with that postulated suspicion. More generally, to the extent that divided power poses less threat of tyranny than unified power, the division of power mandated by constitutional federalism poses fewer risks than mere decentralization.[130]

LIMITATIONS OF THE LIBERAL POLITICAL MODEL. On the other hand, states may interfere with the implementation of federal directives that would reduce tyranny. States could be tyrannic, and to the extent that federalism provides a protected realm for state activity, it creates a realm protected for tyranny. Does local tyranny or national tyranny present the greater threat? Whether as a contingent, historical accident or as a necessary feature of political theory, one may conclude that states, rather than the national government, pose the greatest threat of the oppressive exercise of public power. Certainly, the history of race in the United States suggests caution in assuming that conferring authority on states reduces the unjustified use of coercive power. When the threat is tyranny, federalism may be the problem, not the solution.[131]

THE LIMITATIONS OF THE DUALIST APPROACH

Dualist theories of federalism identify important values, but they do not address the resolution of the conflicts that commonly arise. The theories focus on the reasons for separating state and federal authority, not on how to reconcile them. The families of arguments discussed above can accept a large realm of coextensive authority; many matters may be subject to concurrent regulation by the state and national governments. For the arguments to realize fully the identified values of constitutional federalism, however, some subject areas must be reserved to states and kept out of the hands of the federal government. Lines must be drawn.

In the economic model, federalism ensures competition and innovation by prohibiting the federal government from creating a monopoly. Federalism functions only because states are prevented from colluding and freeing policy choices from regulatory competition. The policies must be defined by subject area. The areas of permissible and impermissible federal regulation must be demarcated. The republican model understands federalism as guaranteeing meaningful self-governance by ensuring that certain decisions are made at the local level. Certain topics must be reserved for nonnational decisions so as to safeguard meaningful political participation. Again, the areas reserved for local control must be defined. The liberal model prevents tyranny by prohibiting the federal government from intruding into certain policy matters. Defining the realm in which state action must be protected—so as to prevent national tyranny—becomes crucial.

But how are the boundaries to be defined? Push the border of the protected state enclave a bit in one direction, and some benefits are enhanced, and some risks likewise increase. A larger realm for state action leads to more choice, competition, self-government, and protection from national tyranny, but also enhances the possibility of externalities, violations of rights of national citizenship, denial of full local political participation for some groups, and state tyranny. Push the border a bit in the other direction, and the benefits and risks diminish. A federalism of line drawing leads to a kind of zero sum situation. The resulting conflict in values cannot be resolved. Given the dualist premises, the antinomies of federalism are unavoidable.

The landmark federal education legislation, the No Child Left Behind Act of 2001 (NCLB),[132] illustrates the difficulty in applying these dualist conceptualizations to actual issues of federalism. The economic perspective promotes the values of choice and competition. NCLB is in a sense a truth-in-labeling law, through which the federal government tries to force states to provide the information necessary to allow parents to make informed choices.[133] In this way, the federal influence seeks to allow market forces to come into play.[134] Here, federal intervention in education promotes competition. NCLB also represents an effort to promote a national right to an adequate education. From the republican perspective, NCLB could be criticized as an instance of the national government intruding into the participatory democratic processes of the local school districts. On the other hand, NCLB also could be understood as an attempt to empower local communities by providing greater information and accountability than states have been willing to demand. Political participation also requires a minimal level of education. The liberal approach could identify NCLB as an example of federal tyranny in the important area of education. By contrast, NCLB could be a national effort to prevent local tyranny. Education can be conceived as a national right that requires federal protection against local disparagement.[135] The Clinton administration defended federal intervention in education as fighting the "tyranny of low expectations,"[136] and President George W. Bush similarly derided the "soft bigotry of low expectations."[137]

Overall, NCLB illustrates the shortcomings of the dualist project. Dualist federalism claims to advance certain values by separating state and federal authority. These values are genuinely important. However, NCLB suggests that in the contemporary United States these values can best be promoted, and competing concerns minimized, through the concurrent exercise of state and federal power. The proper question is not where to draw the line between state and federal realms, but how to harness the dynamic interaction of state and federal power. Dualist federalism has no resources to address that issue. The problem with dualist federalism is not the values it designates, but the method it seeks to employ. Dividing state and federal spheres of authority cannot achieve the significant benefits that dualism identifies.

THE FRUITLESS DEBATE ABOUT STATE DISTINCTIVENESS

Another unfortunate symptom of the persistence of dualism is the continued debate about the distinctiveness of states. The need to ground a differentiation between the national and local leads to unsupportable claims of regional difference. Scratch a debate about federalism, and you find a dispute about the character of states. Defenders and opponents of federalism quickly resort to arguments about the cultural uniqueness of states.[138] It is the dualist conception of federalism that makes these arguments about cultural distinctiveness so important. To justify separating state and federal realms and creating enclaves protected from federal regulation, dualism seeks to endow states with strong identities. As recipients of such special privileges, states must constitute more than mere geographical entities; they must be integral communities of value.

The distinctiveness of state communities would help to justify both the need to draw lines between state and federal authority and the particular location of the boundary. A community is defined by reference to its other. For dualists, with regard to at least some issues, those inside a state's boundaries generally share a set of values, which differ from the values of outsiders who live in other states. From this communal perspective, the goal of federalism is to identify the issues characterized by internal homogeneity and external difference. These distinguishing issues help to define the boundaries of state authority. Matters of distinctive local concern are assigned to state governments, and federal intrusion in these areas is prohibited. In this conception, the states constitute separate spaces of value, and their boundaries must be respected.

From a dualist perspective, much is at stake in the distinctiveness debate. As both the advocates of federalism and their nationalist counterparts understand federalism in dualist terms, they both rely on assertions about distinctive state identities to buttress their claims. Their disagreement stems from their divergent views on the extent to which states do serve as loci of distinctive values.

For critics of federalism, such as Dean Rubin, the distinctiveness debate provides a prime line of attack. Dean Rubin insists that states do not exhibit distinctive values. He asserts that the United States generally manifests a cultural uniformity. That relative homogenization, he asserts, undermines the possibility of federalism in the United States.[139] The only relevant political community for Rubin is the nation. Because states do not constitute political communities, federalism must rest on false and feeble foundations.[140] Professor Mark Tushnet agrees. Tushnet expresses skepticism about the potential of federalism in the contemporary United States because he asserts that federalism entails a fundamental plurality of values. Tushnet does not see an affirmation of value pluralism in the United States, and he therefore deprecates the potential of federalism.[141]

By contrast, Professor Daniel Elazar, one of the champions of American federalism, asserted that states were sufficiently different so as to form distinctive civil societies.[142] Other scholars who write sympathetically about federalism also insist on the cultural distinctiveness of individual states.[143] Along similar lines, some commentators urge that communal sentiments within states should be cultivated so as to supply the necessary foundations for federalism.[144]

As discussed in chapter 1, this characterization of states as distinctive communities of value rings hollow today. Nationalizing trends in the United States are increasing, and the variety that does exist does not track geographical boundaries. Americans receive progressively more of their news from national news organizations that tend to focus on national events and to cover those events similarly. The ubiquity of national chains for fast food, clothing, and home improvement has reduced local commercial variation. Cultural phenomena and even sports that used to be regionally oriented are expanding throughout the nation. You can read about it in one of the 798 Barnes & Noble bookstores, spread across all fifty states (or just go to Amazon.com).[145] Accordingly, many claims of state uniqueness are vastly overblown.[146] Of course, some aspects of state distinctiveness undoubtedly remain. "Don't mess with Texas" captures a certain cultural self-identification. "Don't mess with Rhode Island" lacks the same resonance; the slogan becomes less confrontational and more environmental. Overall, though, it is increasingly difficult to identify people's home state based on their cultural preferences. The dichotomous coding of "red" and "blue" states masks vast underlying differences that belie claims of states as meaningful units of cultural analysis. At high levels of abstraction some differences may appear, but when one tries to establish distinctions with any specificity, the evidence proves most elusive. The best evidence suggests a "purple" America where state borders do not define deep ideological divisions. It is difficult to prove that no cultural differences exist, but it is even harder to define what the differences are in a way that would be useful for constitutional analysis.

As the preceding chapters suggest, claims of regional distinctiveness rest on weak, or certainly weakening, foundations. More important, these arguments about state peculiarity are wholly unnecessary. From a dualist perspective, connecting states to distinctive values helps to justify drawing lines between state and federal authority. However, these celebrations of state difference belong to the federalism of the past. Scholars who attempt to link federalism to claims about state cultural integrity make the Trent Lott error. They mistake the Old Federalism for contemporary federalism, which does not presuppose fundamental difference among the values of the states. Contemporary federalism can coexist with the reality of increasing homogeneity and the concomitant decline in regional identities.

In any event, even if one believes in the persistence of significant regional variation about important values, the ambiguity of the concept of state distinctiveness renders it useless as a guide to demarcating zones of state and federal authority. Arguments about state character cannot yield determinate boundaries between state and federal power. The state distinctiveness debates exemplify the trenchant observation that constitutional theorist Alexander Bickel made in a different context: "No answer is what the wrong question begets. . . ."[147] A theory of federalism that depends on a notion of states as distinct cultural units rests on weak foundations indeed. A theory that could move beyond this mainstay of dualist federalism would be a significant advance.

The theory of polyphonic federalism represents my alternative to dualist federalism. Before explaining the theory in the next chapter, though, I would like to review some other efforts to avoid the traps of dualist federalism. While I believe these attempts are ultimately unsuccessful, or at least incomplete, they offer valuable insights in analyzing the problems of dualism and in exploring the tenacious hold of dualism even on those who seek to advance beyond it.

Attempts to Move Beyond Dualist Federalism

Other scholars have recognized the limitations of dualist conceptions of federalism and have attempted to overcome dualist assumptions. Dualism, however, has proved hard to avoid in discussions of federalism. Here I review three such efforts, namely, process federalism, empowerment federalism, and cooperative federalism.

PROCESS FEDERALISM

Some scholars have sought to advance the values of federalism by focusing on the process by which governmental decisions are made, rather than on the substantive reach of federal regulations. Through this emphasis on process, the theories try to avoid the dualist project of defining particular subjects of exclusive state authority. These theories, however, either fail to address important decisions about the allocation of power or else fall back on dualist premises when they do provide such guidance.

The Political Safeguards of Federalism

The argument for the political safeguards of federalism represents the most well-known and enduring effort to challenge the judicial enforcement of dualist federalism.[148] Under the political safeguards theory, the national political process properly resolves all of the tensions underlying federalism. According to this theory, Congress embodies the states actually exercising their decision-making authority. The political safeguards perspective denies the sharp distinction between the states and the national government. The values of federalism are served by having the states participate and represent their interests in the national political process. Further constitutional, specifically judicial, protection is not necessary. It is the states themselves, acting through Congress, that determine the allocation of governmental authority.

Objections to this theory are longstanding. However, it is useful to review first the central positive contribution of the theory. From 1937 until 1995, the United States Supreme Court did not strike down any acts of Congress as exceeding the scope of Congress's Commerce Clause authority. Even after 1995, judicial protection of federalism is quite modest. Nevertheless, the states remain as vital policymaking organs. State interests have fared quite well, even in the absence of judicial reinforcements.[149] Whatever the reason for the strength of states, states retain much power and influence over important decisions. This fact of the political history of the United States casts serious doubt on the need for substantial judicial protection of state authority.

Despite this important contribution, the political safeguards theory suffers from two significant weaknesses. First, it is not clear that state interests are fully represented in the national political process.[150] With the popular election of senators, states are not represented directly in Congress. Many have argued that the senators and members of Congress become part of a national governing body, losing any ties to state interests.[151] Second, even if the states are adequately represented in Congress, the problem of the people remains. Federalism promises that by protecting states it will protect individuals. The ultimate beneficiary of federalism is the people, not the states.[152] However, the structural protection of state interests might not translate into protection for the people. Without constitutional boundaries to restrict them, the states and the national government may work together in ways that could be detrimental to the people. For example, state officials may collude with the national government to avoid accepting responsibility for their actions.[153]

For present purposes, though, the most significant problem with the political safeguards approach is that it is fundamentally a theory of judicial review, not a theory of federalism. The political safeguards argument explains why courts should not draw lines between the state and federal government; instead, the courts should defer to congressional judgments. However, the theory does not tell Congress how it should make the allocational decisions. The political safeguards approach tells courts not to interfere with NCLB, but does not help Congress design the law. Moreover, even with regard to courts, the theory fails to give guidance in resolving some federalism disputes that inevitably require judicial resolution, such as those raising issues of preemption. The political safeguards approach does not tell courts whether to allow state tort suits to supplement the federal regulation of airbags in cases like *Geier*, nor does it advise courts whether to allow states to require disclosure of information about Holocaust-era insurance policies in cases like *Garamendi*.

The issue of the institutional allocation of authority between the courts and Congress is crucial. However, the institutional competence decision must follow from a normative theory of federalism. The institutional decision cannot simply replace the need for a theory of federalism. A theory that sheds no light on NCLB, *Geier*, or *Garamendi* leaves crucial issues unaddressed.

Contemporary Process Federalism

In the wake of the Supreme Court's renewed interest in federalism, scholars have again formulated theories of federalism centering on the political process.[154] In the most extended scholarly response to the attack on federalism by Rubin and his coauthor Feeley, Professor Vicki Jackson sought to save federalism by rejecting theories of enclaves of state regulation protected from federal interference. Jackson asserted that federalism need not preserve certain areas for exclusive state jurisdiction, but could instead rely on the structural protection of dual levels of government.[155] This move from a categorical concept of areas of national and local authority to a structural notion of dual, overlapping levels of government is very promising.

Jackson clearly wishes to reject strict, categorical notions of dual federalism. Her theory focuses more on the process by which Congress considers the interests of states, and even then her standard is very deferential. She urges that in the lawmaking process Congress take seriously the limits on its authority, and she does not contemplate substantial judicial enforcement of federalism.[156] In the end, though, Jackson does not fully distance herself from the effort to delineate special areas of state activity. All that she does is to soften judicial enforcement of such borders. The boundaries still exist, even if it is up to Congress in the first instance to locate them. Her theory assumes a line between federal and state realms and some judicial supervision of this border.

Ultimately, Jackson finds certain areas in which the states enjoy special, albeit procedural, protection. She insists that "it is possible to identify greater and lesser degrees of connection between enumerated powers and regulated conduct."[157] Those areas characterized by "lesser degrees of connection" receive greater protection from federal interference. Operating within the dualist paradigm, this process-based theory retains a substantive, dualist core. Jackson makes this dualism explicit: "To make political safeguards of federalism work, some sense of enforceable lines must linger."[158] Other process-based theories similarly rely on some notion of particular areas in which federal intrusion arouses special scrutiny.[159]

This gentle federalism cannot evade the perils of dualism. Process theories rely on boundaries protecting some areas from federal regulation; these theories just erect more permeable, process-related barricades at the frontier. Nevertheless, at some point, a court may prohibit the federal government from acting. Such a judicial ruling may promote interstate competition or deny rights of national citizenship; it may promote republican self-governance or permit local exclusion; it may check national tyranny or immunize local oppression. Still focused on separating state and federal spheres, Jackson's theory does not explain how to manage the inevitable interconnection of state and federal authority.

A further indication of the underlying dualism in Jackson's work is her attack on Rubin and Feeley's denial of state cultural distinctiveness. Jackson's language is measured and moderate. In the end, though, she must defend some notion of states as integral communities of value. She writes,

> Although correct in emphasizing the successful development of a strong sense of national identity, in suggesting that the only relevant "political community" is the national one Rubin and Feeley may underestimate the positive importance of state or regional identifications felt by some citizens (perhaps not well represented among the ranks of law professors).[160]

For a theory that retains strong dualist elements, the allure of distinctive state communities proves irresistible. To bolster the claim for limiting national power, Jackson relies on the notion that states really do form cultural units. As in other dualist accounts, she seeks some justification for drawing lines between state and federal power.

FEDERALISM AS EMPOWERMENT

Some scholars, notably Professor Erwin Chemerinsky, have suggested the possibility of a federalism that does not make subject matter distinctions between state and federal power.[161] In this conception, the federal government and the states are just different sources of power, with no specially protected state domain. In this twin-engine form of federalism, the federal government can address exactly the same issues as the state government. Principles of federalism do not function to limit federal or state power; rather, they serve to enhance both state and federal authority. Federalism stands for a robust view of the empowerment of government at the state and federal levels.

This empowerment view constitutes a decisive break with dual federalism. Federalism no longer focuses on drawing lines between state and federal domains of authority. States function simply as loci of power; only bare facts of geography distinguish one state from another or a state from the national government. The territorial bounds of the authority of the various states and the federal government may differ. The subject matter of their authority does not.

This view of federalism avoids many of the problems that plague dual federalism and its progeny. The quixotic quest to distinguish matters of local interest from matters of national concern can cease. Similarly, federalism as empowerment need not seek to locate, or create, the cultural essence that corresponds to the different states. The independent-minded Texan, the pioneering Oregonian, and the avant-garde New Yorker can continue to exist as stereotypes, but without the need to give them the legal weight they cannot possibly bear. Federalism as empowerment avoids the need to hypothesize such state-based ideal types or to attempt to deploy judicial authority to fashion them.

Accepting the full concurrence of state and federal power represents the first step in moving beyond dualist federalism. The next step, however, requires a theory of how to resolve tensions that arise due to the overlap of state and federal power.[162] For all its shortcomings, dual federalism had a solution to this problem: the unauthorized assertion of power must yield. In pure forms of dual federalism, conflict between state and federal authority could occur only if one of the governments exceeded its legitimate scope. If state and federal authority constitute mutually exclusive realms of governance, then conflict can occur only if one entity is on the wrong side of the border.

In an empowerment view, the state and federal governments are always acting within the legitimate scope of their authority. Federalism as empowerment offers no theory on how to harness creatively the tensions and potential conflicts between state and federal law. The theory does not tell Congress how to manage the state-federal overlap. Empowerment federalism has nothing to say about the No Child Left Behind Act, other than that courts should keep their hands off it. Even with regard to the judiciary, empowerment federalism provides insufficient guidance. Preemption and dormant Commerce Clause cases do arise. The courts cannot simply stay out of these areas. However, federalism as empowerment does not advise courts on how to resolve the conflicts.[163]

COOPERATIVE FEDERALISM

Process federalism and empowerment federalism provide normative accounts of federalism, generally focused on limiting judicial interference. As discussed above, they give little direction to other branches of government. Cooperative federalism, by contrast, has focused primarily on nonjudicial actors. What cooperative federalism lacks is an adequately specified normative theory.

Tracing back to the New Deal, or perhaps earlier,[164] cooperative federalism acknowledges and endorses the close relationships between the state and national governments in a variety of areas. State implementation of federal regulatory regimes provides a prime example of the operation of cooperative federalism.[165] The term arose out of the recognition that the separation of state and national authority assumed in dual federalism did not accurately describe the actual interaction of state and national governments. The perceived need for such cooperation and the longstanding judicial acquiescence in these cooperative arrangements gave the concept strong normative force. Cooperative federalism seeks to legitimate in theory the state-federal partnerships that in fact pervade governmental operations.

While an essential corrective to dual federalism, cooperative federalism gives an incomplete specification of federal-state relations. Cooperative federalism blesses the voluntary interaction of state and national governments. The theory does little to sort out the conflicts that may arise in that relationship. The interaction of state and national authority may be competitive, or even confrontational. Cooperative federalism contributes little to an understanding or resolution of these conflicts. Recognizing this problem, Daniel Elazar called for a normative theory of cooperative federalism.[166] Little work has been done, though, to flesh out the constitutional framework of such a theory.

That lack of specification contributes to an instability in cooperative federalism. The theory resists the separation of state and federal, but does not ensure that the two governments play well together.[167] Some scholars have found that cooperative federalism has become a coercive federalism of national mandate.[168] Others charge that it constitutes a collusive relationship lacking in the competitive dynamic so important to federalism.[169] Because cooperative federalism accepts the general notion of a federal-state partnership, but does not provide for rules of engagement, the theory provides no resources for monitoring federal-state relations.

Cooperative federalism thus marks the end of dual federalism, but does not itself provide a replacement. Dualism has a theory of the proper relationship of the state and federal governments and of the courts in enforcing it. Cooperative federalism lacks that kind of comprehensive vision. The theory acknowledges the centrality of federal-state partnerships, but has little to say about refereeing conflicts that may arise.

In this chapter I have highlighted the centrality of dualism to contemporary judicial and academic accounts of federalism. I also have discussed the problems that a dualist conception of federalism causes from a policy perspective and the difficulty of addressing these concerns from within a dualist mindset. Various theorists have attempted to move beyond a dualist approach to federalism, and these efforts provide helpful guidance in constructing a new model. The current alternatives, however, fail to offer a means for managing the pervasive overlap of state and federal power. In the next chapter, I explain a reconceptualization of federalism, which I call polyphonic federalism. Polyphonic federalism moves beyond dualist premises and offers a framework for addressing the complex, interactive, and potentially adversarial relationship of the states and the federal government.

CHAPTER FOUR

Federalism as Polyphony

Chapter 3 argued that discussions of the values of federalism have not thrown off the shackles of federalism past. These debates remain mired in the dualist dilemma of where to draw the line between state and federal authority. No Child Left Behind (NCLB)[1] provides but one illustration of how the evolution of society has made that question impossible to answer. The state and national governments both have important roles to play, but the attempt to draw some firm boundary between them is doomed to fail. Like Trent Lott and the Rehnquist Court, these debates attempt to apply old precepts of dualist federalism to the contemporary world. That effort to fit contemporary federalism into dualist categories cannot succeed. As I have suggested in previous chapters, the key to understanding contemporary federalism is to embrace the overlap of state and federal authority. That concurrence is not an aberration to be shunned, but a core reality to be accepted and theorized.

This chapter develops an alternative to the dualist conception of federalism, an alternative that better corresponds to the social realities of contemporary society and the needs of modern governance. I term this conception "polyphonic." The chapter begins by exploring the metaphor of polyphony and contrasting it with the dominant tropes of dualist federalism, and then further defines the nature and implications of the polyphonic conception. I argue first that systems like polyphonic federalism, which involve the overlap of different sources of power, are more innovative and resilient than systems like dualist federalism, which entail the compartmentalization of various kinds of power. Second, I argue that the interaction of state and federal power better advances the substantive goals generally associated with federalism, including efficiency, democratic participation, and liberty.

The Metaphors of Federalism

THE SPATIAL METAPHORS OF DUALIST FEDERALISM

The dualist perspective lends itself well to spatial metaphors. A core and periphery of state power exist, and a core and periphery of federal power exist. At the peripheries, concurrent state and federal control is permitted, but a core remains, free from intrusion by the other government. Federalism then becomes an exercise in line drawing, determining which kinds of activities belong to the state or federal regions and deciding where the boundary lies between core and periphery. Different people urge that the lines be drawn in different places. The underlying focus on line drawing, however, remains pervasive.

From a dualist perspective, the central metaphors of federalism are visual and spatial. Federalism is understood in terms of territory or, sometimes, as a layer cake of federal, state, and perhaps local authority.[2] Attempts to move beyond traditional notions of dual federalism retain that visual/spatial aspect. Morton Grodzins wrote of the need to replace the layer cake image with that of a marble cake.[3] But whether state government is viewed as a solid layer of authority or as a rich vein of power running throughout a federal confection, the basic dualism remains.[4] Federal power and state power exist next to each other; they are adjoining, not coinciding.

Spatial metaphors come naturally to the discussion of governmental power. Political authority generally follows geographical boundaries. Within a particular region, a particular government enjoys sovereignty, and the boundaries between different governments tend to be geographical. In many, perhaps most situations, the concept of a region, realm, or zone of authority is not a metaphor, but a legal reality. The authority of the sheriff ends at the county line; local law extends to the geographical frontier, but not beyond. The idea of federalism, itself, constituted a challenge to the modern notion of a single governmental entity exercising exclusive political authority over a given territory.[5] Yet dualism and the urge for governmental authority defined, at least metaphorically, by geography continue.

This book contends that the spatial conception of federalism is misguided. The dualist notion of federalism leads to unfortunate doctrinal conundrums. Mired in dualism, the courts have been unable to articulate coherent principles for topics, such as federal preemption, that inevitably involve the interplay of state and federal law. The dualist approach also has given rise to fruitless theoretical discussions. All that dualist federalism can do is to move the line between state and federal authority in one direction or another. Dualism contains no resources to mediate the conflicts between state and federal power. Awarding a region to the national government enhances some values, while bestowing it on the states promotes other values. Dualist federalism is a zero sum game, a battle over territory that demands a victor. Dualist federalism has no principles to allow a sharing or overlap of authority.

FROM SPATIAL TO AURAL METAPHORS

To understand contemporary federalism, it will be useful to move beyond the spatial metaphors of dualism. The key trope that I propose is polyphony. Polyphony has been defined as "the simultaneous and harmonious combination of a number of individual melodic lines."[6] The fugues of Johann Sebastian Bach and the canon of Johann Pachelbel are prominent examples of polyphonic compositions. One of the central advantages of the metaphor of polyphony is its aurality. It is difficult to imagine two items occupying the same space, without displacing each other or combining into a single new, unified whole. The choice is a marble cake or a stew. Sound, on the other hand, can combine into new melodies, without losing its individual character. Professor Bernard Hibbitts has explained the distinction as follows:

> [S]ound may be considered multivariate insofar as different sounds can be simultaneously combined in the same space without suppressing their component parts. Thus it has been noted that "music is not like vision." Unlike visual colors, musical tones "may be combined without losing their individuality. What you end up with is a chord, something new, which has its own sound but in which the individual tones are also distinct and identifiable. It's not a blending . . . but something of a different order."[7]

It was for this reason that Mikhail Bakhtin used the concept of polyphony in his literary theory. He explained, "The essence of polyphony is precisely in the fact that the voices remain independent and, as such, are combined in a unity of a higher order than in homophony."[8] Polyphony is especially apt for federalism because it is used specifically for musical compositions including several parts of equal importance.[9] Polyphony is sometimes contrasted with counterpoint. Counterpoint refers to a composition in which the parts are graduated by rank.[10] Polyphony thus communicates the independence and autonomy of state and of federal authorities.

Aurality also emphasizes the diachronic nature of an interactive conception of federalism. From a polyphonic perspective, federalism is a process that evolves over time, an ongoing relationship among various sources of power. Federalism is best understood not as a static set of power relationships, but as the dynamic output of a system in which multiple powers interact with each other. Like a musical composition, federalism exists in time; it unfolds over time.[11] A "snapshot" of federalism, like a "snapshot" of music, will miss a central component of the phenomenon.

From Dualism to Polyphony

In addition to its aurality, polyphony also emphasizes multiplicity. Polyphony entails many voices. Recognizing the power of the metaphor, Professor Harold Berman has invoked it to describe pluralism in Western legal culture. He begins his discussion of pluralism with this musical reference: "It may be useful to draw an analogy between the development of law, so conceived, and the development of music. From the eleventh and twelfth centuries on, monophonic music, reflected chiefly in the Gregorian chant, was gradually supplanted by polyphonic styles."[12] He continues by noting the significance of plurality in Western legal culture.[13] Amelie Oksenberg Rorty has similarly found polyphony to be a useful concept for evoking political pluralism.[14]

Polyphony thus highlights the key features of federalism. It shifts the focus away from dualism's concern with protecting state or federal turf. Instead, federalism is about the interaction of multiple independent voices. These characteristics allow a polyphonic conception to avoid the trap of dualism, while still reaping the benefits of federalism.

THE POLYPHONIC ALTERNATIVE

In the polyphonic conception, federalism is characterized by the existence of multiple, independent sources of political authority. The scope of this political authority is not defined by subject matter. No kind of conduct is categorically beyond the boundaries of state or federal jurisdiction; the federal and state governments function as alternative centers of power. In the first instance, any matter is presumptively within the authority of the federal government and of a state government. Full concurrent power is the norm. A polyphonic conception of federalism thus resists the idea of defining enclaves of state power protected from federal intrusion. Like federalism as empowerment, polyphonic federalism rejects the dualist vestiges of dual federalism. Unlike federalism as empowerment, polyphonic federalism focuses on facilitating and structuring the interaction of state and federal governments.

Whereas dualist federalisms insist on dividing state and federal realms of authority, the key elements of polyphonic federalism are the protection of the institutional integrity of multiple sources of power and the promotion of the dynamic interaction of those centers of authority. Rather than asking whether some activity belongs on the state or federal side of a line, polyphonic federalism asks how the overlapping power of the state and federal governments can best address a particular issue.

The aural metaphor of polyphony is designed to capture that concept of complex concurrence. The state and federal governments occupy the same place at the same time, yet they maintain their institutional identities. This concept does not translate well into spacial categories. If some spacial metaphor is desired, a polyphonic conception of federalism is much closer to Daniel Elazar's concept of a matrix of power than to a marble cake or layer cake.[15] The individual generators remain distinct, but the power flows freely among the different nodes of authority. What receives constitutional protection is the overall system, rather than a monopoly over any particular subject area.

The polyphonic conception remains federalist. As in dualist conceptions of federalism, the allocation of authority between the states and the national government has constitutional status. That allocation differs between the polyphonic and dualist approaches, but the constitutional recognition of independent state and federal authority remains. The continuing integrity of the constituent voices ensures that the concept retains its federalist cast. Neither the federal government nor the states can eliminate the independent lawmaking authority of the other. Though its powers are broad, Congress cannot destroy the institutional integrity of states. It is in that sense that one can affirm the classic statement that the United States is an "indestructible Union, composed of indestructible states."[16] The continued functioning of each state's political apparatus receives constitutional protection. Congress cannot prevent a state legislature from meeting and enacting laws, nor can Congress eliminate the state judiciary and its function of interpreting and enforcing those laws. The anti-commandeering doctrine of *New York v. United States*[17] and *Printz v. United States*[18] thus does recognize an important element of federalism. The federal government would violate constitutional principles of federalism if it assumed control over the state governmental process.[19]

Although the state political process enjoys constitutional protection, the particular outputs of that process do not. From the polyphonic perspective, no state legislation is immunized from the potentially preemptive effects of federal enactments. Congress does not face limits on the subject matter of its regulatory authority. In no area of regulation can the states be assured of supremacy. Congress could enact laws effectively federalizing a domain, preventing state legislation in that realm from taking effect.

Before proceeding to elaborate further a polyphonic theory, it is worthwhile to pause to consider a potential objection. Does the possibility of comprehensive federal regulation render the protection of state political processes illusory? Some have so claimed. Relying on the concept of a state-federal competition for the affections of the people, some scholars insist that states must retain some privileged realm of authority.[20] From this perspective, states must have some constitutionally protected area in which to prove their worth. If the federal government could oust states of all regulatory authority, these scholars worry, the competitive balance of federalism would break down.

Like other dualist responses, this argument ignores the reality of contemporary intergovernmental relations and instead looks to some idealized dual federal past. Today, vast realms of crucial activity lie in areas of concurrent state-federal jurisdiction. The "commercial/noncommercial" or "local/national" or any other test that could be applied does not track areas of important authority. The federal government exercises significant power in fields such as family law,[21] education,[22] and crime.[23] If states must prove themselves, then they must prove themselves in areas where Congress could regulate but has left room for states. Protected enclaves of state authority will not be substantial enough to allow states to woo the people. Even given current dualist doctrines, states must prove their appeal in areas other than the very few domains, such as the regulation of guns in schools[24] or gender-motivated violence,[25] that receive constitutional protection.

Polyphonic federalism accepts that reality. The challenge that polyphony addresses is how to use the interaction of state and federal power to promote important values.

The Values of Polyphony

In its embrace of overlapping state and federal power, polyphonic federalism advances a conception of intergovernmental relations that accords with the realities of contemporary society. In the United States, the distinction between the "truly local" and the "truly national" has disappeared. A conception of federalism that rests on such a distinction has no foundation. Through the interaction of multiple sources of power, polyphonic federalism advances two sets of values. First, polyphony supports systemic principles of plurality, dialogue, and redundancy. As discussed below, systems characterized by these features are more innovative and resilient than systems, like dualism, that rely on compartmentalization of functions. In general, then, a polyphonic system is superior to a dualist one. Second, more specifically, the polyphonic conception of federalism promotes the classic federalism values of choice and competition, self-governance, and prevention of tyranny. As discussed in chapter 3, dualist federalism claims to advance these values. However the dualist mechanism of seeking to separate state and federal power fails to achieve these goals.

This section first discusses the systemic benefits—and potential pitfalls—of polyphony and then turns to polyphony's capacity to promote the values generally associated with federalism.

THE ADVANTAGES OF A POLYPHONIC SYSTEM

In emphasizing the interconnection of state and federal power, the polyphonic conception supports plurality, dialogue, and redundancy. These gains come at a price. The intermingling of state and federal authority may impair the goals of uniformity, finality, and hierarchical accountability. This section assesses the benefits and the costs.

Plurality, Dialogue, Redundancy

With the overlap of federal and state power comes the possibility of multiple approaches to a particular problem. The different institutional frameworks in which state and federal governments operate give them varying perspectives. Their different geographical scope also may give them divergent strengths and weaknesses. Some solutions may work better when imposed nationally, while others function more efficiently on a local scale.[26] The states and the federal government may attempt differing approaches to address particular issues. For example, many methods exist for trying to ensure environmental protection and workplace safety. The federal government may impose some firm national baselines, while the states may experiment with additional safeguards or alternative implementation schemes. Complex problems can benefit from a variety of approaches.

In addition simply to increasing the opportunities for legal protection, the concurrence of federal and state authority provides a valuable opportunity for dialogue. The states and the federal government can attempt alternative means of preventing employment discrimination or defining the fundamental right to privacy. Dialogue magnifies the value of plurality. Not only can each government try different responses to common problems, but the different regulators can learn from each other. In their account of democratic experimentalism, Professors Michael Dorf and Charles Sabel have emphasized the importance of bottom-up problem solving.[27] Regulators can learn from the best practices of other regulatory regimes.

Professor Kirsten Engel's theory of "dynamic" federalism conceives of a similar ongoing, dialectical process.[28] The interaction of state and federal regulators may produce a regulatory scheme superior to what either level of government would produce on its own. Engel has demonstrated how the development of national low emission vehicle standards built on such a productive dialogue. California developed its own standards to require the sales of lower emission cars. Other states considered adopting the California standards, which led the federal Environmental Protection Agency to work with the auto industry to produce alternative regulations, more stringent than the existing national standards. The resulting regulatory scheme represented an advance on what state or federal regulators had conceived on their own.[29]

Along with her coauthor David Adelman, Engel has further developed the dynamic model of federalism by analogy to ecosystems.[30] Adelman and Engel build on the concept of "complex adaptive systems," which evolve through a combination of optimizing processes and trial and error. Trial and error ensures elements of randomness and diversity in the system. Complex adaptive systems are constantly open to change and variation; they avoid becoming fixated at one, invariable state. Even if such a state would represent a temporary point of optimization, remaining fixed at that point would render the system fragile as conditions change.

Adelman and Engel contrast a complex adaptive system with one based on strict optimization. Given conditions of complexity and variability, Adelman and Engel argue that complex adaptive systems are more resilient and innovative than systems based on a single point of optimization. Adelman and Engel liken a complex adaptive system to a diversified portfolio; instead of the pure optimization strategy of pursuing short-term growth, diversification reduces the risk of catastrophe and offers better long-term promise. Drawing on the analogy of natural ecosystems, Adelman and Engel advocate regulatory solutions that incorporate multiple levels of governance, as opposed to policies that seek to identify a single, most efficient level of regulation. As Adelman and Engel's work highlights, the features of polyphonic federalism that I identify are well supported by studies of natural systems.

Dialogue facilitates regulatory innovation. The optimal regulatory scheme develops and changes over time, with constant interaction from a variety of forces, including information generated by other regimes. State tort suits may produce information of great value to federal regulators.[31] Again, like a musical composition, federalism consists in multiple participants contributing to an unfolding, dynamic process.

The interplay between state and federal courts in crafting protection for rights of sexual intimacy provides a salient example. In the 1986 case of *Bowers v. Hardwick*,[32] the United States Supreme Court found that a state criminal prosecution for homosexual sexual relations did not violate the Fourteenth Amendment. Subsequent state court cases interpreting state constitutions noted that decision and sometimes offered alternative approaches, finding fundamental rights to intimate homosexual conduct.[33] When the United States Supreme Court revisited the issue in *Lawrence v. Texas*[34] in 2003, the Court reflected on the diverse opinions expressed by state courts.[35] The state court cases figured in the Court's acknowledgment of changing social attitudes toward homosexual conduct. The state voices contributed to the Court's decision to overrule *Bowers* and extend constitutional protection to intimate homosexual conduct. Similarly, in its rejection of applying the death penalty to crimes committed by juveniles, the United States Supreme Court relied in part on the abolition of the juvenile death penalty in some states.[36] In these and other areas, state laws have served as models for federal laws and have guided their interpretation.[37]

Indeed, even if Congress does mandate a uniform policy denying effect to state law, state action may nevertheless have a valuable role to play in a federalist system. State enactments that conflict with federal law may constitute important symbols of opposition.[38] Even if a state policy cannot become legally binding, the existence of a potential alternative system reminds officials and citizens of the possibility of choosing other solutions. A state law can provide an important protest, a powerful criticism of the federal approach. That kind of officially stated opposition can, in time, help to transform federal policy. That change might take the form of adopting the state alternative, or the federal government might simply allow local variance.

Redundancy is an important value in complex systems. Yochai Benkler has noted the array of benefits that flow from redundancy, especially when the multiple layers afford distinctive perspectives:

> [R]edundancy provides important values in terms of the robustness and innovativeness of a system. Having different people produce the same component makes the production system more resistant to occasional failures. Moreover, having different people with different experience and creative approaches

attack the same problem will likely lead to an evolutionary model of innovation where alternative solutions present themselves. . . .[39]

Redundancy makes systems both more resilient and more innovative. Polyphonic federalism embraces the overlap of federal and state authority to take advantage of these benefits.

State and federal law may provide alternative forms of relief. To a large extent, redundant protection currently constitutes the norm. Potential victims of securities fraud or police abuse can seek help from state or federal law. The United States Supreme Court, for example, has often stated that the main federal civil rights cause of action under 28 U.S.C. § 1983 stands as a supplement, not as a replacement, for state law remedies.[40] State and federal constitutions both safeguard fundamental rights.

The potential regulatory redundancy constitutes a fail-safe mechanism, an additional source of protection if one or the other government should fail to offer adequate safeguards.[41] The lapse may occur because one government does not address an issue at all or because it fails to enforce regulations that facially apply. The civil enforcement provisions of the Violence Against Women Act (VAWA),[42] for example, extended federal authority to gender-motivated acts of violence. State law covered these acts as well, but Congress enacted the law in response to a perception that states did not adequately enforce the laws on their books. The fate of Christy Brzonkala, discussed in chapter 3, illustrates the need for redundancy. After she was allegedly raped by members of the football team at Virginia Tech and neither the school nor the state took remedial action, VAWA seemed a welcome alternative avenue of relief.[43] VAWA appeared to offer a way to bridge the remedial gap, to ensure some kind of response to the alleged crime. Rather than focus on that valuable redundancy, the Court applied its dualist conception of federalism and held that Brzonkala's rape was a local matter beyond the constitutional reach of the federal government.[44]

Counter-Values: Uniformity, Finality, and Hierarchical Accountability
If two regulatory heads are better than one, it may still be the case that sometimes too many regulatory chefs spoil the broth. Overlap has its costs. Concurrent jurisdiction may threaten significant principles of uniformity, finality, and hierarchical accountability.

Uniformity in law serves as an important value. To the extent that state and federal law both apply, parties may be subject to conflicting obligations. Certainly their lives become more complicated. Keeping track of multiple obligations may tax individuals and firms, especially those operating in more than one state. The problem of multijurisdictional transactions is endemic to federalism itself, but a polyphonic regime expands the possibility for federal and state conflict within a single state. Complicated issues of federal preemption may arise.

A related concern is the finality of legal proceedings. Finality constitutes a crucial legal value.[45] A definite and certain resolution of regulatory disputes enables individuals and firms to continue to lead their lives and conduct their affairs free from legal uncertainty. Dialogue between state and federal actors represents suspension of finality. The resolution of federal issues may be the prelude to protracted state proceedings. Courts have developed capacious rules of preclusion to encourage the simultaneous adjudication of state and federal claims. Other enforcement processes, however, tend to proceed along parallel, or serial, paths, rather than together. If federal and state regulations both apply, federal and state authorities may each seek to enforce the laws in separate, uncoordinated proceedings.

When the United States Supreme Court has sought to justify dividing state and federal realms, it has concentrated less on problems of uniformity and finality and more on potential issues of accountability. Indeed, concerns for accountability appear in both the Commerce Clause[46] and the anti-commandeering[47] branches of the Court's federalism jurisprudence. Members of the Court have asserted that the failure to protect a realm of state autonomy creates confusion among the citizenry. The overlap of state and federal authority prevents citizens from understanding where ultimate responsibility lies. When citizens object to government policies, should they direct their ire at their state capital or at Washington, D.C.? Justices have asserted that this blurring of lines of accountability becomes particularly acute with regard to areas that traditionally have been subject primarily to state rather than federal regulation, such as family law, education, and crime.[48] In these fields, citizens expect that states will retain ultimate control. Federal regulation in these areas presents a substantial danger of confusing citizens and undermining governmental accountability.

Scholars have questioned the empirical underpinnings of this line of argument. Are people really so easily confused?[49] Moreover, given the extensive overlap of state and federal power in so many areas, how important is it that some area of state exclusivity be maintained? Citizens would need a fairly sharp sense of discernment to know which would be the few areas in which Washington was immune from responsibility. One might well suppose that the creeping federalization of family law,[50] education,[51] and crime[52] has sufficiently blurred the boundaries of traditional areas of state authority to render them of little conceptual use.

Further, even if the concept of traditional areas of state regulation retains some cogency, the Court's attempt at line drawing has done little to protect these domains. The distinction between commercial and noncommercial activity simply does not define the relevant boundaries. As was apparent as far back as *Gibbons v. Ogden*,[53] many areas of traditional state concern involve commercial activity. As *Gibbons* recognized almost two hundred years ago, state health and safety regulations apply to commercial activities that are clearly within the scope of potential federal regulation.[54] Indeed, one of the most significant methods of state regulation has been through common law tort actions. Recently, however, the United States Supreme Court has held various state tort actions impliedly preempted by federal law.[55] This kind of preemption of state court activity, in addition to other forms of federal preemption, invades spheres that seem as likely as any other to be associated with ultimate state authority.[56]

Thus, if preserving clear channels of accountability is a genuine concern, the attempt to draw lines around state domains does little to address it. In the complex commercial society of the United States, the overlap of actual and potential state and federal regulation is too extensive. The point is not to deny that accountability is ever a relevant concern. Rather, the dualist attempt to draw lines between state and federal authority does not represent an effective means of guaranteeing accountability. A polyphonic account asks how states and the national government might best work together to promote political accountability, consistent with the other values of polyphony.

The challenge for a polyphonic account of federalism is how and when to promote the values of plurality, dialogue, and redundancy without undermining important concerns for uniformity, finality, and hierarchical accountability. That challenge may be difficult, but the polyphonic account at least identifies the proper values for managing the overlap of federal and state power.

For example, as discussed earlier, the dualist approach provides little guidance in assessing the No Child Left Behind law. Polyphony provides at least a framework for analysis. NCLB constitutes a joint state-federal effort to improve education. States have some discretion in implementing the program, subject to various federal guidelines. NCLB should allow states to learn from each other and from the national government. The national government also can build on the best practices of the states. The federal government may grant waivers from its guidelines and learn from the experiences of states that depart from the rules.[57] Subject to federal baselines, the states can vary their practices, and practices can evolve over time.

NCLB seeks to minimize the areas in which the federal government imposes a uniform and final answer. At the same time, the concurrent actions of the state and national governments give redundant protection for educational achievement. Consistent with the polyphonic framework, NCLB focuses centrally on issues of accountability.[58] Unlike a dualist approach, NCLB does not assume that providing an exclusive realm of state authority best promotes accountability. Instead, the act seeks to advance accountability directly by imposing federal reporting requirements on state and local school boards. The act tries to hold local school authorities accountable, and states have proved themselves most willing to point their fingers at the federal government if they perceive hardships caused by the federally mandated regime.[59]

This analysis rests to some extent on an optimistic account of NCLB. Some aspects of NCLB, especially the reliance on particular high-stakes tests, have been criticized for squelching local variation.[60] In other words, NCLB may be too monophonic. The central point remains, though, that the polyphonic approach highlights the relevant concerns. The dualist framework of dividing state and federal power does not provide similar illumination. Complex problems require more than moving the state-federal line in one direction or another.

Federalism issues arise with great frequency in the United States today. Should each state develop its own approach to the use of marijuana for medical purposes, or should there be a uniform national policy?[61] Should each state's judicial system offer alternative remedies for classes of potential victims, or should the national court system provide a uniform venue for large multistate actions?[62] Such questions remain difficult, but the polyphonic account at least identifies the proper values for managing the overlap of federal and state power. The nature of these values also suggests which governmental bodies should be managing the potential allocational conflicts and which should not.

POLYPHONY AND THE VALUES OF FEDERALISM

The previous section discusses the advantages of a polyphonic system. Though I focus on the benefits of a polyphonic understanding of the relationship of the states and the federal government, the arguments apply more broadly. In a variety of contexts, systems that rely on multiple sources of power prove more resilient and innovative than systems that have a single source of authority. In this way, polyphonic federalism is like the market or the personal computer, a decentralized, multiunit alternative to purely centralized functioning.

Through the dynamic interaction of state and federal authority, polyphonic federalism also advances the goals traditionally associated with federalism, including responsive and efficient policies, republican self-governance, and the prevention of tyranny. Though these aims are common to both the polyphonic and the dualist approaches, the polyphonic methods of promoting them would differ greatly from those employed by dualist federalism.

Independent state power means that states could pursue their own policy preferences. Under the polyphonic conception, interstate competition would still occur, and states could still serve as laboratories of innovation. Federalism would not, however, act as an antitrust principle, protecting against interstate collusion. If states managed to capture federal authority and impose uniform federal regulation as a way to squelch competition, no judicial intervention would inhibit them. Nevertheless, a polyphonic conception might well lead to more competition. States would be freed to experiment in some areas of policymaking that are currently preempted under dualist judicial review. Even under the Rehnquist Court's federalism decisions, the judicially enforceable limits on federal power remain weak. Our constitutional system simply provides very little protection against the federalization of policy decisions.

As discussed earlier, the most significant issues relating to state policy experimentation occur in the context of federal preemption and the dormant Commerce Clause. Here, the polyphonic conception would empower states. Polyphonic federalism understands the overlap and competition of state and federal authority to be the norm. Once federalism is understood as working through state-federal interaction, rather than through state-federal separation, neither the federal regulation of noncommercial areas nor the overlap of state and federal regulations serves as a cause for alarm. Neither should usually elicit judicial interference. In this way, polyphonic federalism would endow the states with more real policy discretion, even as it removes the slight barrier that the Court has erected in giving the states exclusive control in some small areas. A comparison of the cases in which the Court has limited federal activity in the name of federalism with the cases in which the Court has used preemption or the dormant Commerce Clause to invalidate state actions suggests that less judicial interference would give more policy prerogative to the states.[63]

Polyphonic federalism guarantees the integrity of state institutions, ensuring that loci of local self-governance would exist and would provide fora for political participation. These participatory institutions would continue to keep habits of civic engagement strong. Indeed, maintaining the state policymaking apparatus serves as a crucial element of a polyphonic regime. States must have their own voices. As with the economic approach, with regard to the republican perspective, the polyphonic conception would eliminate some formal safeguards, while offering more real power to the states. In the polyphonic view, no particular policy area would fall under the exclusive control of local democratic institutions. The federal government could undertake its preferred initiatives, no matter what the outcome of local deliberations. No constitutional barrier would prevent broad federal programs that would render the state legislature a debating society, with little policy control. On the other hand, the narrower view of federal preemption and the dormant Commerce Clause entailed in the polyphonic conception would almost certainly lead to much greater real policy discretion.

The polyphonic conception would yield the greatest benefits in protecting against tyranny. Dualist conceptions understand federalism to prevent tyranny by limiting the power of the national government. In this view, safeguarding a sphere of independent state authority inhibits the central government's ability to oppress the people. This classically liberal defense of federalism seems quite out of step with modern experience. In the United States, the actual protection against governmental overreaching has come from the individual rights portion of the United States Constitution, rather than from any limits on the scope of federal power. Moreover, it has been the federal government that has been most active in protecting against governmental abuses and the state governments that have been the sources of oppression. The Civil Rights Act of 1964[64] and the Voting Rights Act[65] are prime illustrations of the central role of the national government in fighting tyranny. Claims to protect enclaves of state authority served to impede, rather than promote, the protection of individuals.

Polyphonic federalism recognizes that safeguarding individual rights may well require affirmative governmental action. States and the national government can cooperate and compete to ensure the best realization of individual liberty. In the contemporary United States, oppression often comes not from the absence of an abstract right, but rather from failures of implementation. The promise of a remedy for every right traces to the beginnings of the Republic and beyond.[66] Nevertheless, problems of enforceability remain; remedial gaps exist. Here, the advantages of polyphonic federalism become prominent. Polyphonic federalism understands state and federal courts, like other state and federal institutions, to engage in an overlapping and competitive relationship. As discussed in later chapters, that kind of interaction contains the greatest promise for the fullest vindication of state and federal rights in the contemporary United States.

So far this chapter has discussed the advantages of polyphonic systems and has argued that, given the integrated national society of the contemporary United States, a polyphonic rather than a dualist approach best promotes the values of federalism, including innovative and responsive governance, democratic participation, and prevention of tyranny. Is it still possible that even in United States today, dualism might better protect some right in some circumstances? Certainly. One could imagine a situation in which a state seeks to safeguard some important value, but the federal government overrides the state protection. Even with an emerging national consensus on many important issues, some areas of controversy remain. As discussed in chapter 1, issues of sexual identity, including homosexual marriage, continue to divide the country. In that area, or in some other, one could imagine a state providing more "protection" than the federal government. Depending on one's understanding of the issue, "protection" might take a variety of forms and might be more "protective" of the rights of gays and lesbians or of those defending "traditional" social arrangements. Opponents of the state's choice might go to Congress and seek preemptive federal legislation to override the state law. Dualism offers a hope of a court's blocking this end run around local preference. If a dualist court were to define the particular area of state policy as "truly local," then the state law would receive judicially enforced constitutional protection against interference from the federal government.

Is dualism thus vindicated? No. Several important qualifications should be kept in mind. First, whether any particular area would be defined as "truly local" is uncertain. The lack of social referent for this label renders the category unpredictable in application. A second, and related point, is that the expansive understanding of Congress's power to bribe or cajole states through its spending decisions saps the constitutional safeguard of real force. Even under a dualist conception, Congress can achieve almost any goal it truly seeks to accomplish. The Court speaks of the "truly local," but the Constitution affords to Congress broad powers over spending and commercial regulation. Money and economic activity flow freely without regard to notions of "local" or "national." Given the integrated national economy, the concepts of "local" and national" do not fit with the actual constitutional allocation of authority. The Constitution does not follow the Court's map of authority.

More generally, a constitutional system cannot provide perfect answers in every situation. In the modest words of the Framers, the goal is a "more perfect Union."[67] Absolute perfection is unattainable in this world. A well-functioning constitution establishes structures that are optimal over the broad range of cases. I have explained why, overall, polyphonic systems perform well and why in the contemporary United States polyphonic federalism is likely to provide better protection for rights than dualist federalism. A potential counterexample based on the most contentious issue in contemporary moral debate does not negate the larger claim. If one was certain of what rights deserved vindication and of which level of government would provide the optimal level of protection, then one would want control over that area given to that government. Such foreknowledge, however, is impossible; nor is it likely that one government would remain the best rights champion over the course of time, nor is there reason to believe that it is one level of government rather than an interaction of multiple layers of governance that would best ensure rights at any given time. Indeed, as this book explains, many reasons suggest that interaction rather than isolation will be the best strategy.

Methodological Comparison: From Dualism to Polyphony

To give further definition to the concept of polyphonic federalism, this section turns to a consideration of some key methodological issues. Comparison with the dualist conception of federalism serves to highlight some of the important features of the polyphonic perspective.

A FEDERALISM OF STRUCTURE

A significant similarity between the polyphonic and the dualist conceptions of federalism lies in their reliance on structural arguments. The focus of my argument is structural and pragmatic, rather than textual or originalist. My main concern lies in examining the theoretical and doctrinal problems that accompany dualist understandings of federalism and in proposing an alternative that avoids these difficulties and better accords with the actual operation of governments in the United States today. The polyphonic conception of federalism, I contend, more accurately describes the allocation of authority between states and the national government. Polyphony also provides a normatively more attractive approach to regulating the distribution of political power.

The polyphonic approach does not derive directly from the text of the Constitution. It is not an interpretation of the language of the Interstate Commerce Clause[68] and the Necessary and Proper Clause.[69] The polyphonic approach may well be consistent with a variety of interpretations of those provisions,[70] but for present purposes, structure, not text, provides the primary constitutional foundation. The United States Constitution contemplates a system with important and independent roles for the states and for the national government. Polyphonic federalism adheres to that conception.

In its reliance on structural inferences from the Constitution, the polyphonic perspective differs little from dualism. Contemporary visions of dualist federalism have similarly limited textual support. The United States Supreme Court does use the word "commercial" to tie its analysis to the constitutional grant of authority to Congress to regulate "Commerce . . . among the several States."[71] The focus of the Supreme Court's concern, however, does not lie with some essential definition of commerce. The Court has acknowledged the difficulty in divining what constitutes "commerce."[72] Nor does the Court seem interested in pursuing an originalist inquiry into the meaning of "commerce" at the time of the framing. Justice Thomas alone has urged such a course.[73] Legal scholars differ on where such an inquiry would lead.[74]

Rather, the Court seeks some way to distinguish the "truly local" from the "truly national."[75] The reliance on the distinction between commercial and noncommercial activity is a means of achieving that goal. The weight of the Court's argument is structural, not textual. The terms "truly local" and "truly national" do not appear in the Constitution. Indeed, the word "federalism" does not itself appear in the document. The Court's overriding imperative is to find some boundary to federal authority. It is crucial to distinguish here between original meaning and original expectation. The Framers of the Constitution likely did not expect that the federal government would exercise powers essentially concurrent with those of the states. The Framers likely did not expect that the states and the national government would evolve into modern administrative states with all manner of regulation. That is to say, the Framers were not clairvoyant. As Jack Balkin has explained at length, though, originalism should look to the meaning of the constitutional text, not to the applications expected by the Framers.[76]

Again, my argument for polyphony—like the Court's support for dualism—rests not on originalist but on structural principles. A focus on the interrelationship, rather than the separation, of state and federal authority can achieve the goals usually ascribed to federalism, and other goals as well, with greater theoretical clarity and fewer doctrinal burdens.

FORMALISM AND FUNCTIONALISM

Although polyphony and dualism share a structural orientation, their methods differ in important respects. Dualism is fundamentally a formalist approach to the allocation of power between the states and the national government. Dualism claims to advance a variety of values, but it does so through drawing lines. Dualism attempts to deploy categorical distinctions, such as commercial/noncommercial and "truly local"/"truly national." It turns out, however, that drawing lines does not clearly accomplish these goals. Creating protected enclaves of state authority does not realize the aims of economic, republican, or liberal theory; nor can the boundaries of state authority be clearly defined.

As is apparent from the foregoing discussion, polyphonic federalism also could be analyzed in terms of the tension between a set of values and a set of counter-values. The polyphonic conception, though, avoids the formalist rigidity of dualism. Instead, the goal is to find a functional balance of federal and state authority. Polyphony embraces the tension; it does not seek to avoid it by resorting to other categorical distinctions. Accordingly, the tensions do not become irreconcilable antinomies. Doctrinal structures can accommodate plurality, dialogue, and redundancy, while also fostering uniformity, finality, and hierarchical accountability. The overlap of state and federal authority can be managed so as to recognize both sets of values. Indeed, in some instances, one set of values can be promoted without threatening the other.

The dualist perspective, by contrast, conceives of the states and the national government as neighbors. Some areas may be subject to their joint use, but some are not. The states and the national government each enjoy a constitutionally protected space. The boundaries of the protected domains must be drawn somewhere. The more area given to the state, the more area that must be taken away from the national government. In the polyphonic perspective, the states and the national government are not neighbors. The concept of polyphony seeks to avoid such spatial metaphors and their attendant dualism. If property law is to provide guidance, the appropriate relationship would be closer to a joint tenancy. The states and the federal government generally enjoy a joint, undivided interest. Conflicts will occur, but as the following chapters illustrate, it is through the conflicts that federalism works. State and federal interaction and confrontation are part of the system; they are harnessed to advance the goals of federalism.

THE ROLE OF COURTS

Judicial administrability serves as one of the chief justifications for the Court's attempt to construct a dualist approach using distinctions such as commercial/noncommercial. One suspects that this concern for judicially applicable rules helps to explain the persistence of dualist notions of federalism in the courts, while cooperative federalism long has been the norm in the administrative relations of the states and the national government. Drawing lines is something that courts can do, and applying categorical distinctions seems well suited to the judicial role. In this manner, the Court is retracing the historical evolution of the Commerce Clause doctrine. The New Deal Court's move from a formal to a functional analysis of Commerce Clause questions led to a greater deference to Congress. In cases such as *Wickard*, the wheat case, the Court recognized that Congress had a much greater capacity to evaluate an activity's practical effect on interstate commerce.[77] Seeking a larger judicial role, while recognizing the problem of institutional competence, the Rehnquist Court returned to a categorical framework. By reinstituting formal characterizations of activities, the Court has sought to move Commerce Clause jurisprudence into a posture more amenable to judicial enforcement.

It may be that active judicial supervision can succeed only with relatively rigid, if arbitrary, lines. If that analysis is correct, however, it is the active judicial intervention that must cease. The polyphonic conception of federalism rejects drawing lines between state and federal power. Polyphony ends the search for the "truly local" and the "truly national." It substitutes the functional considerations of plurality, dialogue, and redundancy, along with the countervailing concerns for uniformity, finality, and accountability. The substitution of functional for formal criteria entails a diminished role for courts. Legislatures can do a much better job than courts in trying to sort out the relevant considerations. Therefore, courts should defer to this legislative calculus.

Whether concurrent regulation of guns in schools or gender-motivated violence promotes or hinders the values of federalism is a question for Congress, not for the courts. Accordingly, the dualist project of *Lopez* and *Morrison* should be abandoned as pointless efforts to safeguard a truly local sphere that does not exist and cannot be created. Few other existing precedents would need to be revised because the Court so rarely has actually located such privileged domains of local power. The courts should return to their pre-*Lopez* posture of deference to the relative institutional competence of Congress.

Some state-federal interactions, however, demand judicial supervision. Preemption and dormant Commerce Clause issues arise when Congress has not clearly spoken. In such instances, the courts must interpret a statutory scheme or the constitutional principle of a national market. Indeed, these kinds of controversies currently constitute the bulk of the federalism cases in the courts.[78] In a polyphonic conception, courts would still have to review these alleged state infringements on national prerogative. The standard that the courts would apply, however, would be much more sympathetic to concurrent state and federal regulation.

The United States Constitution has an important structural role in regulating the interaction of state and federal governments. One of the significant ways in which the Constitution sets the framework for that interaction is through background principles of interpretation. Interpretive rules governing federal-state interaction figure centrally in the polyphonic account. The Supreme Court recently has fashioned several "plain statement" rules to protect the constitutional values of federalism.[79] These rules recognize a role for the Constitution in setting principles of interpretation. Many of the important questions of federalism relate to the content of those rules.

In the polyphonic conception, courts should apply a background presumption that state power and federal power can coexist.[80] In the absence of evidence to the contrary, courts should not strike down state laws because they operate in the same field as federal law. This presumption would apply in both the preemption and the dormant Commerce Clause settings. Both involve situations in which the courts must decide whether to permit state regulation in an area in which Congress could, but has not, clearly excluded the states. Courts should not be in the business of eliminating state regulatory plans in the name of creating uniform federal regulatory policy. The existence of multiple overlapping regimes of regulation represents one of the important consequences of federalism. Such concurrence promotes plurality, dialogue, and redundancy. The presumption of concurrence would decrease implied preemption of state laws that stand as an "obstacle" to the achievement of federal purposes.

The presumption of concurrence also would limit the scope of the Court's doctrine voiding nondiscriminatory state laws that impose an undue burden on commerce. The Court currently applies a balancing test to such laws,[81] and the presumption in favor of concurrent regulation would serve as a factor weighing against the invalidation of state law. Such a presumption could be overcome by contrary evidence of an unusual need for uniformity.

The presumption of concurrence would leave large areas of preemption and dormant Commerce Clause doctrine unchanged. Congress could expressly preempt state law. States still could not discriminate against commerce from other states.[82] In the absence of congressional guidance, though, the presumption would lead the courts toward a greater acceptance of concurrent state regulation. The values of polyphonic federalism, then, correspond to deferential review when Congress clearly has decided to regulate an area. In conditions of less certainty, such as preemption and the dormant Commerce Clause, the courts would be more accommodating of state action.

Polyphony Applied: Reconsidering Preemption

Preemption is inherently monophonic. When a federal law preempts a state law, the state voice is silenced. Only the federal regulation remains. Chapter 3 discussed the lingering dualism in the current Supreme Court's approach to preemption. Preemption fits well into a dualist conception. If the federal government has intervened in a particular area, state regulation in that area is viewed with suspicion. Preemption helps to keep lines of authority clear.

To explore further the implications of polyphonic federalism, I now offer an alternative account of preemption. One of the chief deficiencies in the Court's preemption jurisprudence lies in the failure to appreciate the value of concurrent state and federal regulation. The Court gives lip service to the concept that preemption should be limited to particular areas, but the Court conceives this principle in dualist terms. In *Rice v. Santa Fe Elevator Corp.*, the Supreme Court used dualist language in declaring an "assumption" against preemption: "[W]e start with the assumption that the historic police powers of the States were not to be superseded by the Federal Act unless that was the clear and manifest purpose of Congress."[83]

Rice's reference to "historic police powers" has assumed a talismanic quality, meriting repetition throughout the Court's preemption jurisprudence.[84] It is not clear, however, that this *Rice* presumption against preemption has a dispositive effect on the outcome of actual cases.[85] In *Rice*, the Court held that the federal law did preempt state law. *Rice* often is cited in dissent from decisions holding state law preempted.[86] Moreover, the decision offers no sympathy for concurrent regulation. *Rice* does not recognize the benefits of polyphony. To the contrary, *Rice* affirms the dualist principle that the federal government should tread lightly when it walks in areas reserved for state authority.

From the polyphonic perspective, the problem of federal preemption of state law lies in its eliminating the advantages of regulatory overlap. Preemption is "jurispathic," erasing the benefits of concurrent legal regimes.[87] The negation of state law destroys plurality, dialogue, and redundancy. These losses occur whether the effect of the preemptive federal law is to replace the state regulations with a comprehensive, national scheme or to forestall all regulation. Whether there is one set of regulations or none, the possibilities for experimentation, for dynamic interaction and learning, and for the fail-safe benefits of multiple regulators all disappear. The polyphonic account acknowledges the potential benefits of preemption, in terms of uniformity, finality, and accountability. The polyphonic framework thus provides a coherent, functional method for analyzing preemption.

THE UNAVOIDABILITY OF INTERSTATE EFFECTS: NO STATE IS AN ISLAND

Preemption can be understood as a way to promote accountability by prohibiting states from shifting costs to other states.[88] This defense of preemption, though, fails to account for the reality of overlapping fields of regulation. Regulations rarely, if ever, have effects solely within a single jurisdiction. In the United States, interstate movement is pervasive. People travel from state to state, and firms do business in multiple states. Indeed, the facilitation of interstate movement and commerce provided a central motive for the decision to replace the Articles of Confederation with the United States Constitution.[89] Regulating people and firms who operate in more than one jurisdiction will inevitably have interstate effects. The costs and benefits will travel with the regulated entity. Laws that touch the stream of commerce in one state will have downstream and upstream effects. Rules that increase the cost of doing business in one state will have an impact on the production and management that may occur elsewhere. Laws in one state will influence the products and profits throughout the United States. In this sense, every state law has effects outside the state, and no state can resist the incursion of laws from other states.

In the contemporary context, the development of the Internet helps to crystallize the diminished importance of territoriality.[90] On the World Wide Web, the concept of territory loses its traditional referent. Business and social life transpire in a place not defined by physical geography. Amazon. com has actual physical facilities, but those seem far removed from the shopping center it provides. Ebay is not really in the East Bay, and MySpace and Second Life create real spaces that do not correspond to existing political boundaries.

Spillover effects, then, are pervasive. A state's actions will produce effects that pour over its borders in all directions. Such spillovers, moreover, are not limited to the economic realm. The social and moral policies of one state may have an impact on people all over the United States. Whatever the recognition policy in the various states, the ability of gay and lesbian couples to receive official validation of their marriages or partnerships in some states may have significant effects in other states, especially, but not exclusively, those in which the couples choose to live. The abortion policies, the alcohol sale policies, the firearms policies, and many other policies of neighboring states may have an impact on the social fabric of a particular state. Executions in one state may give rise to feelings of moral horror or satisfaction in others. As became especially clear in 2000, the electoral policies of one state may determine the outcome of an election for president of the United States. As long as state borders exist, spillover effects will exist.

If preemption is contemplated as an antidote to spillovers, some theory must differentiate among different kinds of extraterritorial impacts. It cannot be the mere existence of interstate effects that triggers preemption. Rather, certain kinds of cross-border incursions must elicit special scrutiny. A concern among many preemption scholars is that states may seek to shift costs onto out-of-state businesses, while retaining benefits for those within the state.[91]

Such conduct is theoretically possible. Real firms do exist in particular locations. Corporations are incorporated in particular states and have offices and perhaps factories in specific locations. State legislatures, agencies, or courts could seek to identify out-of-state firms and target them for costly regulation. Somewhat more benignly, state regulators might act with selective indifference, showing concern for the costs that regulations impose within the state, but ignoring the potential costs that fall on out-of-state parties. The potential inefficiency and inequity of calculating in-state benefits, without concern for out-of-state costs, might justify the promulgation of a uniform federal rule, which would avoid that tendency to predation.[92]

The diffuse nature of firm ownership, however, renders such cost-shifting difficult. The state of incorporation reflects merely a choice of law to govern internal corporate affairs, rather than any substantial connection to that state. Factories and offices do exist in specific states, but the overall economic beneficiaries of firms tend to be widely dispersed.[93] The stockholders, individual and institutional, and other stakeholders of a firm have no necessary geographical relationship with that firm. In sum, the diminished significance of territorial boundaries makes it much more difficult for regulators or courts to identify the true outsider, who would be the appropriate target for cost externalization.

The prevalence of attempted cost shifting is an empirical question. Professors Eric Helland and Alexander Tabarrok have undertaken several studies of the potential judicial targeting of out-of-state defendants. Their research suggests that defendants who are out-of-state firms are subject to larger damage awards in states using partisan judicial elections.[94] Interestingly, their results highlight the differential outcomes in the ten states in which judges are elected on partisan ballots. The key finding is not that out-of-state firms generally fare worse in tort litigation, but that such firms fare worse only in states with partisan election systems.[95] Indeed, the bias against out-of-state defendants disappeared when the study examined cases decided by federal courts, sitting in diversity.[96] The Helland and Tabarrok studies strongly suggest that it is not the law or the juries that may target out-of-state firms, but rather judges selected through partisan elections. Cost shifting appears to result from particular electoral structures, rather than from substantive state policies.

More generally, it is not clear why out-of-state businesses cannot protect their interests adequately in the state political process. Such firms individually or collectively are well situated to make their arguments known through advertising and campaign contributions. With regard to judicial elections, firms have become more active in protecting their interests. The United States Chamber of Commerce and other business organizations recently have intervened with growing vigor to elect pro-business candidates.[97] These efforts may reverse even the residual out-of-state bias that Helland and Tabarrok detected in states with partisan judicial elections.

To the extent that a normative theory of impermissible spillover effects is needed, one relatively well-developed doctrine appears suited to answer that call. The dormant Commerce Clause functions exactly to negate state laws that discriminate against interstate commerce or impermissibly burden interstate commerce. That doctrine targets a small subset of state actions with interstate effects and subjects them to harsh treatment, invalidating them without the need for any congressional action in the area. The normative underpinnings of the doctrine appear with clarity in various judicial opinions. Justice John Paul Stevens, for example, is one of the justices least likely to find state regulations preempted by federal law, but he has an active and robust view of the scope of the dormant Commerce Clause.[98] Protecting the free flow of commerce from partisan interference stands as a normative goal of supreme importance. In more extreme cases, the Due Process Clause restricts the ability of states to regulate truly out-of-state conduct.[99] The potential for spillover effects does not, by itself, justify broad preemption of state law.

A distinct though related concern arises specifically from the problem of standard products designed for a national market.[100] Complying with varying regulatory regimes in different states might eliminate economies of scale and raise the price of the product everywhere. In addition, the manufacturer as a practical matter might be compelled to design the product in accordance with the standards of the most populous state or group of states. A small state might never be able to influence the safety features of such a product. In such circumstances, the arguments against a preemptive national standard diminish. The choice is not between plural standards and a single standard, but between a single standard set by California and a single standard set by a national process.

Even in this situation, a preemptive federal standard may not be the best solution. The federal government can facilitate greater regulatory uniformity without simply displacing state law. Acting as a coordinator, rather than as a command-and-control regulator, the federal government can encourage states to work toward uniform laws. Similarly, the federal government could urge states to devise their own regulatory systems and then give all states the option of choosing from a short menu of sister-state regulatory alternatives. Or the federal government could require state regulations to follow a general federal framework designed to reduce interstate conflict. This option could include a requirement to seek federal approval before implementing a plan.[101] All of these schemes would promote plurality, dialogue, and redundancy. The resulting regulations would reflect a dynamic, bottom-up system. However, by limiting the number of choices, this plan would afford some measure of uniformity, or at least constrained diversity.

Finally, concerns for uniformity should never lead to the elimination of a state compensatory scheme without the substitution of an alternative, individual remedy. State tort systems have regulatory impacts, but they serve other purposes as well. Of particular relevance to the study of preemption, tort law administered by courts seeks both to deter certain forms of conduct and to compensate victims. Much tort scholarship focuses on the role of private lawsuits in regulating risk-creating behavior.[102] Tort law, however, also seeks to redress harms to individuals[103] and to advance goals of corrective justice.[104] While the regulatory function of tort law might duplicate the role of federal regulations, the redress and corrective justice functions do not. Most agency risk regulation proceeds at the systemic level. Preempting state tort suits with federal administrative standards would thus greatly reduce the plurality of legal voices. Preemptive federal action would not merely replace a state voice with a federal voice or replace one form of risk regulation with another. Federal preemption would completely eliminate the individual voice of redress and corrective justice. The federalist system offers the possibility of both federal regulation of systemic risks and state redress for harmed individuals. Polyphonic federalism allows both voices to sing.

Federal regulators should be cautious before decreeing that a category of accident victims must bear their own losses because of the larger needs of the national economy. Some benchmark must be fashioned to define what constitutes a compensable harm. Nevertheless, that benchmark may not match the regulatory goals of the overall program. Regulators may also decide that the best course of action is to promote a uniform national design standard, while making provisions to compensate all who suffer harm, even if that standard is met.[105] It certainly would be reasonable to decide, for example, that auto manufacturers should not be required to install airbags, without necessarily deciding that no auto manufacturer should be found liable if someone is injured because of the absence of an airbag. At least a court should not assume that a decision not to impose a requirement is necessarily a decision to preempt a compensatory tort action.

NATIONAL UNIFORMITY AND THE POST-WESTPHALIAN ORDER

The federal interest in uniformity, especially in foreign policy matters, provides another justification for preemption.[106] The federal government certainly has the power to dictate the foreign policy of the United States, and the United States Supreme Court has construed broadly the congressional desire to prohibit states from developing their own foreign policies.[107] Throughout the world, however, regulatory authority increasingly is exercised by supranational and subnational bodies. The nation-state no longer functions as the sole source of law. In this way, a post-Westphalian order is emerging. Federalism and globalization are creating alternative nodes of power. The polyphonic conception of federalism accords with global trends to look beyond the nation-state for the exercise of power.

Under the Westphalian system, the sovereign state is the principal political unit.[108] While the nation-state certainly retains its central role in contemporary politics, that dominance is waning. Supranational bodies such as the European Union, the World Trade Organization, and entities devised by the North American Free Trade Agreement exercise significant power. Subnational units do as well. Consider again Governor Arnold Schwarzenegger's description of California as "the modern equivalent of the ancient city-states of Athens and Sparta."[109] This comment captures a decidedly non-Westphalian conception of the nation-state. The Westphalian nation-state is not supposed to include autonomous city-states.

As in the domestic context, it is the emerging global consensus on a broad range of powerful issues that creates the precondition for such devolution of authority onto nonnational entities. Goals are widely shared. Subnational and supranational units work individually and together to explore different means to reach generally accepted ends.

These nonnational entities have been especially active in the area of climate change. The federal government has undertaken little action to mitigate the effect of greenhouse gases and global warming. For example, the United States refused to ratify the Kyoto Protocol, which concerned global warming.[110] In the face of inaction by the national government, states and regions have attempted to address climate change. California has undertaken various initiatives designed to control the output of carbon dioxide.[111] Seven northeastern and mid-Atlantic states entered into a memorandum of understanding regarding a plan to cut carbon dioxide emissions through a cap and trade plan. Other organizations of governors are working to develop their own regional plans to reduce greenhouse gases.[112]

In an even more direct threat to the primacy of the nation-state, various states have worked with Canadian provinces on devising plans to address climate change. In 2001, the Conference of New England Governors and Eastern Canadian Premiers adopted a "climate action plan," which included specific targets for the reduction of greenhouses gases. A less formal organization, known as "Powering the Plains," includes representatives from North Dakota, South Dakota, Iowa, Minnesota, Wisconsin, and Manitoba. The group is collaborating on alternative fuel projects.[113]

Professor Kirsten Engel has published a series of articles explaining the value of these regional environmental efforts.[114] While these collaborations may have little impact on climate change overall, they may promote a variety of benefits. These projects may develop innovative solutions to common problems and may prod the national government into action. These efforts illustrate the value of plurality, dialogue, and redundancy. The state regulatory process provides information to the United States and affords a fail-safe mechanism should national regulations be absent or fall short of desired goals.

Global subnational initiatives exist outside of the environmental context as well. Professor Judith Resnik has documented the transnational

story of groups seeking to gain local support for the Convention to Eliminate All Forms of Discrimination Against Women (CEDAW).[115] The United
States has not ratified CEDAW. Several transnational nongovernmental organizations, including Amnesty International and the General Federation
of Women's Clubs, encouraged states and localities to endorse CEDAW.
Resnik reports that "[a]s of 2004, forty-four cities, eighteen counties, and
sixteen states have passed or considered legislation relating to CEDAW."[116]

San Francisco has gone further and sought to implement some of the
provisions of CEDAW by investigating and issuing reports relating to systematic discrimination against women.[117] Similarly, Los Angeles adopted an
ordinance noting the "continuing need . . . to protect the human rights of
women and girls by addressing discrimination, including violence, against
them and to implement, locally, the principles of CEDAW."[118]

These examples indicate that states and localities can interact directly
with international organizations and conventions. These global-regarding
activities may have some capacity to spur the United States to action, or at
least mitigate to some small degree the perceived harms of federal inaction.
These state and local initiatives do not contradict the foreign policy of the
United States government. Rather, states and localities have taken positions
in situations in which the national government has declined to make a
commitment. Prohibiting these kinds of actions by state and local governments would promote national uniformity, but would not advance any
independent federal interest. Applying broad doctrines of preemption to
prohibit these efforts to think globally/act locally with global effects would
achieve little benefit and risk broad losses. If significant federal interests do
exist, Congress or the president should clearly articulate the nature of these
interests and the necessity for their preemptive scope. The unique functions
of the nation-state are diminishing in number, and contemporary doctrines
of preemption should not try to recapture the lost world in which nation-
states alone exercised significant prerogatives.[119] The polyphonic approach
understands federalism within the United States in the context of these
global trends.

CHAPTER FIVE

The Benefits of Intersystemic Adjudication

Once one understands the interaction of state and federal authority as the
core of federalism, one can gain new insights into the relationships among
a variety of governmental institutions. The interrelationship of state and
federal legislative and regulatory schemes was highlighted in the discussion
of preemption.[1] This chapter and chapter 6 explore the implications for the
judicial system of the polyphonic conception of federalism.

Some of the key features of this legal regime have been discussed already.
The courts would not invoke categories such as economic and noneconomic
as part of an effort to divide state and federal authority. The courts would
not broadly construe principles of preemption so as to forestall concurrent
state and federal regulatory regimes. Some of the most important aspects of
polyphony, though, will be realized in the rules governing the jurisdiction
of state and federal courts. These sometimes arcane principles play a large
role in guaranteeing important values, including the vindication of human
rights.

An important element of the polyphonic conception of federalism is
a recognition of the particular place of courts in realizing the promise of
federalism. As compared with dualism, courts have less of a role as refer-
ees. Courts do not draw and police lines between state and federal authority. Instead, courts themselves participate in promoting plurality, dialogue,
and redundancy. As Professor James Gardner has emphasized, courts act as
"agents of federalism."[2] The presumption of concurrence applies to courts
as well as to state and federal legislative and regulatory bodies. In the judicial arena, too, the interaction of state and federal authority promotes the
goals of federalism.

An examination of the implications of polyphony for principles of judicial jurisdiction casts light on an area that should be but often is not

connected to larger debates about federalism.[3] Discussions of federalism generally focus on the regulatory authority of Congress and of the states. State and federal courts, though, also play significant roles in realizing the benefits of federalism. Further, arguments about the jurisdiction of the federal and state courts often occur without an appreciation of the larger framework of federalism. This chapter and chapter 6 attempt to remedy these omissions by integrating the analysis of judicial jurisdiction into an overall conception of federalism.

As will become apparent, the structure of judicial federalism resembles that of regulatory federalism in important respects. Much of the existing jurisdictional rhetoric repeats dualist principles of separating state and federal authority. At the same time, in actual practice, the jurisdiction of the federal and state courts overlaps and intertwines. Thus, as with my previous treatment of regulatory federalism, my account of jurisdiction is both descriptive and prescriptive. These chapters call attention to important, and often underappreciated, elements of jurisdictional polyphony. Further, building on the conception of polyphonic federalism I have been developing, I ground and defend these jurisdictional interactions. Exercises of jurisdiction that seem aberrant from a dualist point of view turn out to be principled and beneficial when viewed from a polyphonic perspective.

Polyphonic federalism points the way to an important use of courts to implement rights. The redundancy of state and federal court systems provides a significant advantage of judicial federalism in the United States.[4] If one system fails in its promise to protect rights, the other remains ready to intervene. Intersystemic adjudication, in which a court defined by one political system implements the laws of another system, represents the flowering of polyphonic federalism in the judicial realm. This chapter illustrates how intersystemic adjudication could fulfill the promise of polyphony.

Unlike most other federalist polities, the United States maintains a fully developed dual court system, with federal trial and appellate courts and state trial and appellate benches in every state.[5] Most other federalist systems employ a single set of lower courts, generally identified with the subnational units, which hear cases raising issues of national or subnational law.[6] Given the dual judicial system in the United States, cases must be allocated among state and federal courts. This distributional decision involves an important question of federalism, how power should be assigned among states and the national government. The different structural features of state and federal courts in the United States magnify the importance of the choice. The electoral accountability of most state judges, in contrast to federal judges, may give the state and federal courts different perspectives on issues, particularly those relating to hotly contested matters of public policy.[7]

The existence of a dual court system creates the possibility of allocating cases based on the law at issue. Federal questions could be sent to federal court and state questions to state court, though of course cases raising both kinds of issues would pose allocational difficulties. Instead, in the United States, the jurisdictions of the state and federal courts overlap extensively. Issues of state law commonly arise in and are adjudicated by federal courts; issues of federal law commonly arise in and are adjudicated by state courts.

Such intersystemic adjudication occurs in all federalist polities. Indeed, the absence of dual judiciaries necessitates the practice. If all lower courts are subnational courts, much application of federal law will take place in nonfederal courts. The existence of a dual judicial system with largely overlapping jurisdiction, however, gives a distinctive cast to intersystemic adjudication in the United States. The same issue may arise in state and in federal court, and litigants have the ability to choose their preferred forum for the adjudication of the issue in their specific case.

From a dualist perspective, intersystemic adjudication constitutes a necessary evil. Consistent with the attempt to divide state from federal power, dualists argue that the courts of a particular legal system should interpret the law of that jurisdiction.[8] Intersystemic adjudication raises the specter of judicial usurpation. Courts would be shaping the law of a different political system. Within a polyphonic framework, intersystemic adjudication does not pose this peril. Rather, under certain circumstances, intersystemic adjudication can further the values of plurality, dialogue, and redundancy. Just as the overlap of state and federal regulatory authority may be pernicious in some circumstances, so too may intersystemic adjudication be inappropriate in certain cases. Matching the court to the law being applied does advance important goals in some instances. However, intersystemic adjudication stands as an underappreciated practice in the system of judicial federalism in the United States. My goal in this and succeeding chapters is to apply the polyphonic approach to analyze the issue of judicial jurisdiction and thereby to explore some of the benefits of polyphony produced by intersystemic adjudication.

In this regard, it is useful to keep in mind one of the most significant issues that intersystemic adjudication can be useful in addressing. A fundamental legal problem is the potential gap between right and remedy. It is not so much the broad definition of rights as the practical ability of enforcement that guarantees the full potential of a liberal democratic system. The problem of closing remedial gaps appeared in the most famous decision in the canon of constitutional law in the United States. In 1803 in *Marbury v. Madison*, Chief Justice Marshall famously declared a remedial imperative:

> The very essence of civil liberty certainly consists in the right of every individual to claim the protection of the laws, whenever he receives an injury. One of the first duties of government is to afford that protection. . . .
>
> The government of the United States has been emphatically termed a government of laws, and not of men. It will certainly cease to deserve this high appellation, if the laws furnish no remedy for the violation of a vested legal right.[9]

Federalism can ensure that the government of the United States continues to deserve the "high appellation" of "a government of laws." As discussed in this chapter and in chapter 6, intersystemic adjudication can provide a redundancy that bridges the remedial gap.

Jurisdiction and Judicial Federalism

DUAL AND UNITARY SYSTEMS OF JUDICIAL FEDERALISM

The United States Constitution did not mandate a dual court system. At the Constitutional Convention, the concept of a federal supreme court had wide acceptance. The delegates disagreed, however, on the need for lower federal courts. Some delegates argued that the state courts would suffice for lower courts and that additional federal courts would encroach on the states and cause unnecessary additional expense. James Madison and James Wilson proposed that the Constitution permit, but not require, lower federal courts. The delegates agreed to this plan, which became known as the "Madisonian Compromise."[10] Article III of the Constitution vests federal jurisdiction in the Supreme Court "and in such inferior Courts as the Congress may from time to time ordain and establish."[11] Thus, the Constitutional Convention left it to Congress to decide whether to create a complete federal court structure.

After the Constitution was ratified, the new Congress quickly implemented the authority to create lower federal courts.[12] Members of Congress apparently felt it prudent to establish trial courts to further the purposes of the grants of federal jurisdiction in Article III, including uniformity in admiralty law, the enforcement of federal law and the collection of federal revenue, adjudicating disputes relating to foreign affairs, and the provision of more impartial tribunals for disputes between different states and their citizens.[13] It is instructive to note as well the jurisdiction that Congress chose not to confer on the federal courts. In 1789, Congress granted the lower federal courts jurisdiction over the enforcement of revenue laws and federal criminal laws, but not generally over cases arising under federal law.[14] Article III clearly created the possibility that lower federal courts could exercise jurisdiction over federal questions. The first Congress, though, chose not to use its authority to grant that jurisdiction. Aside from a brief, soon repealed grant of jurisdiction in 1801, Congress did not give lower federal courts jurisdiction over such general federal question cases until 1875.[15] An embrace of intersystemic adjudication thus dates from the birth of federal courts. Citizens from different states could bring their state law disputes into federal court, and disputes involving issues of federal law would commonly begin in lower state courts.

The existence of a dual court system creates issues of interpretive authority. What tribunal will be the authoritative interpreter of state law, and what tribunal will be the authoritative interpreter of federal law? Here as well, other countries have adopted systems different from that in the United States. Ensuring the enforcement of national law represents an important concern in federal systems generally. Rather than setting up a dual court system, other countries have addressed this problem by alternate methods, such as establishing some specialized federal courts, exercising control over the selection of provincial judges, or providing a right of appeal to a federal court.[16] The difference between the dual judicial system of the United States and the more unitary judicial systems of other federalist nations becomes even more stark when viewed from the top of the judicial pyramid. The United States Supreme Court stands as the ultimate interpreter of federal law, reviewing issues of federal law that arise in lower federal courts or in state courts.[17] In exercising its appellate authority over state courts, however, the United States Supreme Court does not generally review questions of state law.[18] The highest court of each state is understood to render the authoritative interpretation of that state's law.

In reviewing state court decisions, the United States Supreme Court has consistently deferred to state court interpretations of state law. Only if a state court's reading of state law potentially leads to a violation of federal law has the Court sought to second-guess the state court.[19] The treatment of state law issues arising in federal court, however, has been a focus of substantial controversy. Here, the issue is not the Supreme Court's exercise of appellate jurisdiction over a particular ruling of a state court. Rather, the question is whether federal courts must follow state court precedent when interpreting state law, or alternatively, may the federal courts reach their own, independent conclusions on the meaning of state law. Courts generally follow the interpretation of the appellate court that sits in review of their judgment. Interpretive deference follows from the knowledge that deviation will lead to appellate reversal. However, no appeal lies from the lower federal court to the state courts. A federal court's interpretation of state law will never be reviewed by a state court. How have federal courts understood their responsibilities in this setting?

A fair summary would be that federal courts long have understood state courts to be the authoritative interpreters of "state law." The main historical debate focused on what counted as state law. State constitutions, state statutes, and state laws governing local matters, such as property disputes, generally fell safely within the category of "state law."[20] The highest state court served as the definitive interpreter of these matters, and federal courts were bound to follow these precedents. In *Swift v. Tyson*[21] in 1842, the United States Supreme Court held that other matters of nonfederal law, especially in commercial areas, would be treated not as a species of state law, but as a kind of general common law. Justice Joseph Story declared that "the law respecting negotiable instruments may be truly declared in the languages of Cicero, adopted by Lord Mansfield . . . to be in a great measure, not the law of a single country only, but of the commercial world."[22] State courts did not serve as the definitive interpreters of this general, nonfederal law, and federal courts could reach an independent construction of these matters.[23]

This system eventually gave rise to perceived inequities. The common law applied by a state court might vary from the common law applied by the federal courts located in the same state. Parties could shop for their preferred law by moving between state and federal court. Further, because of the requirements of diversity jurisdiction, corporations often had a greater ability to choose between the state and federal forum. The *Swift* system helped to guarantee interstate uniformity, as federal courts throughout the land applied the same general common law. However, the lack of uniformity within a given state made the system unsustainable. The problems of state and federal courts applying different general common law grew as federal courts treated more issues as general common law questions rather than matters of "state law." By expanding the conception of general common law, the federal courts assumed greater interpretive independence from state courts.[24]

In *Erie Railroad Co. v. Tompkins*,[25] the United States Supreme Court ended this trifurcated regime of federal law, general law, and state law. All nonfederal law became state law, subject to authoritative construction by the highest state court. For matters of state law, then, the United States Supreme Court is not supreme. Judicial interpretive supremacy rests with the highest court of each state.[26] Every federal court, including the United States Supreme Court, must defer to the highest state court's interpretation of state law.

In Australia and Canada, by contrast, a federal high court serves as the ultimate interpreter of both national and subnational law.[27] Commentators credit the existence of a single final interpreter with creating a greater sense of the unity of the law.[28] Statutory law differs among the states and territories, but the federal high court serves as a unifying force. The absence of parallel court systems decreases the possibility of interpretive divergence between state and federal tribunals,[29] and the single high court structure diminishes the variations in the law among the various states.

ALLOCATING ISSUES BETWEEN PARALLEL COURT SYSTEMS

Unlike these other models, the system of judicial federalism in the United States involves parallel state and federal interpretive tracks, and no single court exercises interpretive authority over both. This arrangement enhances the importance of the choice of forum, and the existence of extensive areas of overlapping jurisdiction makes forum choice common. The state and federal paths lead to different destinations. Eventually, the authoritative interpreter—either the United States Supreme Court or the highest court in the state—will resolve contested issues, and that determination will enjoy binding authority in both systems. That definitive resolution, however, may be a long time in coming. Doctrines must determine in which of the independent, available tracks the case will proceed.

For the most part, subject matter jurisdiction is a matter of legislative right, not judicial grace. A federal court cannot refuse to hear a properly filed state law diversity case, nor may a state court close its doors to a federal question. Congress exercises its discretion in deciding how much of the constitutionally defined federal judicial power it will confer on the lower federal courts and how much concurrent jurisdiction will be permitted to the state courts. Once that decision is made, courts exercise their statutorily granted jurisdiction. Congress, not the courts, owns the key to the federal courthouse. To a large extent, Congress has lent those keys to the litigants. When state and federal courts enjoy concurrent jurisdiction, either litigant generally may opt for the federal forum.[30] The plaintiff may file in state or federal court, and the defendant may exercise the right to remove a case from state court to federal court. Judges must accept the cases properly brought before them.

Within the broad scope of federal jurisdiction, though, doctrines do exist to allow federal courts to have some say over the allocation of state and federal issues. Particularly intricate questions arise when a single case involves state and federal elements. The resolution of a state law question may serve as a necessary prerequisite to a federal claim. A plaintiff, for example, may assert that a state statute violates the federal Constitution. A federal court would have to decide the meaning of the challenged enactment before it could assess its constitutionality. Alternatively, a state law claim for recovery might come within the supplemental jurisdiction of the federal court.[31] Under the current supplemental jurisdiction statute, as well as under prior judicially crafted rules, a plaintiff filing a federal claim in federal court may include any state law claims that arise from the same transaction or occurrence as the federal claim. For example, misconduct by a local police officer may give rise to claims under both federal civil rights laws and state tort laws. The existence of the federal issue would allow the plaintiff to bring both state and federal claims in a federal court and invoke the supplemental jurisdiction of the federal court over the state law claim.

Supplemental jurisdiction allows for the efficient packaging of related claims, and it helps to preserve the availability of a federal forum for a federal claim. In the absence of supplemental jurisdiction, a plaintiff would face the choice of filing the state and federal claims together in state court or of splitting the claims between state and federal court. The claim-splitting alternative could be costly and could occasion preclusion obstacles if parallel issues were adjudicated in the two proceedings. Once a tribunal, either state or federal, decided an issue, that judgment would be binding in the other proceeding. Supplemental jurisdiction allows a federal forum for the federal claim without the hazards and inefficiencies of parallel litigation.[32] Supplemental jurisdiction, which opens the federal courthouse to related state law claims, provides yet another example of the pervasiveness of intersystemic adjudication.

The Values and Counter-Values of Intersystemic Adjudication

This section explores the potential advantages and disadvantages of intersystemic adjudication. To illustrate the principles involved, this section focuses on one of the most controversial examples of intersystemic adjudication, federal court interpretation of state constitutions. Federal court interpretation of state law generally presents a contested instance of intersystemic adjudication. It was the perceived abuse of this power that led to the *Erie* decision, which stripped federal courts of their ability to characterize nonfederal matters as general law, rather than as state law. Federal court interpretation of state constitutions introduces yet another level of controversy. Courts understand state constitutions to enjoy an especially intimate connection to the state.[33] Federal interpretation of the state charters thus may appear as the height of federal intrusion. To defend intersystemic adjudication in this context is to confront the most serious arguments against the interpretive practice.

State constitutional litigation also represents one of the most important areas for the vindication of individual rights. Each state has its own constitution, and these charters generally protect a broad panoply of rights. Some of the state provisions parallel those in the federal Constitution, guaranteeing due process, equal protection, free speech, and similar core values. Some state constitutions protect a broader range of rights. One area of particular recent interest has been state constitutional guarantees of education. All states rely to some extent on local financing of their public school systems. This scheme often results in enormous inequality of resources, as students in wealthier areas enjoy greater funding than students in poorer locations. In *San Antonio Independent School District v. Rodriguez*,[34] the United States Supreme Court upheld the constitutionality of this financing method. In the wake of *Rodriguez*, advocates of educational equality brought state constitutional challenges to the district-based funding system. Plaintiffs relied both on the Equal Protection Clauses of state constitutions and on the Education Clauses, which are present in the constitutions of all states.[35] The plaintiffs seeking greater funding have prevailed in approximately half the states.[36] The interplay of this state constitutional litigation and federal efforts to enhance education provides a fascinating example of polyphonic federalism.

For present purposes, though, it is more useful to focus on state constitutional provisions that mirror the federal Constitution. Even if the language of the state charter duplicates that in the federal Constitution, the state constitution remains part of state law. State courts may interpret the language in state constitutions to safeguard rights broader or different from those protected by the federal Constitution. The Georgia Constitution, for example, contains a provision that essentially duplicates the Fourteenth Amendment of the United States Constitution in prohibiting the deprivation of "life, liberty, or property" without "due process of law."[37] In *Bowers v. Hardwick*[38] in 1986, the United States Supreme Court held that the Due

Process Clause of the federal Constitution did not protect sodomy. *Bowers* was overruled by the 2003 decision in *Lawrence v. Texas*.[39] In the meantime, though, in *Powell v. State*[40] in 1998, the Georgia Supreme Court ruled that the Due Process Clause of the Georgia Constitution did include a right to privacy that protected sodomy. The Georgia Supreme Court ruling was especially notable because *Bowers* concerned the same Georgia statute as *Powell*. Thus, the Georgia sodomy statute did not violate the Due Process Clause of the federal Constitution, but it did violate the Due Process Clause of the Georgia Constitution.

Because of this possibility of broader state protections, plaintiffs seeking to vindicate individual rights may wish to assert claims under both the state and the federal constitutions. Supplemental jurisdiction allows the plaintiff to bring both constitutional claims together in federal court. Such dual constitutional challenges are increasingly common.[41] Certainly, they do not occur with the frequency of other sorts of supplemental state claims brought in federal court. However, because state constitutional claims generally present an assertion of individual rights against a state defendant, such claims raise issues both more fundamental to individual liberties and more central to state autonomy than the state law claims typically asserted in federal litigation. These dual claims present a particularly interesting and significant example of intersystemic adjudication.

DOCTRINAL BACKGROUND OF DUAL CONSTITUTIONAL CLAIMS

Before turning directly to the polyphonic framework, it is necessary to review some of the current doctrinal background. Federal courts clearly have jurisdiction over the dual constitutional challenges, but they have choices in the manner and order in which they address the various claims, and those choices have importance for the litigants and the court system. Because of concerns for separation of powers and federalism, cases raising dual constitutional challenges implicate a complex thicket of doctrines. These doctrines reflect varying attempts to harmonize three, sometimes conflicting, principles.

First is the "avoidance" principle. Avoiding unnecessary federal constitutional rulings has been a longstanding tenet of the federal courts. The United States Supreme Court's constitutional interpretations can be overturned only by constitutional amendment or by the Court's overruling a prior case. Because its constitutional judgments are so difficult to change, the Court has adopted a practice of deciding cases on other grounds, if possible. Avoiding constitutional adjudication allows for further democratic deliberation. Elected representatives can continue to debate the merits of a proposal, unfettered by constitutional constraints. If, for example, the Court rests its holding on the interpretation of a statute, the legislature will have the opportunity to decide whether to enact the statute in a different form. The constitutional issue might disappear without the need for an authoritative adjudication that would establish binding authority over a range of future cases.[42]

The second principle, which I call the "local interpretation" principle, suggests that state courts should be the primary interpreters of state law.[43] State courts will have more experience and expertise in the interpretation of the law of their state. Further, when state courts address state law issues, authoritative resolution may be obtained in that case. The highest court of the state can clarify the status of the law and apply it to the parties. By contrast, when a federal court adjudicates a question of state law, authoritative interpretation will not be possible in that case. If the state courts interpret the state law differently in a different proceeding, the parties in the prior federal case will not have the benefit of that authoritative ruling.

The third principle, which I term the "open door" principle, holds that a federal forum should be available for a federal claim. Barriers that pose obstacles to asserting federal claims in federal court would violate this principle. Following the Civil War, Congress enacted several statutes to open the federal courts to federal claims. Congress first granted jurisdiction for civil rights claims[44] and then, in 1875, conferred jurisdiction on federal courts for all federal claims, subject only to an amount-in-controversy requirement.[45] Federal courts, with life-tenured judges, may provide a more hospitable setting for the assertion of individual rights. The insulation from politics, along with a potentially more national perspective, may be especially attractive for constitutional litigation, which often targets state officers.[46]

The avoidance, local interpretation, and open door principles all reflect important jurisdictional policies. Complying with any two of the principles does not pose much problem. Following all three proves difficult. Consider the example of a challenge to a public religious display. A plaintiff might bring suit in federal court asserting that the display violates both the Establishment Clause of the United States Constitution and a similarly worded provision of the state constitution.

Let's start with the first two principles. To honor the avoidance principle, federal courts should base their rulings on the state claim, not the federal constitutional issue. In the religious display example, the federal courts should try to resolve the litigation on the basis of the state religion clause, rather than the federal Establishment Clause. In accordance with the local interpretation principle, federal courts should not themselves adjudicate the state issue, but should instead seek the guidance of state courts. The doctrine of *Pullman* abstention[47] allows the federal court to achieve these goals. *Pullman* abstention comes into play when novel or unsettled questions of state law arise in a federal constitutional case. In these circumstances, the federal court can require the claimant to file a suit in state court to seek clarification of state law. The plaintiff would file suit in state court seeking a resolution of the state constitutional claim. The federal suit remains in abeyance while the claimant proceeds with the state court litigation. After the state law issue is clarified, the claimant can return to federal court for adjudication of any federal issues that remain. So, if the plaintiff receives an unfavorable ruling on the state provision, the federal court will remain open for the renewed Establishment Clause challenge. State certification statutes provide a speedier alternative to abstention. These provisions allow federal courts to refer state law issues directly to state courts for resolution, rather than forcing the claimant to initiate an independent lawsuit.[48]

Although *Pullman* abstention vindicates the avoidance and local interpretation principles, the open door principle does not fare as well. Routing dual constitutional challenges through state court delays the adjudication of the federal claim, thereby burdening access to the federal forum. The resolution of the Establishment Clause issue will be delayed by the state court litigation on the state constitutional claim. Professor Robert Pushaw has noted that *Pullman* abstention imposes an especially unfair burden in civil rights cases, as civil rights plaintiffs disproportionately have limited means and may not have the resources necessary for successive trials in state and federal courts.[49] Certification, when available, ameliorates but does not wholly obviate the problem of delay. The delay entailed in abstention or certification provides a powerful incentive for the plaintiff to submit state and federal claims to the state court for resolution.

Alternatively, under the doctrine developed in *Siler v. Louisville & Nashville Railroad Co.*,[50] federal courts could first adjudicate the state constitutional claim so as to avoid reaching, if possible, the federal constitutional issue. If the state law ground disposes of the case, then the court has succeeded in resolving the dispute without the potential rigidity of federal constitutional adjudication. This procedure also avoids burdening access to the federal forum. The plaintiffs might or might not prevail on the state claim, but if unsuccessful on the state claim, they could expect a simultaneous ruling on the federal Establishment Clause issue, avoiding the delays of certification or abstention. This approach complies with the avoidance and open door principles, but at the cost of violating the local interpretation principle because it is the federal court that is adjudicating the state constitutional claim.

Finally, the federal court could rule first on the federal constitutional claim. If that claim fails, the court could turn to the state claim, or it could even refuse to decide the state law issue. Under the supplemental jurisdiction statute, as well as under previous case law, a court retains some discretion to dismiss supplemental claims. The current version of the supplemental jurisdiction statute lists potential grounds for dismissal, including that "the claim raises a novel or complex issue of State law."[51] State constitutional law questions might well satisfy this provision. In any event, whether it actually refuses to entertain the supplemental state constitutional claim or merely first adjudicates the federal constitutional issue, the federal court would be deciding, rather than avoiding, the federal constitutional issue. Beginning with the adjudication of the federal constitutional claim satisfies two, but only two, of the three guiding principles. The court would neither impose a barrier to the federal forum nor transgress the local interpretation principle. What suffers is the canon of avoiding federal constitutional adjudication.

The three principles evade easy harmonization. Federal courts cannot avoid federal constitutional rulings, while also leaving state law issues to the state courts, and ensuring that federal courts remain hospitable forums for federal claims. If a court cannot satisfy all three principles, the question is which should take priority. The proper manner for resolving these dual constitutional claims implicates significant issues of federalism. How should important state and federal claims be allocated among state and federal courts? Specifically, how should courts understand the benefits and disadvantages of intersystemic adjudication?

PROTECTING INDIVIDUAL RIGHTS THROUGH INTERSYSTEMIC ADJUDICATION

Having reviewed the doctrinal landscape, I now turn to an evaluation of intersystemic adjudication. The "local interpretation" principle discussed above counsels against intersystemic adjudication. This section takes issues with that principle by examining intersystemic adjudication through the lens of polyphonic federalism. I focus on the three overlapping values—plurality, dialogue, and redundancy—and on the corresponding set of counter-values—uniformity, finality, and hierarchical accountability—that intersystemic adjudication may hinder. My argument is not that federal courts always should adjudicate state constitutional claims within their jurisdiction, but that federal courts sometimes should do so, rather than automatically giving priority to the local interpretation principle.

Plurality/Uniformity

State individual rights guarantees may be subject to several interpretations. Federal court adjudication of state constitutional claims allows for additional exploration of these meanings. The federal court never will provide the definitive construction of the state provision. The federal court interpretation may be helpful, however, in contributing to the discussion of the best way to realize the underlying constitutional value. Federal judges can contribute to a plurality of legal meaning, which provides a rich background for the investigation of fundamental rights.

Federal judges are rooted in an institutional context different from that of state judges. They are chosen by different means and enjoy tenure on different terms from state judges. Federal judges will thus be able to offer a perspective that differs from that of state judges. A useful dialogue may ensue between state and federal judges over the proper interpretation of a fundamental right. Immersion in state constitutional debates also may prove useful to federal judges in interpreting the federal Constitution. Examining state precedent may enrich a court's understanding of the sources and meaning of fundamental rights that exist in both state and federal documents.[52] State and federal courts can engage in a valuable dialogue over the meaning of state and federal constitutional guarantees.[53]

Plurality does come at a cost. Uniformity in interpretation also serves as an important value.[54] When a federal court interprets the state constitution, it creates the possibility of multiple meanings. The state constitution will have an interpretation in the federal system and may have a different interpretation in the state system, until the state supreme court resolves the conflict. This plurality could be unsettling and confusing. Parties may win or lose depending on the forum hearing the case. This kind of disparate result is the price of pluralism. Is the game worth the candle? While she served on the United States Supreme Court, Justice Sandra Day O'Connor commented on the similar problem that arises from diverse interpretations of federal law:

> While uniformity is a necessary and desirable goal, its immediate achievement is not always possible. Nor is immediate action necessarily desirable. Part of the beauty of our federalism is the diversity of viewpoint it brings to bear on legal problems. State court judges may have a different approach

to a problem than might a federal judge. .... Under our system, the 50 state supreme courts, 13 United States Circuit Courts of Appeals, and countless trial and intermediate appellate courts may bring diverse experiences to bear on questions that, because of the Supremacy Clause, they must answer in common.

When those courts encounter an unresolved question of federal law, their differing perspectives may lead them to different conclusions. The resulting divergence provides a valuable moment in the law—a moment of dialogue among different jurists in which they may share their views on a common issue. There can be no doubt that the dialogue is a profitable one or that the Court on which I sit listens to the voices in the debate. Indeed, it is not all that infrequent that the Supreme Court will, despite the existence of a conflict on an issue of federal law, decline to review a case so that other voices may be heard on the subject before the issue is resolved once and for all. The benefits of dialogue can, for at least a limited time, outweigh the immediate need for uniformity.[55]

In recognizing the benefit of interpretive plurality, I assume that state and federal constitutional rights share important features. When a state constitution and the federal Constitution both talk about due process or equality, those meanings might be distinct; that is a premise of allowing the state provision to be interpreted independently of the federal.[56] The meanings, however, are not incommensurable. The state and federal charters invoke shared values. The contours of the specific rights may vary, but the ideals the provisions embody are sufficiently similar for federal and state courts to engage in a profitable dialogue. To put the issue slightly differently, the question is whether the state and federal constitutions correspond to one interpretive community or many. Are states so radically different that their constitutions invoke fundamental values that diverge from those of the nation as a whole? The dual federalist premise of separating areas of state and federal regulation might suggest a foundational divide about fundamental values. Dual federalism protected states from federal intrusion into such areas. In that framework, perhaps the states and the national government had little to share about safeguarding important liberties. The polyphonic approach builds on the concept of a generally integrated, national understanding of important values. When citizens across the United States seek "equality," they are pursuing the same value, although questions may arise about its meaning and application in particular settings. As Professor Paul Kahn put it, "There is not one equality in Connecticut and another in Texas, or even Utah."[57] Differences among citizens remain, but state boundaries do not demarcate regions of fundamentally different cultures. The more one recognizes the emergence of a national community, the more likely it is that dialogue will be helpful.

Dialogue/Finality

A related paired opposition that Justice O'Connor's comments invoke is that of finality and dialogue. Finality is a significant legal value.[58] The law has an important settlement function. Sometimes it is more important that a matter be settled than that it be settled right. A federal court's interpretation of a state constitution will never carry that guarantee of final resolution. The same issue might arise in a different case in state court, and the federal court's interpretation of the state constitution will have no binding effect. The flip side of lack of finality is the possibility of dialogue. What makes a conversation possible is the absence of a final authority. The federal courts can express their opinions on state constitutions, and lower state courts can express their opinions. They can listen to each other and learn from each other. The state supreme court can learn from the dialogue until it decides to end the discussion by rendering an authoritative interpretation. The perils of finality are reflected in part in the doctrine of seeking to avoid federal constitutional adjudication. It is well established by the avoidance principle discussed earlier that courts will not rely on federal constitutional grounds if other grounds are available.

It is useful in this regard to remember that the power of a state high court to give a definitive opinion does not mean that it will necessarily give the best interpretation. Sometimes finality is more important than correctness, but that possibility recognizes the distinction between the last word and the best word. Justice Jackson's famous caution in *Brown v. Allen* seems apt here: "We are not final because we are infallible, but we are infallible only because we are final."[59] Justice Jackson referred to the United States Supreme Court, but the observation applies more generally to ultimate interpreters, be they a state or a federal high court. When the necessarily fallible state high court does give the last word, it can benefit from other views on the topic.

Redundancy/Hierarchical Accountability

To place the same opposition in a kind of organizational perspective, when federal courts interpret state law, hierarchical accountability always will be absent. On the organizational chart of the interpretation of state law, the state's highest court sits at the top. Its authority is ultimate. Federal courts stand outside this chain of command in the sense that no appeal lies from their decisions to the ultimate interpreters. Once the state supreme court speaks, the federal court must listen. With regard to the decision in the specific case at issue before a federal court, however, the state court will never speak. A federal appellate court, in particular, will have little accountability. No state court review is possible, and review by the United States Supreme Court, while theoretically possible, would in practice be unlikely.[60] From an organizational perspective, this arrangement frustrates authoritative interpretation.

It is worth contemplating the possibility of error. The federal courts might incorrectly construe the state charter. Correction of such an error may take some time and provides no relief to the parties in the first litigation. Of course, the problem of error is pervasive. The state court may misinterpret the state constitution just as the federal court might misinterpret the state constitution. The comparison of these problems raises difficult questions. One concern is for the qualitative characteristics of the error. For reasons of federalism, a federal court's misinterpreting the state constitution might be an error of a categorically greater magnitude than the same misinterpretation by the state court. My scratching the paint on my neighbor's car may be more serious than putting a big dent in my own. This kind of categorical concern relates to the legitimacy of the overall enterprise of federal court interpretation of state law, a subject that I address below. Inherent in the process of interpretation is the possibility of error. If the enterprise of federal court interpretation of state constitutions is legitimate, then errors are no greater threat here than in other forms of interpretation.

Is a federal court more likely than a state court to misinterpret the state constitution? Again, it is important to distinguish between deviation from what the state high court might eventually hold and incorrect interpretation. The more one understands federalism to protect distinctive state enclaves, the more federal court interpretation of state constitutions appears problematic. How can a federal court really understand the spirit of the state community? If one rejects this kind of romantic nationalist view of the state and thinks of a state constitution as more about achieving widely shared values, then the risk of error diminishes. A federal judge would be able to draw on a common background of constitutional principles in realizing the values referenced in the state constitution.

Moreover, this structure enables a different organizational virtue, that of redundancy.[61] The existence of parallel lines of authority means that a blockage or error in one will not affect the other; they do not intersect. If one path for realizing state constitutional rights does not work, an alternative path exists. If for some reason the lower state courts do not properly recognize a state constitutional right, resort may be had to the federal courts. This kind of redundancy is one of the chief results of the system of judicial federalism that exists in the United States.

The different institutional structures of the state and federal courts may enhance the value of redundancy. State and federal courts differ in many ways.[62] Extensive debates have focused on whether this organizational variation hinders state courts in the enforcement of fundamental rights. Evidence appears to support the conclusion that electoral pressures render state courts less sympathetic to specific kinds of individual rights claims.[63] Other scholars argue that state courts may be more receptive to certain kinds of arguments about individual rights.[64] From the perspective of redundancy, the key issue is that federal and state courts differ. Redundancy allows parties to enjoy the potential benefits of both.

APPLYING THE POLYPHONIC FRAMEWORK TO
DUAL CONSTITUTIONAL CLAIMS

The role of federal courts in interpreting the California Constitution illustrates some of the productive possibilities that a polyphonic approach allows. The California Constitution contains a No Preference Clause,[65] which the California courts have construed to sweep more broadly than the federal Establishment Clause in requiring government neutrality concerning religion.[66] Federal courts have applied the No Preference Clause in controversial cases, involving such matters as crosses on public property and on city insignia.[67] One notable, long-running dispute concerns crosses on public property on Mt. Helix and Mt. Soledad in the San Diego area. Erected in 1925, the Mt. Helix cross stands thirty-six feet tall. The Mt. Soledad cross dates from 1954 and is forty-three feet tall. Both crosses are made of concrete and serve as local landmarks.[68] In 1991, a federal judge held that the crosses violated the No Preference Clause of the California Constitution, and he prohibited their continued presence on public property.[69] The ruling triggered sharp public reaction, including protest marches and angry letters to newspapers.[70] The claimed status of the Mt. Soledad cross as a veteran's memorial engendered particular outrage.[71] The attorney for the City of San Diego charged that opponents of the cross "shame the memory of those valiant men and women who fought and died to preserve" freedom of religion, and he chastised the opponents for "ignor[ing] the rights of the majority."[72] Not surprisingly, some of the attacks were directed at the district judge, Gordon Thompson Jr. The judge was accused of "judicial tyranny,"[73] and one writer asserted, "The judge would have us exchange the 'reactionary' Christian moral behavior, respect for others and tolerance, with politically correct moral relativism and the primacy of the judiciary, with judges and lawyers as the new high priests."[74]

In sum, the cross litigation presented exactly the kind of situation in which political insulation could be expected to assist a judge in protecting minority rights. Indeed, one commentator insisted that the controversy demonstrated the importance of protecting judges from political reprisal:

> [T]he ruckus [Judge Thompson's] ruling has stirred up may provide a timely reminder of why federal judges enjoy lifetime tenure. . . . If we really believe that majority rule aims to protect the rights of a minority, this judicial freedom from retribution seems essential. Thompson was free to make a finding on crosses—and on the law—without regard to its inevitable unpopularity.[75]

A California Superior Court judge, subject to election,[76] also might have braved public outcry. Nevertheless, the cross controversy certainly illustrates how federal judges' insulation might allow them to play a particularly valuable role in state constitutional adjudication.[77] Nor is there any indication that the federal courts are disrupting the development of California law.[78] The California courts have not disagreed with the federal interpretation of the No Preference Clause and have in fact relied on the Ninth Circuit's interpretation of some provisions of the California Constitution.[79]

The federal courts will never provide a definitive interpretation of the California Constitution. Nevertheless, federal judges may contribute to a discussion of values embodied in the California charter. The state courts of California remain free to interpret the California Constitution as they see fit. The legislature and the people of California can amend the Constitution to clarify its meaning. Indeed, the California Constitution has been amended with great frequency.[80] In this way, federal court interpretation of state constitutions resembles the kind of constitutional interpretation that is the global norm around the world. Most constitutions around the world are much easier to amend than the Constitution of the United States.[81] At the same time, it is unusual for judges to face elections, as do most state court judges in the United States.[82] Having unelected judges interpret a constitution that is reasonably subject to amendment is a common situation in other countries. Federal court interpretation of state constitutions brings that practice to the United States.

The denouement of the cross controversy illustrated some other ways in which contemporary federalism reflects the interaction of state and federal law. The Mt. Helix part of the dispute ended relatively quickly. After a mere decade of litigation, the parties agreed to a settlement in which San Diego County transferred ownership of the 3.2 acre site to a private foundation.[83] The cross thus no longer stood on public property. The controversy surrounding the Mt. Soledad cross lasted much longer. The City of San Diego attempted to avoid the judge's ruling by selling just the piece of land on which the cross and war memorial stood. The plaintiffs claimed that transferring only the ground under the offending site was a sham that could not cure the violation of the California Constitution. A series of judicial rulings and revised sale plans followed. Finally, the defenders of the Mt. Soledad cross went to the federal government to escape the consequences of the federal judge's interpretation of the state constitution. At the behest of local federal legislators, the United States Congress in 2006 enacted legislation exercising the power of eminent domain and immediately transferring the cross and war memorial to the United States Department of Defense.[84] The original plaintiffs then filed suit in federal court challenging the legislation as violating the Establishment Clause of the First Amendment to the United States Constitution.[85]

The saga of the Mt. Soledad cross illustrates the power, as well as the complexity, of polyphonic federalism. Federalism allows California to maintain an independent constitutional system with protections against government endorsement of religion broader than those found in the United States Constitution. A dual court system meant that this state constitutional provision could be enforced by a federal judge against a city in California. By invoking the federal forum to bring a controversial challenge to a cross, the plaintiffs took advantage of the insulation afforded to federal judges under the United States Constitution. By permitting this kind of federal court jurisdiction, the national government effectively assisted the state in implementing state law. The defenders of the cross might have attempted to change the state constitution. Instead, these defenders, including some city officials, sought the intervention of the federal government to circumvent the state law. At that point, the federal government functioned as an additional line of protection for the cross. Expressing national values, the national government enacted legislation to assist the local politicians in maintaining the cross. Finally, the original plaintiffs returned to federal court to invoke the constitutional values of the United States to prevent the federal legislature and executive from intervening to protect a religious symbol.

At the end of the process, as at the beginning, the insulated federal courts stand ready to enforce fundamental state or federal law, even in the face of current political unpopularity. The legislative and executive branches of the federal government provide alternative avenues for the pursuit of policy preferences. These layers of governance constitute the core of federalism in the contemporary United States.

THE LIMITS OF INTERSYSTEMIC ADJUDICATION

Intersystemic adjudication has its costs. My argument is not that all dual constitutional claims belong in federal court. I seek to make the more modest claim that intersystemic adjudication may provide benefits, even when it places state constitutional claims in federal court. With regard to some dual constitutional claims, the advantages of plurality, dialogue, and redundancy will not outweigh the foregone opportunity for uniformity, finality, and accountability.

One situation in which the potential benefits of intersystemic adjudication do not justify the costs occurs when definitive state court authority has determined that the state constitutional provision means the same as its federal analog. As discussed above, when confronting state constitutional language that duplicates text in the federal Constitution, state courts enjoy the freedom to interpret the state constitution differently from the federal. Instead, however, state courts may engage in "lockstep" interpretation and construe their charter to have the same meaning as the federal. If the state clause has been interpreted to mean the same as the federal, the state provision has no independent significance. It merely serves as a referent to the federal clause. Essentially, only a question of federal law presents itself. What does the federal Constitution mean? The state constitution will trail dutifully behind.

In these cases, the federal court should decide the federal question because that issue will be dispositive. Avoidance of the federal constitutional issue is impossible. Purporting to rest only on state grounds would be disingenuous and potentially confusing because the interpretation of the state constitution would be an indirect interpretation of the federal Constitution. The better practice would be to opt for directness and clarity. Abstention would delay federal adjudication by unnecessarily diverting the federal claim through state court and would be pointless because the state court could not interpret the state constitution without construing the federal Constitution. In such cases, the federal court cannot avoid the federal constitutional issue. The federal court then is free to decide the federal constitutional issue. With regard to lockstep provisions, plurality, dialogue, and redundancy cannot occur. Only one law, federal law, is involved in the case. When the state constitution remains silent, only a federal monologue is possible. To be clear, state court interpretations of federal law may indeed be beneficial by providing an additional view from an alternative perspective. So, state court construction of lockstep provisions may help elucidate the meaning of the federal Constitution. However, when federal or state courts interpret a lockstep provision, they should make clear that they are offering their interpretation of federal law. Federal constitutional adjudication is unavoidable, and in the case of claims brought in federal court the local interpretation and the open door principles indicate that the federal court should decide the federal constitutional question.

Another setting inhospitable for polyphony occurs when the state constitution addresses a narrow issue without an analog in the federal charter. If the provision reflects a uniquely local interest, the federal courts will have little expertise or experience to contribute. In *Reetz v. Bozanich*,[86] for example, the plaintiffs alleged that new Alaskan fishing regulations violated their rights under the Equal Protection Clause of the Fourteenth Amendment and under the Fishery Clauses of the Alaska Constitution. The relevant provisions of the Alaska Constitution included, "Wherever occurring in their natural state, fish, wildlife, and waters are reserved to the people for common use"[87] and "No exclusive right or special privilege of fishery shall be created or authorized in the natural waters of the State."[88] Noting that the state constitutional provisions had never been interpreted by Alaska courts, the Supreme Court held that the federal courts should invoke *Pullman* abstention and await guidance from the state courts on the proper construction of those clauses.

This kind of state provision focuses on a local matter about which federal courts have little to add. Alaska courts undoubtedly have much greater experience with the law and norms of fishing in Alaska. The federal voice has no part in this inquiry. On such narrow issues of local concern, a state monologue is appropriate.

Intersystemic Adjudication and the Values of Federalism

By focusing on a particular aspect of polyphonic federalism—the embrace of intersystemic adjudication—this chapter has illustrated the benefits of polyphony. It is now useful to review the way in which these examples of polyphonic federalism advance the goals of federalism highlighted by the economic, republican, and liberal perspectives that were outlined in chapter 3. As discussed below, federal court interpretation of state constitutions also promotes these traditional federalism values, including responsive and efficient policies, republican self-governance, and the prevention of tyranny.

The federal court interpretation would have little impact on interstate competition. With or without an active interpretive role for the federal courts, different states could offer divergent packages of state constitutional rights. Federal court interpretation would, though, enhance intrastate competition between the state and federal courts. The highest court of the state will eventually provide the definitive judicial interpretation of the state constitution. Until that ruling, though, the state and the federal courts can attempt their own constructions of the constitutional provision. The dual court systems can serve as laboratories in which different interpretations of the same provision are tested.

An appreciation of the republican perspective requires careful attention to the workings of state government. In the republican model, each state constitution represents the product of participatory self-governance. Citizens deliberate over their communal interests and then enshrine important principles in the state constitution. Respect for republican self-governance requires respect for the state constitution. From this perspective, federal courts might seem like interpretive interlopers, giving an unwanted national spin to the outcome of local deliberation.

Such a view of federal courts, however, mistakes the state courts for the state constitution. Honoring the state constitution is essential to realizing republican values. State courts, though, do not enjoy a monopoly over correct constitutional interpretation. Any court, state or federal, might misinterpret the state constitution. In this regard, even the highest state court has no special privilege. The interpretation of the highest state court is authoritative, and it must be followed by state and federal courts. That finality does not mean that the interpretation of the state high court is necessarily the best, just the last.[89] What is most important from the republican perspective is that the state constitution be interpreted correctly. The state and federal courts can participate in this process together. Producing the best interpretation is the best realization of republican values.

Federal court interpretation of state constitutions can play a valuable role in safeguarding against governmental tyranny. The state constitution is a prime way in which the people of the state protect themselves from the power of the state government. State individual rights guarantees have become an increasingly significant force in protecting human rights in the states.[90] State court enforcement of state constitutional rights, however, has at times proved disappointing.[91] State courts generally are accountable to the voters in the state. To the extent that the constitutional provision protects an individual against a majoritarian decision, that electoral vulnerability may distort the interpretive process. In these circumstances, the more insulated federal judiciary may provide a valuable alternative perspective on a state constitutional issue. By participating in the process of state constitutional interpretation, federal courts can help to prevent state tyranny.

Legitimacy of Intersystemic Adjudication

So far, this chapter has explained some of the practical benefits of intersystemic adjudication in general, and of federal courts interpreting state constitutions in particular. In addressing these topics, though, it is necessary to confront the argument that intersystemic adjudication runs counter to central organizing principles of our constitutional system. Another way of posing this objection is to say that the foregoing account details some of the strategic advantages that a federal forum may bring to certain parties, but that underlying postulates of the constitutional system in the United States undermine the legitimacy of these arguments.

CHALLENGES: THE SPIRIT OF *ERIE*

The decision of the United States Supreme Court in *Erie* has served as a focus of scholarly resistance to intersystemic adjudication. *Erie* directly rejected one form of intersystemic adjudication that had arisen: federal courts independently interpreting state common law. More generally, commentators have found *Erie* to embody three principles that individually and in combination could be taken to oppose intersystemic adjudication. These principles are positivism, realism, and federalism.[92]

On one level, *Erie* held that in cases in which federal law did not supply a rule of decision, federal courts were bound to apply the common law as it would be applied by state courts. After *Erie*, federal courts could no longer enforce general common law in preference to the common law of the particular state. The holding of *Erie* and its overruling of *Swift v. Tyson* do not directly relate to federal court interpretation of state constitutions. In all of the discussions of the role of federal courts in interpreting state constitutions, no one doubts that federal courts must follow the rulings of the highest court of the state. The state high court definitively interprets state law, including the state constitution, and the federal courts are bound to follow that construction. Indeed, even before *Erie*, federal courts were theoretically required to follow state courts' interpretations of positive enactments, such as state constitutions.[93] Only with regard to state common law did federal courts enjoy the prerogative of independent interpretation.

In practice, federal courts sometimes did not defer to state court interpretations of the state constitution in the pre-*Erie* period.[94] In *Township of Pine Grove v. Talcott*,[95] for example, the United States Supreme Court confronted the question whether a state statute violated the state constitution. The Michigan Supreme Court had adjudicated this question on two occasions. The United States Supreme Court, though, refused to follow those opinions. The Court reviewed and rejected the Michigan court's interpretation of its own constitution. The United States Supreme Court stated: "With all respect for the eminent tribunal by which the judgments were pronounced, we must be permitted to say that they are not satisfactory to our minds. We think the dissenting opinion in the one first decided is unanswered."[96] The Supreme Court thus sided with the dissent and rejected the state supreme court's interpretation of state law. In another case, *Gelpcke v. City of Dubuque*, the Court memorably summed up its refusal to accept certain state court interpretations of state law: "We shall never immolate truth, justice, and the law, because a State tribunal has erected the altar and decreed the sacrifice."[97]

To be clear, I am not advocating a return to *Gelpcke*. The state supreme courts should retain the authority to render binding interpretations of state law. It may be that the state supreme courts will interpret state law badly. However, uniformity, finality, and hierarchical accountability remain critical values. Mere error does not deprive their judgments of authority. Until the state supreme court has spoken, though, the federal courts and state courts can engage in a constructive dialogue. *Erie* stands for the principle that once the state supreme court interprets state law, the judicial conversation must stop. Obedience must follow. *Erie* does not decree that the conversation between state and federal courts can never begin.

What stands in the way of intersystemic adjudication is not *Erie*, but the larger jurisprudential commitments that *Erie* has been understood to embody. Critics of intersystemic adjudication rely in particular on certain versions of legal positivism and legal realism that *Erie* arguably presupposes. The positivist theme is that all law must have a foundation in some identifiable authority. *Erie* identified as a central flaw in the preexisting *Swift* system the existence of general common law that was in some sense neither state law nor federal law. After *Erie*, common law is either state law or federal law and is authoritatively construed by state courts or by the United States Supreme Court, respectively.

The legal realist component of *Erie* recognized that judges make law as much as they "find" it. Accordingly, the law reflected in state court decisions is as much the law of the state as is the product of the legislature.[98] Both legislatures and courts make law, and it makes no sense for federal courts to distinguish between these different sources when determining the content of nonfederal law.[99] The federal courts must follow the state supreme court's authoritative construction of state law, whether that law takes the form of statutes or judge-made common law.

The federalism theme emphasizes the corresponding point that while state courts are agents of the state government, federal courts are agents of the federal government.[100] For federal courts to impose their interpretation of common law principles in preference to state court interpretation represents the federal government invading the domain of the states. Federalism entails an allocation of authority between the state governments and the federal government. The *Swift*-era practice of federal courts independently interpreting general common law constituted an intrusion by the federal government into an area properly belonging to the states.[101]

Some scholars have combined these principles into an indictment of intersystemic adjudication. They argue that federal courts' interpreting state law represents exactly the kind of federal intrusion into state affairs that *Erie* sought to end. Intersystemic adjudication in this view is equivalent to the federal government setting up mini-federal legislatures to create state law. Professor Bradford Clark, for example, has stated that a federal court's interpreting state law is like the *Swift*-era practice of federal courts' making general common law: "In either case, a federal court's practice of 'indulg[ing] in lawmaking by decisions' necessarily interferes with the sovereign prerogative of the states to decide both *whether* and *how* to regulate the conduct of the parties."[102] This argument would apply equally to state court interpretation of federal law. State courts interpreting federal law would be setting themselves up as mini-Congresses engaging in the illegitimate creation of federal law. What this parallel suggests is that the force of Clark's argument lies not in the question whether a court's rulings have a lawmaking effect, but rather in the question whether such lawmaking is authorized.

Of course, given the existence of diversity jurisdiction and supplemental jurisdiction, scholars generally do not claim that federal courts should never interpret state law. Some scholars do urge, though, that federal court interpretation of state law be minimized through devices such as abstention and certification.[103]

DEFENSES

This section defends the legitimacy of intersystemic adjudication. It agrees that *Erie* stands for a modern recognition of the insights of positivism and legal realism. It also agrees that *Erie* defines important issues of judicial federalism. I argue, however, that the critique developed previously misstates the implications of positivism, realism, and federalism.

Distinction between Law and Judicial Interpretation

The key error of the critique of the legitimacy of intersystemic adjudication lies in its false attribution of exclusivity to the roles of state courts. One can accept the realist insight that when state courts interpret state law, they in effect make law. One also can accept the positivist concern for locating the authority underlying law. The decisions of state courts are law because state courts are authorized by the lawmaking authority, the state, to make the law. In this sense, the state courts are lawmaking agents duly authorized by the states.

If one believes that the exclusive legitimate judicial source of state law-making is a state court, then federal interpretation of state law is a kind of usurpation. If state law is whatever the state court says it is, then the federal courts are operating with a substantial legitimacy deficit. The federal courts would necessarily be derivative. State courts would be making the pure, essential state law, and federal courts would be attempting to determine its content through a glass darkly. Professor Barry Friedman, a leading scholar of jurisdiction, appears to take this position.[104] He criticizes an argument that I had made that, in certain circumstances, federal courts might render a "more impartial" reading of state law than would state courts.[105] My argument referred to some of the fears of bias raised in the context of diversity litigation, as well as to studies of political pressures experienced by state judges subject to electoral scrutiny. Professor Friedman responds, "It is difficult to know exactly what 'more impartial' means in this sentence. The only 'reading' of a state constitution that can be authoritative is that rendered by its highest court."[106] I take it that a "more impartial" reading is more likely to be correct than a "less impartial" (or more partial) reading. Professor Friedman does not deny the potential for a federal court to be more impartial, nor does he deny the link between impartiality and correctness. Instead, he asserts that only the highest state court can be "authoritative." But it is this equation of "authoritative" and "correct" that I challenge.

The interpretation of state law rendered by the state's highest court must be followed by state and federal courts. Nevertheless, that interpretation may not be the best construction of the provision at issue. Fear of electoral repercussions, for example, might shape a state court's interpretation of the law. The opinion of a federal court interpreting the same item might provide a useful perspective, perhaps compensating for the perceived unpopularity of following a particular course. Potential bias does not make a decision less authoritative; it just makes it less likely to be correct. Federal courts also are subject to political pressures and have no monopoly on interpretive skill. The different perspective of the federal court, though, might assist the state court in its search for the best interpretation.

If instead of equating state law with the opinion of the state court, one takes the slightly more modest position that state courts participate in the creation of state law, then there is nothing necessarily illegitimate about federal courts participating in the process as well. This argument applies to state common law, but applies with even more force to state constitutional law.

In interpreting the state constitution, it seems much more apt to say that a state court participates in the making of the law, rather than to say that the state constitution is nothing more than what the state court says it is. The literature on constitutional interpretation outside the courts is large and growing. The main thrust of this scholarship, which has focused on the federal Constitution, is that one need not understand courts to be the exclusive interpreters of the federal Constitution. Other governmental officials interpret the Constitution as well.[107] A great deal of what the president does is to interpret the Constitution. A special unit in the Department of Justice, the Office of Legal Counsel, gives opinions to the president about the constitutionality of laws. A great deal of what Congress should do is to interpret the Constitution. In the federal constitutional context, the main debate is about supremacy. Should the United States Supreme Court be supreme in the interpretation of the federal Constitution?[108] In the state court/federal court context, supremacy is not at issue. With regard to state law, the state high court is supreme, at least with respect to federal courts.

The debate about exclusivity recognizes conceptual space between a constitution and what the court says it means. It is not conceptually incoherent to say that the United States Supreme Court misinterpreted the Constitution. In the case of state constitutions, plural interpretation seems an even greater practical necessity. Given the long, complex nature of state constitutions and the many activities of state government, state constitutional issues arise with great frequency. The interpretation of state attorneys general and other state officials will, in many areas, determine the meaning of the state constitution with practical finality.[109] Given the necessarily plural nature of state constitutional interpretation, a federal role does little to diminish the goals of finality and uniformity.

Once one recognizes that the state high court does not enjoy the exclusive authority to interpret the state constitution, the role of the federal court comes into focus. Federal intervention can contribute to an understanding of the meaning of the state constitution. The federal court is not an outsider, an interloper. Rather, federalism gives to the federal court the ability to speak about the state constitution as well as, under current understandings, the obligation to follow the state supreme court once that interpretation has been established.[110]

In sum, Erie clarified that the state high court was the supreme interpreter of state law. This result followed from particular understandings of federalism, probably buttressed by jurisprudential commitments to realism and positivism. Positivism meant that all law was state law or federal law. General common law was therefore really state law. Realism reinforced that conclusion. If common law was state law, then the state high court enjoyed the right of authoritative interpretation. However, neither Erie nor a broader notion of the spirit of Erie made the state supreme court the exclusive interpreter of state law. So when a federal court interprets a state constitution, it does not usurp state authority. As with other instances of polyphonic federalism, the federal and state courts can participate together in the protection of fundamental rights.

Erie *and the New Deal*

This understanding of Erie and of the kind of judicial federalism implied by Erie finds support in the larger context of 1938, when Erie was decided. Erie stands as part of the moment that witnessed the end of dual federalism. During this period, the Supreme Court recognized the difficulty of distinguishing categorically between national and local affairs, and it largely stopped trying to do so.[111] Decisions from this period unleashed the federal government to pursue a wide variety of aims that might at one point have been understood to be within the exclusive province of the states. *Wickard v. Filburn*,[112] the wheat case discussed in chapter 2, is emblematic. In that ruling, the Court held that congressional power to regulate interstate commerce included the authority to prohibit a farmer from growing too much wheat for home consumption. At the same time, the United States Supreme Court allowed the state and federal governments to pursue social welfare aims that previously had been denied to them.[113]

Some of the social goals were being advanced by state courts through the course of common law development. Using their power to declare general common law, the federal courts sometimes had impeded these state law developments. *Erie* was an effort to prevent the federal courts from interfering with the social policy being developed by the state courts. As with other instances of the decline of dual federalism, *Erie* then was really about empowering states and state courts.

Erie also raises the issue of the appropriate separation of the state and federal court systems. *Erie* certainly responded to a perception of excessive federal court meddling in matters appropriately decided by state courts. The grounds of complaint, though, related not to federal courts adjudicating state-law issues, but to the nondeferential manner in which federal courts treated state court precedents. *Erie* need not stand for the necessity of rigidly separating the appropriate domains of state and federal courts. *Erie* came at a time when dual federalism was being rejected in favor of more cooperative models, and the decision need not be understood as enforcing a regime of dual judicial federalism. With the decline of dual federalism, the state and federal governments exercise overlapping regulatory authority. Intersystemic adjudication represents an overlap of judicial authority. Just as state and federal governments may engage in cooperative, competitive, or even conflictual relationships, so may state and federal courts. *Erie* did not mandate the end of such judicial interaction.

CHAPTER SIX

State Courts as Enforcers of Federal Law

Chapter 5 used the example of federal court interpretation of state law to illustrate the benefits of intersystemic adjudication. This chapter focuses on state court enforcement of federal law. Here, too, a dualist conception threatens to undermine important advantages of federalism. A principle of keeping federal matters in federal court would obstruct the values served by polyphonic federalism. This chapter notes how the polyphonic perspective fosters an appreciation for the benefits of intersystemic adjudication. State court enforcement of federal law can play a significant role in promoting the goals of federalism. Such intersystemic adjudication leads to a more innovative and resilient jurisdictional system and also safeguards human rights.

State Court Enforcement of Federal Rights

Affording a remedy for the violation of a right is a longstanding promise of the judicial system in the United States.[1] That promise, however, is sometimes not fulfilled. Federal law may provide rights without remedies. This gap between right and remedy presents an important opportunity for the state courts to step into the breach. The ability of state courts to fill a hole in the provision of remedies for federal rights represents a significant feature of jurisdictional federalism, at least when federalism is understood in polyphonic terms.

A remedial gap may arise for several reasons. This section considers the recurrent problem posed by the Supreme Court's narrow construction of the jurisdiction of the federal courts. Because of that interpretation, both the standing doctrine and the doctrine of state sovereign immunity pose significant obstacles to the full realization of rights. State courts may be necessary to provide remedies for the violation of federal rights.

STATE STANDING FOR FEDERAL RIGHTS

The federal standing doctrine provides a prime illustration of the possibilities for state courts to vindicate federal rights. The United States Supreme Court has adopted a restrictive understanding of the kinds of matters that come within the jurisdiction conferred on federal courts by the United States Constitution. In accordance with this narrow conception of the "case or controversy" requirement of Article III, the Court has applied the doctrine of standing so as to limit the suits that may be brought in federal court. These standing restrictions impair the enforcement of federal rights. In fulfillment of the polyphonic conception of federalism, state courts can serve as alternative forums for the vindication of these federal rights.

The Supreme Court has developed a complex body of standing doctrine. One especially significant element that the Court has propounded is that the plaintiff must establish concrete, particularized harm, rather than a generalized grievance.[2] The Court has further clarified that Congress may not circumvent this constitutional requirement by statutorily conferring standing on citizens.[3] Under the Court's standing doctrine, even if Congress wishes to grant citizens broad authority to bring suit to enforce federal statutes, the Constitution stands as a barrier. For Congress to designate citizen monitors in this way, the Court has held, infringes on the president's constitutional authority to "take Care that the Laws be faithfully executed."[4]

The Supreme Court's standing cases have been subject to substantial academic criticism.[5] This doctrine has the effect of making it more difficult to implement federal laws. In certain contexts, the standing hurdles may be especially onerous. With regard to environmental protections, for example, the beneficiaries of the legislation may be quite diffuse. The violation of environmental safeguards may be unlikely to cause concrete injury to any specific person.[6] Congress clearly has the authority to enact such statutes. However, the standing doctrine may obstruct their enforcement. Because of the standing doctrine, environmental laws may provide rights without remedies, at least in federal court.

Polyphonic federalism points the way to a federalist solution to this problem. The limitations of Article III of the Unites States Constitution do not apply to state courts. Accordingly, state courts can enforce the federal laws without the obstacle of federal standing requirements.[7] Intersystemic adjudication can fill this remedial gap.

The practice of state courts' entertaining federal claims that could not be heard in federal court has sparked academic controversy.[8] These scholarly debates implicate the core concerns of polyphonic federalism. From a dualist point of view, it might seem odd to allow state courts to adjudicate federal claims in accordance with state rules of standing. For a dualist, it may appear that national rights should be adjudicated according to national rules. From a functional perspective, applying state standing rules to federal claims results in substantial complexity. The discussions highlight the tension between plurality, dialogue, and redundancy on the one hand and uniformity, finality, and hierarchical accountability on the other. A key concern relates to the reviewability of the state court adjudication in the United States Supreme Court.

Under current law, the reviewability of the state court determination turns on which side prevails in state court. If a plaintiff who would not have standing under Article III in federal court succeeds in vindicating a federal right, the defendant will be able to seek review in the United States Supreme Court. In *ASARCO Inc. v. Kadish*,[9] the Court reasoned that the adverse ruling on the issue of federal law confers on the defendant an injury cognizable under Article III. In effect, being subject to the unfavorable ruling gives the defendant standing for Article III purposes.[10] However, the reasoning of *ASARCO* would not extend to a decision of a state court rejecting a federal claim. Thus, if a non-Article III plaintiff receives an adverse judgment on a matter of federal law, no Supreme Court review is available. In this situation, the state court's interpretation of federal law is final and unreviewable.

Adopting a dualist perspective, scholars such as Judge William Fletcher and Professor Paul Freund have emphasized the resulting threat to the uniformity of federal law.[11] The need for a uniform interpretation of federal law has stood as a central justification for the appellate jurisdiction of the United States Supreme Court over state courts.[12] The existence of an unreviewable state court interpretation of federal law threatens to undermine that uniformity. The uncertainty of reviewing the state court judgment leads to problems of finality as well. Without Supreme Court review, debates about the issue will continue. Indeed, litigation about that particular matter may persist. Other state courts may honor the state court judgment, prohibiting relitigation of the underlying matter; federal courts, however, will not give such preclusive effect to a state court's unreviewable judgment on a matter of federal law.[13] For related reasons, hierarchical accountability also may suffer. The United States Supreme Court, the authoritative judicial interpreter of federal law, may be unable to address a particular federal issue.

The normal lines of authority guaranteeing the opportunity for review by the ultimate interpreter will be broken.[14] For a time at least, the United States Supreme Court may lose its ability to control the interpretation of federal law.

The possibility of plural interpretation and the value of dialogue constitute the flip side of lack of uniformity and lack of finality. The state court interpretation of federal law may be considered by other courts, state and federal. Just as the different institutional setting of the state court enabled it to exercise jurisdiction over the case, so too that different structural matrix may provide a valuable alternative perspective on the issue of federal law.

The polyphonic value that appears with most salience in the standing setting is redundancy. The alternative state standing regime provides another mechanism for the vindication of federal rights. If the federal courts underenforce federal rights through restrictive application of standing requirements, the state courts can provide a valuable outlet, helping to implement federal rights that might otherwise not be enforced.

Of course, underenforcement may be in the eye of the beholder. Perhaps state court rules provide too broad a swath of enforcement capabilities. Here, it is useful to remember the kind of state-federal relationship at issue. One kind of interaction is between state and federal courts, as each system grapples with the meaning of federal law. The state courts and the United States Congress also may engage in a useful partnership. At least with regard to the statutory matters that constitute the central concern of this section, Congress has substantial discretion in determining the scope of the right. Congress decides what rights a statute will entail and has broad authority over the enforcement of the statute. Congress could specify that only a certain category of people has authority to bring enforcement suits. Congress could confer exclusive jurisdiction on the federal courts to enforce the statute. However, if the statute confers broad standing and does not limit the jurisdiction to federal court, Congress (or at least the statute's proponents) may want the broadest possible enforcement, including in state court if necessary. In this way, the state courts and Congress act as partners in realizing federal statutory rights.

THE SPECIAL PROBLEM OF REMEDIES AGAINST THE FEDERAL GOVERNMENT

The state court bypass does not provide a full alternative to federal court jurisdiction. In many instances, the plaintiffs seek to constrain the action of the federal government itself. Much environmental litigation, for example, seeks to force the Secretary of the Interior to follow a particular interpretation of an environmental statute.[15] State court actions against federal officials pose special problems for federalism.

Historical Perspective

Before 1850, state courts exercised the power to issue writs of mandamus and writs of habeas corpus against federal officials. Underage enlistment in the federal armed forces provided a recurring setting for these state court orders. On numerous occasions, state court judges issued writs of habeas corpus ordering federal military officials to discharge minors.[16] In the context of a property dispute, the Supreme Court held in 1821 that state courts could not issue writs of mandamus against federal officials.[17] However, the practice of granting writs of habeas corpus continued.

The controversy over slavery brought these state writs into sharp conflict with national policy. The Fugitive Slave Act of 1850 expanded the power of federal courts and federal marshals to return escaped slaves and to punish those who aided the escapees.[18] Under that law, Sherman Booth, a Wisconsin abolitionist, was taken into federal custody on charges of helping a fugitive slave escape from a federal deputy. The Wisconsin Supreme Court issued a writ of habeas corpus ordering the release of Booth. The United States marshal, Stephen Ableman, sought review of the writ in the United States Supreme Court. In *Ableman v. Booth*,[19] the United States Supreme Court reversed the state supreme court. The United States Supreme Court held that the state court was without authority to interfere with the federal judicial process. In *Tarble's Case* in 1872,[20] the United States Supreme Court reaffirmed the holding of *Ableman*, this time in the more traditional context of a state court writ to release a minor from the federal armed forces.

Current Applications

More recently, the Supreme Court held that state judges may not enjoin litigation in federal courts.[21] Although the Court has not directly addressed whether state courts may issue injunctions against federal officials, the historical background places this power in substantial doubt.[22] Even if state court remedies are limited in this way, suits challenging federal action may nevertheless give state courts a valuable voice. Plaintiffs lacking Article III standing might still come to state court for a declaratory judgment on the meaning of federal law. To be sure, these actions too face jurisdictional questions. In some circumstances, courts have treated declaratory judgments as essentially the same as injunctions,[23] potentially subjecting them to the same prohibition. Properly viewed, however, declaratory relief is significantly less intrusive and should be permissible, even if injunctions are barred.

Alternatively, state courts could issue advisory opinions on the meaning of federal law. Although Article III prohibits federal courts from giving advisory opinions, courts in some states have a long tradition of issuing such opinions.[24] A state court advisory opinion would offer no direct relief to a plaintiff challenging the action of the federal government. A well-reasoned opinion might, though, help to persuade the federal government to abide by that interpretation of federal law. Such an advisory opinion at a minimum would serve as a rallying point for opposition to the conduct of the federal government.

In an ideal world, the president would take care that the federal statutes were faithfully executed. In an ideal world, the United States Supreme Court might reform its doctrines governing standing in federal court.[25] Federalism, though, presents a solution for this world. The existence of parallel state and federal court systems provides a crucial alternative means for the enforcement of federal or state rights. The polyphonic conception of federalism emphasizes that possibility.

SOVEREIGN IMMUNITY AFTER ALDEN

Federal doctrines of sovereign immunity present another area in which state courts have a significant opportunity to assist in implementing federal rights. Recent decisions of the United States Supreme Court have given states a new and vital role in enforcing federal rights. Since the 1985 decision in *Garcia v. San Antonio Metropolitan Transit Authority*,[26] it has been clear that Congress can regulate the activity of state governments, just as it can regulate private parties. However, if the state violates the law, cases such as *Alden v. Maine*[27] and *Seminole Tribe v. Florida*[28] establish that the federal government cannot grant a private remedy for the person wronged. Underlying principles of state sovereignty, the Supreme Court held, prevent Congress from providing for private suits for money damages against unconsenting states in state or federal court.[29] As discussed in chapter 3, that was the fate the befell Patricia Garrett. Even if Alabama fired her based on her undergoing cancer treatment, an action that violates a valid federal law, she still cannot recover back pay.[30]

Garrett and those in her position may seek injunctions against the state.[31] Injunctions, however, do not always provide the necessary relief; Garrett needed her back pay.[32] If the federal right arises from the Fourteenth Amendment to the United States Constitution, Congress can override the states' immunity and allow a monetary remedy.[33] Many important federal rights, though, do not rest on the Fourteenth Amendment. In enacting the Fair Labor Standards Act,[34] the Age Discrimination in Employment Act,[35] and the Americans with Disabilities Act,[36] for example, Congress used its Commerce Clause authority to grant rights broader than the federal constitutional minimum. Under the Supreme Court's rulings, Congress cannot provide a private damages remedy to vindicate these rights.[37]

In upholding principles of state sovereignty, the Supreme Court emphasized that the restriction on congressional authority extended only to the remedy, not to the right itself. The states remain obligated to obey the underlying law. Whether or not the employee can sue for back pay, for example, a state university cannot discriminate against the employee based on age, disability, or pregnancy. These recent Supreme Court decisions thus constitute a kind of devolution of remedial power. The states must follow federal law, but the Supreme Court has conferred on the states, rather than on the national government, the mandate to establish the necessary remedial scheme. In *Alden*, Justice Kennedy explained this devolution as follows:

> The constitutional privilege of a State to assert its sovereign immunity in its own courts does not confer upon the State a concomitant right to disregard the Constitution or valid federal law. The States and their officers are bound by obligations imposed by the Constitution and by federal statutes that comport with the constitutional design. We are unwilling to assume the States will refuse to honor the Constitution or obey the binding laws of the United States. The good faith of the States thus provides an important assurance that "[t]his Constitution, and the Laws of the United States which shall be made in Pursuance thereof . . . shall be the supreme Law of the Land." U.S. Const., Art. VI.[38]

Alden and *Seminole Tribe* establish a remedial gap and a remedial challenge. As a matter of federal law, there may be rights without effective remedies. The authority to bridge this gap is delegated to the states. The supremacy of federal law depends in large measure on the "good faith" of the states.

From the perspective of the states, a crucial question is which branch of government should be responsible for guaranteeing the enforcement of federal law. Surely, all branches have an obligation not to violate federal law. The state legislature must strive to enact legislation that comports with federal requirements, and executive and administrative officials must conform their actions to federal mandates. All state officers must seek to honor individuals' federal rights.[39] One cannot, however, protect rights without providing remedies. A systematic effort to prevent the violation of rights requires a systematic remedial framework. The executive and legislature can help to ensure effective remedies. Most directly, the legislature generally may waive the state's immunity and consent to private suits for damages.[40] Our legal tradition, though, also recognizes a strong role for courts in ensuring remedies.

State courts have sometimes found that claims of sovereign immunity must fall before alleged violations of state constitutional rights.[41] State courts also have invoked right-to-remedy clauses (sometimes called "open courts" clauses) in state constitutions to restrict the ability of the legislature to deny effective remedies for the violation of established rights.[42] The problem of federal rights without remedies presents a strong case for state judicial action. In cases involving state law rights, sovereign immunity could be understood as limiting the domain of the right: State law creates a right to recovery, but also determines that the right may not be asserted against the state. The remedy thus founders on the positivist foundation of the right. What the state gives, the state can take away, at least when the restriction enjoys the traditional status of sovereign immunity.[43] The individual must "take the bitter with the sweet."[44]

Federal rights present different concerns. The federal right does not emanate from the state. The state cannot modify or condition it. Individuals have rights against the state independent of the authority of state law. The question is whether the state is going to deny a remedy for that right. The United States Supreme Court relied on the "good faith" of the states to ensure the enforcement of these rights against the state. Whatever the merit of that decision, the state judiciaries need not rely merely on the "good faith" of the executive and the legislature to realize these rights. Rather, state courts can fulfill their historic function of ensuring that for every right there is a remedy. Indeed, only judicially enforceable remedies can provide a full measure of recognition for the federal rights.[45]

Unlike the standing area, state court solutions to sovereign immunity problems pose little threat to uniformity, finality, or hierarchical accountability. Sovereign immunity does not bar appellate review in the United States Supreme Court of federal issues. If the state court entertains the federal claim against a state official, the United States Supreme Court can give an authoritative resolution of any federal questions that arise. In this instance, the availability of the alternative forum promotes the vindication of federal rights without adverse consequences for federal law.

As with my discussion of standing, my claim here is not that state court adjudication of federal claims is inherently superior to federal court adjudication. The Supreme Court's sovereign immunity jurisprudence has justifiably been subject to severe academic criticism.[46] In an ideal world, federal courts would fully vindicate federal rights against states. A polyphonic conception of federalism emphasizes that the dual court system in the United States provides dual means of enforcing rights. Here again, the state courts can act as partners of Congress in providing important protections for individual liberties. Congress can create the statutory rights, and the state courts can help to ensure effective remedies.

More Polyphonic Federalism in Action: State Criminal Prosecution of Federal Officials

As a kind of coda, it is useful to consider a different sort of example of polyphonic federalism in action. A more rare and dramatic instance of intersystemic adjudication involves a state criminal prosecution of a federal official for violating state law. Such an action is one way in which a state may protect its citizens from having their rights violated by the federal government. This kind of situation arose in connection with the armed confrontation between federal agents and Randy Weaver in Ruby Ridge, Idaho, in 1992.

Randy Weaver was a white supremacist and government separatist who had moved his family into the backwoods of Idaho after service in the Army's Green Berets.[47] In 1991, a sting operation conducted by the Federal Bureau of Alcohol, Tobacco, and Firearms led to Weaver's arrest for selling sawed-off shotguns.[48] Following the arrest, Weaver retreated to his home on Ruby Ridge and did not appear at his trial date.[49] Another warrant was sworn out for Weaver, but no arrest was immediately attempted. Instead, the federal authorities instigated a sixteen-month surveillance operation, costing nearly $1 million, in preparation for effecting the arrest.[50]

On August 21, 1992, during the course of the surveillance operation, six deputy United States marshals entered Weaver's property dressed in camouflage and employing night vision equipment.[51] Later in the morning, the marshals were discovered by a party consisting of Randy Weaver, family friend Kevin Harris, Weaver's fourteen-year-old son Samuel, and Samuel's dog. In the ensuing confrontation, one of the marshals shot Samuel's dog, and Samuel responded by firing at the marshals. The marshals returned fire, striking Samuel once in the arm and once in the back, killing him. At the same time, Harris shot and killed Deputy Marshal William Degan. Harris and Randy Weaver retreated after the exchange. Weaver and his wife, Vicki, later returned to collect their son's body.

By the next morning the Federal Bureau of Investigation had assumed control of the operation, deploying fifty-one agents to surround Weaver's cabin, including Special Agent Lon Horiuchi, a sniper attached to the Hostage Rescue Team.[52] Horiuchi observed Randy Weaver, Weaver's teenage daughter Sara, and Kevin Harris run from the cabin, apparently in response to the sound of a helicopter lifting off nearby. One of the males, Randy Weaver, was carrying a gun. When Weaver made a threatening gesture toward the helicopter, Horiuchi shot and wounded him. The three retreated to the cabin, with Harris coming last and now in possession of the gun. Horiuchi fired at Harris, but the bullet passed through a window pane in the top of the cabin door, striking Vicki Weaver in the head before hitting Harris in the shoulder. Vicki Weaver, who had her infant daughter in her arms, was killed instantly. Ten days later, Harris, Weaver, and Weaver's three children surrendered to the authorities.

The confrontation at Ruby Ridge sparked a barrage of criticism over the manner in which the federal government handled the situation. When the Justice Department decided not to pursue charges against Horiuchi for his role in the death of Vicki Weaver, the local Idaho prosecutor filed a charge of involuntary manslaughter in Boundary County Court.[53] Horiuchi exercised his right to remove the case to federal court and have the state criminal prosecution proceed in a federal forum.[54] The key issue in the case was the scope of the immunity that federal officials should enjoy when undertaking their federal duties. Horiuchi sought to dismiss the charges based on federal immunity. The federal district court did dismiss the charges, and the dismissal was affirmed by a panel of the United States Court of Appeals for the Ninth Circuit. The Ninth Circuit then reheard the case en banc and vacated the panel opinion by a vote of 6–5.[55] With the Ninth Circuit contemplating a further rehearing, the newly elected local prosecutor decided to drop the charges.[56] The prosecutor's action initially met with opposition from Boundary County commissioners, one of whom stated, "The issue that we want to see resolved is not that Mr. Horiuchi is tried. . . . It's the ultimate decision on whether a federal employee has immunity from state law."[57] However, the commissioners later rescinded a resolution calling for the continuance of the action against Horiuchi.[58]

The facts of the case were extraordinary, and the issue of Supremacy Clause immunity arises rarely. Overall, however, the case illustrates the larger point that one of the key ways in which federalism operates in the

United States is through the interaction of state and federal governments. The State of Idaho ended up presenting state criminal charges against a federal official in a federal court. It was through this entwining of federal and state law and institutions that the federalist system in the United States sought to recognize Idaho's interest in protecting its citizens without sacrificing the ability of the United States to protect all its citizens. Although anomalous in many respects, the Horiuchi case is paradigmatic in its presentation of contemporary federalism. Dualist notions of separate spheres of authority and cooperative notions of harmonious interaction do not capture the dynamic, competitive, and conflictual relationships among the states and the federal government that figure centrally in federalism.

The Values of Federalism Revisited

Chapter 5 explained how federal court enforcement of state law advances federalism from the perspective of the economic, republican, and liberal perspectives. I now apply that framework to this chapter's topic, the interpretation of federal law by state courts.

Enforcing federal statutes in state court through broader conceptions of standing, enforcing federal statutes through narrower conceptions of sovereign immunity, and using state criminal prosecution of federal officials present relatively clear examples of promoting the benefits of federalism. From the economic perspective, one observes two components of valuable competition in each instance. First, the state is providing a remedy in competition with the federal remedy. The federal government has offered one product—federal standing, the Eleventh Amendment, and federal prosecutorial discretion—and the states are offering an alternative. Such competition between the states and the federal government may serve a disciplining function. If the state enforcement actions prove popular, the federal courts or the federal government may decide to change their rules. The federal courts may not want to lose control over the development of federal statutory law because plaintiffs are forced into state court. The president, acting through the Department of Justice, may not want to lose control over the prosecution of federal officers. Competition from the states may spur federal action.

Second, the states can compete with each other about the extent to which they will enforce federal law or prosecute federal agents. In each instance, the alternative to state participation is federal monopoly. By giving the states a role in enforcing the law, states have the opportunity to offer varying packages of policies to their citizens. Citizens may favor or disfavor states that vigorously enforce federal law or vigorously prosecute federal agents. Intersystemic adjudication adds an important state component to what would otherwise be purely federal matters.

These state judicial and prosecutorial actions may also promote republican self-governance. These instances of intersystemic adjudication allow the states to exercise control over the administration of federal law. The dualist perspective attempts to reserve some area of exclusive state control, a realm of state hegemony in which the output of state self-governance is guaranteed to take effect. The actual areas of exclusive state control, however, are extremely small. State participation in the enforcement of federal law actually increases the opportunity for citizens of a state to have control over matters affecting their lives. The United States Supreme Court may claim that the boundaries it constructs are to protect states, but they act as much to fence in the states as to fence out the national government. These examples illustrate that the interaction of federal and state authority has a much greater potential to empower citizens. State enforcement of federal law or prosecution of federal officials greatly enhances the self-governance of a state's citizens. In the polyphonic conception, a state's citizens may not be masters of their own domains, but they exercise much greater control over a much greater domain.

These examples of polyphonic federalism show particular strength in thwarting tyranny. The criminal prosecution of Lon Horiuchi constitutes a classic example of a state using its authority to try to check the improper use of federal power. The possibility of a state criminal prosecution may serve as a valuable deterrent to wrongdoing by federal agents. The potential for state action ensures that no individual is above the law.

The state court enforcement of federal law thwarts tyranny as well. An important function of federal law is to prevent state tyranny, but the sovereign immunity doctrines of *Seminole Tribe*[59] and *Alden*[60] threaten to immunize states from the application of federal law. These decisions hinder the enforcement of federal statutes that regulate tyrannic state conduct. State enforcement provides a judicial check that would not otherwise exist on the abusive exercise of state authority. Broadened standing in state court may allow an individual to bring an enforcement action against a state, thus further protecting against the misuse of power by the state. State courts also help to keep the federal government within the bounds of federal law. Whatever the coercive effect on federal officials of state court judgments, state judges can provide an important voice declaring that the federal government is in violation of a federal statute. Moreover, modern liberal theory understands governmental inaction as a potential source of tyranny as well.[61] For a worker in an unsafe plant, for a citizen in a polluted neighborhood, for an employee subject to discrimination in the workplace, government regulation may represent a reprieve from the potential abuses of private power. In this respect, the failure of the federal courts to enforce federal statutes, even against private defendants, may occasion tyranny. Enforcement in state court can address this problem. Multiple channels of enforcement can protect against the tyranny of inaction.

CHAPTER SEVEN

Customary International Law in State and Federal Courts

The preceding chapters have applied the polyphonic conception of federalism to issues involving the overlap of state and federal law and state and federal courts. Though I touched on matters of foreign affairs, such as in discussing the *Garamendi* preemption decision, the focus has been domestic. In the situations examined, the choice facing courts and regulators has been to apply federal law, state law, or both. This chapter expands the domain of discussion to include international law. The effect of international law within the United States has been an increasingly important and controversial subject of legal debate. This topic also helps to illustrate the importance of polyphony. So far in this book, the voices of the states and the federal government have provided the strains of polyphony. International law, however, constitutes another voice. Incorporating international law into the domestic legal system raises many complex issues. With its emphasis on the interplay of multiple, different voices, the polyphonic approach to federalism offers an especially useful framework for addressing international law. Dualist theories have much more difficulty finding a place for the third melody of international law.

The Controversy over Customary International Law

It is well established that some forms of international law function as binding federal law. When the United States enters into a treaty or joins an international convention, following the requisite procedural formalities, including Senate ratification, the provisions of the treaty or convention become federal law. Some disputes remain about when such agreements are "self-executing"[1] and when they require further implementing legislation, but treaty law has the fundamental characteristics of federal law, including invalidating contrary state law and triggering the federal question jurisdiction of the federal courts.

Another kind of international law, "customary international law," arises not from the ratification of a treaty but from the actual practices of states. As one authoritative source puts it, customary international law "results from a general and consistent practice of states followed by them from a sense of legal obligation."[2] Customary international law includes a broad array of rules, including immunity of foreign diplomats, the enforcement of legal judgments and, most controversially, human rights principles.[3]

A fierce debate has arisen recently over the status of customary international law in domestic courts. Does customary international law count as binding federal law in the same manner as ratified treaties? Under the "modern" view, supported by Dean Harold Koh among others, customary international law is federal law, like other federal law.[4] On this conception, customary international law is binding on federal and state courts and preempts contrary state law. By contrast, according to the revisionist position, advanced most forcefully by Professors Curtis Bradley and Jack Goldsmith, customary international law is not, of its own force, a valid source of law. According to the revisionists, customary international law is not federal law unless federal lawmakers make it so.[5] Similarly, Bradley and Goldsmith argue that customary international law is not state law unless state lawmakers make it law. Without further action by authorized bodies in the United States, such as state or federal legislatures, customary international law is not law that is binding in courts in the United States. For the revisionists, customary international law simply does not constitute law in the United States without some further authorizing act.

The passion underlying this debate stems in large measure from its application to human rights litigation. Customary international law includes some human rights norms. Under the modern position, these norms become federal law, binding in state or federal courts. In this manner, human rights law "produced" abroad—through the general and consistent practice of states—automatically is incorporated into United States law without any intervening act by the legislature.

The *Filartiga* case in 1980 illustrated this possibility.[6] As alleged in that litigation, Joel Filartiga was an opponent of long-time Paraguayan leader Alfredo Stroessner. In retaliation for Filartiga's political activities, Norberto Pena-Irala, the inspector general of police in Asuncion, Paraguay, directed the abduction, torture, and murder of Filartiga's son Joelito. Filartiga's daughter, Dolly, subsequently came to the United States and sought political asylum. Dolly and Joel Filartiga learned that Pena was living in the

United States, and they filed suit against him in federal court in New York, seeking damages in connection with Joelito's torture and murder. They brought their action under the Alien Tort Statute, a law first enacted in 1789, which provides, "The district courts shall have original jurisdiction of any civil action by an alien for a tort only, committed in violation of the law of nations or a treaty of the United States."[7] The Filartigas alleged that Pena's torture of Joelito transgressed customary international law and thus constituted a violation of the "law of nations."[8] The action raised jurisdictional questions that required the court to confront directly the status of customary international law. Because the Filartigas and Pena were aliens, the federal court had jurisdiction of this suit only if it raised an issue of federal law. That inquiry in turn depended on whether customary international law was federal law.

In an endorsement of the modern position, the United States Court of Appeals for the Second Circuit affirmed federal jurisdiction, holding that torture violated customary international law and that customary international law formed part of federal common law.[9] The Filartigas eventually received a $10.4 million default judgment against Pena. Pena had in the meantime returned to Paraguay, and the Filartigas never recovered any money.[10] Nevertheless, the case spurred further litigation in courts in the United States to enforce human rights norms. Other lower courts followed the reasoning of *Filartiga*, ruling that customary international law was incorporated into federal common law.[11]

The United States Supreme Court did not join the debate over customary international law for another two decades. The Court finally engaged, but did not resolve, the controversy in its decision in *Sosa v. Alvarez-Machain* in 2004.[12] *Sosa* was the latest stage in a long-running, cross-border dispute. In 1985, Enrique Camarena-Salazar, an agent working for the federal Drug Enforcement Administration (DEA), fell into the hands of drug dealers in Mexico and was tortured and murdered in Guadalajara. The DEA came to believe that a Mexican physician, Humberto Alvarez-Machain, assisted in the torture. The DEA hired several Mexican nationals, including Jose Francisco Sosa, to abduct Alvarez-Machain from his home in Mexico and bring him to the United States, where he was taken into custody and charged with federal crimes. Alvarez-Machain first argued that the illegality of his abduction required dismissal of the criminal charges. In 1992 the United States Supreme Court rejected this argument, ruling that the irregular circumstances of his apprehension did not deprive the federal courts of jurisdiction over him.[13] Accordingly, Alvarez-Machain was tried in the United States. After his criminal trial ended in an acquittal, he sued several people involved in his abduction, including Sosa.[14] Alvarez-Machain's claims included an allegation under the Alien Tort Statute that his abduction violated customary international law.

The civil litigation brought Alvarez-Machain back to the United States Supreme Court, this time as a plaintiff. He lost again. In brief, the Supreme Court held that the Alien Tort Statute did allow claims for some kinds of violations of customary international law, but that Alvarez-Machain's allegations, based on a relatively brief detention, did not fall within the domain of permitted claims.

Both sides of the modern/revisionist debate claimed victory in the *Sosa* decision, leading one commentator to characterize the majority opinion as a "Rorschach blot."[15] The modernists stressed the Supreme Court's affirmation that customary international law could function as binding law without being specifically so designated by Congress.[16] The Court understood the Alien Tort Statute as only conferring jurisdiction.[17] The substantive rights therefore must have come from customary international law, without an authorizing statute. The revisionists emphasized that the Court accepted only a narrow category of customary international law claims, and even then, only in the unusual and limited statutory context of the Alien Tort Statute.[18] Despite the Court's referring to the Alien Tort Statute as merely jurisdictional, the revisionists argue that the Court effectively viewed the statute as the relevant source of rights.[19] The dispute over customary international law continues.

My goal here is not to delve further into the difficult international law issues raised by the debate. Rather, I wish to analyze the underlying federalism concerns and explore how the polyphonic conception can highlight the benefits of various approaches. Under the modern view, customary international law is binding federal law and supersedes any conflicting state law. Under the revisionist view, customary international law is at most state law, depending on the decisions in each state to accept it. While treaty law is federal law, customary international law becomes a species of state law.[20] Both the modern view and the revisionist approach understand customary international law in dualist terms. Customary international law must be state law or federal law. It must fit neatly into one box or the other.

The polyphonic approach developed in this book sheds light on the contrasting positions. The modern view insists on the importance of uniformity and finality. Customary international law must have one meaning throughout the United States, and treating it as federal law best ensures that uniformity. The hierarchical nature of our system for interpreting federal law, with the Supreme Court at the top of the pyramid, ensures that a single meaning will result. Professor Ernest Young has noted the modernists' fear that the revisionist alternative "would invite a cacophony of diverse state interpretations."[21] Cacophony is always the dark underside of polyphony. Further, in the modern account, international law is best understood as a matter for the federal government. States should not meddle in these affairs, certainly not by offering varying interpretations of the demands of customary international law.

The modern approach fails to appreciate the potential benefits of plurality and dialogue. As with other kinds of laws, the participation of multiple interpreters could illuminate the range of possible meanings. The various courts could benefit from reviewing the understandings of other tribunals. Even with peremptory, universal norms, questions may arise about their proper application in particular circumstances. Productive interchange among courts could help to define the meaning of torture or piracy in contemporary settings. In this way, federalism has benefits for the elucidation of customary international law.

This understanding of the contributions of federalism follows from the account of polyphony I have developed. A different situation would arise if, contrary to the arguments presented in this book, federalism were conceived as a way to realize diverse state cultures. What could that kind of diversity contribute to an understanding of the universal principles embodied in customary international law? If instead one recognizes the general consensus on fundamental issues that exists in the United States, state courts have much to contribute. The different state courts can work together to provide the best conception of a shared set of basic principles. The understanding of customary international law can benefit from the wisdom of fifty interpreters who agree on the fundamentals.

Similarly, the modern view accepts the dualist notion that states have no power to act in the area of foreign affairs. As I discussed earlier in connection with the *Garamendi* case, that view of states finds little support in the theory or reality of contemporary politics. States and localities have become active participants in international dialogues. Perhaps some issues do require a final, uniform answer sooner rather than later. For example, foreign dignitaries may require immediate knowledge of their rights and responsibilities in every state. As in other areas, Congress always would retain the authority to federalize customary international law by enacting an appropriate statute.[22] The only question is whether the default rule should favor diversity or federal uniformity.

The revisionist view values accountability above all other possible characteristics of the system. The revisionists focus on the source of law and insist that some lawmaking authority must designate customary international law as state or federal law. The revisionists especially warn against federal courts applying customary international law without an authorizing statute. Concerns for legitimacy underlie the revisionist critique. They understand *Erie* as categorically prohibiting federal common law without a firm grounding in an authoritative text, be it statutory or constitutional. In chapter 5, I offered a more flexible understanding of *Erie*. I argued that the key problem targeted by *Erie* was illegitimate federal court intrusion into state policy development. In the pre-*Erie* period, the federal courts had expanded their conception of general common law to cover a wide array of matters traditionally governed by state law. The federal courts insisted on independent interpretation of tort law and other aspects of state law that were central to state regulatory policy. *Erie* ended that particular practice, but did not prohibit the further development of federal common law in appropriate areas. The very day *Erie* was decided, the Supreme Court also affirmed the use of federal common law to resolve interstate border disputes.[23] Customary international law appears to be an area in which federal courts could contribute a valuable perspective, rather than simply arrogating state law prerogatives.

In a related objection, the revisionists insist that the judicial application of law not traceable to authoritative state or federal institutions violates fundamental principles of democracy. If customary international law is not the product of the federal or state lawmaking processes, how can it be treated as law, consistent with principles of popular sovereignty? To apply customary international law in the United States is to apply law not made by the people to whom it applies. In other words, the customary international law issue presents a special case of the more general problem of intersystemic adjudication. Sometimes courts apply laws that are the product of a different political system. To the extent one values clean lines of jurisdiction and clear boundaries between legal systems, this practice appears deviant and should be suppressed. From a perspective more open to multiple perspectives, intersystemic adjudication seems less threatening.

The revisionist resistance to federal courts' imposing a single binding interpretation of customary international law aligns with the polyphonic perspective. The reasons for the revisionist objections, though, vary substantially from the polyphonic approach. In the polyphonic conception, the problem is not one of legitimacy, but of monologue. From the perspective of polyphony, the concern is not that the federal courts lack the authority to impose a single, uniform interpretation, but that such an imposition would block the benefits of plurality and dialogue. This distinction between the revisionist and polyphonic concerns is critical for determining the best approach to customary international law.

From the polyphonic perspective, what is needed is an intermediate position that treats customary international law as law, but not as preemptive federal law. This kind of approach would promote interchange among state and federal courts. Dean Alexander Aleinikoff, among others, has offered such a conception. He argues that customary international law might function as nonpreemptive federal law.[24] In this view, federal and state courts would apply customary international law, but state courts would not be bound by federal court interpretation of customary international law, and federal courts would not be bound by state court interpretation of customary international law. Customary international law would function like general common law in the pre-*Erie* era. Unlike the modern view, customary international law would not be binding, uniform federal law applicable in both state and federal courts. In contrast to the revisionist position, customary international law would indeed have the status of law without the need for further authorizing legislation.[25] In particular, federal courts would be able to apply customary international law as a kind of federal common law, though without the binding authority on state courts that federal common law usually entails.

This understanding of customary international law as nonpreemptive federal law fits well within a polyphonic framework. State courts and federal courts could develop diverse perspectives and contribute to an ongoing debate about the content and application of customary international law. This approach would allow customary international law to develop in nonuniform ways in state and federal courts. The state and federal courts could engage in a collaborative process of illumination.

Dean Aleinikoff also offers a response to the revisionist criticism of the legitimacy of incorporating customary international law into domestic law. In recognition of the revisionist objections, Dean Aleinikoff proposes an alternative account of legitimacy. He argues that legitimacy need not derive from direct democratic control of the lawmaking process. Such direct control is lacking in many aspects of our political system, including agency rulemaking and judicial review. Instead, Dean Aleinikoff suggests that legitimacy flows from institutions operating in a "field of democratic control."[26] Elements of this field include fair, transparent processes and the ultimate possibility of popular control. It is these kinds of considerations, he argues, "that make the Federal Reserve System, the Environmental Protection Agency, *Marbury v. Madison*, and the United States Congress fully acceptable aspects of an American constitutionalism dedicated to the premise of popular sovereignty."[27] Ultimately, elected officials, answerable to the people, can enact legislation superseding customary international law in the United States. Lawmaking remains in the control of the legislatures.

Though focused on customary international law, Dean Aleinikoff's alternate account of legitimacy has broader application. Intersystemic adjudication generally raises legitimacy concerns. The distinction between applying and fashioning law may be elusive. When federal courts apply state law, they participate in the creation of state law, even though they do not function as part of the state political process. Nor are the federal interpretations of state law subject to state court review on appeal. Similarly, when state courts interpret federal law, they act in a sense as mini-Congresses, establishing federal law. Unlike the case with federal courts and state law, when state courts make federal law, their judgments are subject to review by the United States Supreme Court on appeal. Nevertheless, given the discretionary nature of Supreme Court jurisdiction and the limited size of the Court's docket, state court interpretations of federal law are unlikely to face federal review. The legitimacy of these exercises of intersystemic adjudication, which we largely take for granted, rest on the overall judicial process and its relationship to the electoral process. State and federal courts employ fair, transparent processes, and citizens ultimately retain control over the content of the law in their state and in their nation. As in Dean Aleinikoff's vision, legitimacy rests on the overall functioning of the system within a field of democratic control, rather than on any simple notion of popular sovereignty.

From the perspective of enforcing human rights principles, the Supreme Court's decision in *Sosa* highlights the benefits of Dean Aleinikoff's intermediate approach. The decision in *Sosa* apparently contemplates opening the federal courts to a limited range of human rights claims. Being abducted from one's home and brought to another country for trial, for example, does not qualify. Plaintiffs who, unlike Alvarez-Machain, have claims that fall within the permitted domain may pursue actions in federal courts. But what about others who seek to vindicate human rights? State courts would be an attractive alternative.

The question is whether state courts can interpret customary international law to apply broader human rights principles than those recognized in federal court.[28] Under the modern position, the answer would appear to be negative. If customary international law is binding federal common law, then state courts must conform to the Supreme Court's interpretation. The resolution would be uniform, though uniformly bad for human rights claimants.

By contrast, under the nonpreemptive conception, state courts would remain free to give their own interpretations of customary international law. A state court could incorporate human rights principles that federal courts have declined to recognize. If Alvarez-Machain or the Filartigas find the federal courthouse closed, they can seek relief in state court. Here, as elsewhere, polyphony offers redundancy. Alternative avenues of redress exist. Again, if the existence of multiple interpretations of customary international law became too disruptive, Congress could mandate a uniform, preemptive federal standard. Unless and until Congress felt the need to intervene, however, the fifty state courts could join in the process of articulating and implementing customary international law, including human rights norms.

This conception of customary international law tracks the path that federalism followed in the United States in the second half of the twentieth century. When state autonomy meant the protection of baneful state practices, especially deeply entrenched racism, conferring power on the states seemed antithetical to human rights. Federally imposed uniformity appeared the best way to safeguard citizens throughout the United States. As a national consensus developed on fundamental issues of equality, federalism gained revived credibility. In some areas, states took the lead in promoting civil rights. State governments and state courts came to provide alternative paths to largely shared destinations, rather than blind alleys and circuitous detours; they now participate in active dialogue with the federal government and federal courts about protecting individuals and their rights. When the Supreme Court (re)considered the federal constitutional protection for homosexual sexual intimacy, it noted the existence of state constitutional safeguards.[29] Similarly, in assessing the constitutionality of the death penalty as applied to juveniles, the Court canvassed the state treatment of the question.[30]

States have demonstrated that they are ready to participate in an international dialogue as well. State constitutions give states the ability to define their own conceptions of liberty and equality. States need not slavishly adhere to federal judgments. States cannot confer fewer rights on their citizens, but they can confer more. The intermediate approach to customary international law would offer states that same ability. Unencumbered by a preemptive federal standard, states could offer their own understandings of human rights norms. Plaintiffs would retain the ability to choose the federal forum, but the states would remain as potential alternatives.

Here, as in other areas, forum shopping has winners and losers. Plaintiffs claiming rights under customary international law could choose the most hospitable forum, while defendants would be stuck in the tribunal least favorable to their claims. Polyphonic federalism does not produce symmetry. It favors those seeking to apply the law against defendants. But federalism was never designed to be neutral as to outcomes; it was designed to be liberty enhancing. The understanding of liberty may evolve over time, but that basic feature of federalism remains. Customary international law would provide another potential source of rights protection, which would be greatly magnified by the participation of the states.

CONCLUSION

Throughout this book, I have both identified the federalism that we have—the actual interactions of states and the federal government—and defended a particular conception of governmental organization as the federalism that we should have. Courts represent both positive and negative forces in this normative account. Courts err when they try to impose a dualist legal framework. On the other hand, as chapters 5 and 6 emphasize, courts can and do play an important role in realizing the potential of polyphonic federalism. A key link between the descriptive and normative portions of my argument is an understanding of the relationship of federalism to the changing society in the United States. As forms of social organization have changed, so has federalism. The law has reflected, and should continue to reflect, contemporary social practice. Legal doctrine should harness the creative features of society, rather than fighting a rearguard action to restore concepts of "truly local" and "truly national" that have lost their content.

So, what would the Framers say? This test, a nod to an interpretive theory of original intent, is sometimes employed in constitutional argument. The contention, implicit or explicit, is that a constitutional arrangement cannot be legitimate unless one could imagine the Framers endorsing it. They wrote the document, didn't they? The unspoken accusation is that some bit of interpretive mischief is being attempted and that if only the Framers were still here, they would easily unmask the fraud. The impression conveyed is that someone is seeking to take advantage of the Framers' untimely demise.

Of course, there was no untimely demise. The Framers lived over two hundred years ago. They had seen governments come and go. In a relatively short span of time, they saw colonies become loosely confederated states under the Articles of Confederation, and they then helped form those states into a "more perfect Union"[1] under the Constitution. The Framers well understood the toll that history takes on forms of governmental organization. If they were magically transported into the present, their greatest amazement would likely be that the document they drafted in 1787 retains legal significance, that the Constitution is more than a historical artifact.

As to the interpretation of the Constitution, in a recent federalism case Justice David Souter replied to the "wouldn't the Framers be amazed" line of argument by quoting an earlier justice, Oliver Wendell Holmes Jr. Writing in 1920, Justice Holmes declared:

> [W]hen we are dealing with words that also are a constituent act, like the Constitution of the United States, we must realize that they have called into life a being the development of which could not have been foreseen completely by the most gifted of its begetters. It was enough for them to realize or to hope that they had created an organism; it has taken a century and has cost their successors much sweat and blood to prove that they created a nation. The case before us must be considered in the light of our whole experience and not merely in that of what was said a hundred years ago.[2]

When Justice Holmes wrote of "sweat and blood," his words were more than metaphoric. He had fought in the Civil War and had been wounded in battle. He had experienced the struggles of federalism and the fight to adapt the Constitution to the needs of the Union. The "sweat and blood" of national experience, as well as structural amendments, most notably the Fourteenth Amendment, fundamentally altered that document. The Civil War, the New Deal, and the civil rights movement all changed our understanding of the Constitution and its role in the national life. Federalism played a crucial part in each stage of the constitutional history of the United States. Its role, however, has varied widely over the years. A federal system of government allowed suspicious states to come together in a union, and it provided the flexibility necessary for that nation to endure. The Civil War and the Great Depression tested the strength of the federal union, but federalism proved sufficiently adaptable to allow the nation to survive, though not without sweat and blood.

The success of the federal union of the United States has served as an inspiration to countries around the world, helping to account for the widespread adoption of federalism. Those nations and their challenges differ greatly from those in the United States. Their federalism is not our federalism, but the concept of multiple sources of authority has proved to be an appealing and powerful structure. As I said in the introduction, this book seeks to provide an account of federalism in the contemporary United States, rather than some Universal Theory of Federalism. However, I hope that the conception of federalism I have developed here helps to situate American federalism in a global context. That contemporary global experience is surely instructive. The spread of federalism around the world suggests that its appeal is broader than a particular historical account of a particular nation. Federalism is a powerful organizing principle. A network of coordinated, autonomous actors creates a resilient system, and federalism has allowed governmental organizations to take advantage of that stability.

This book has attempted to place that functional understanding of federalism within the constitutional structure of the United States. As the country has changed, federalism has endured. I have argued that the reason for the survival of federalism has been its ability to adapt. For a time it seemed that the civil rights movement meant the end of federalism, but federalism transformed, survived, and now stands at the center of contemporary struggles for human rights. *Goodridge*,[3] the Massachusetts decision mandating same-sex marriage, demonstrates the importance of federalism to the progressive vision of legal reform. Federalism has come a long way since it served as the rallying cry of the Dixiecrats.

As the nation has changed, as the relationship among the states has changed, so too has the function of federalism. The United States has enjoyed the tremendous benefits of this New Federalism, as the states and the national government engage together to address the complex problems of modern society. The widespread agreement in the United States about the most basic issues of human rights has provided a vital matrix for the flourishing of state and federal interaction. Whatever the issue, be it civil rights, health care, environmental protection, or education, the solution will involve the creative interplay of states and the national government. The concurrent, sometimes conflictual relationship of the states and the federal government has become central to addressing an array of challenges.

The danger this book has identified is a static conception of history that seeks to block this contemporary interplay in the name of restoring a prior conception of dual federalism. Some courts are attempting to reconstruct Maginot lines to protect the states and the federal government from each other. These boundaries in fact safeguard neither, but rather harm both. Drawing lines between the states and the federal government may offer a false hope of harmony and security, but will inevitably sow discord as the governments break out of these artificial constraints. In the unified society of the United States, separating the "truly local" from the "truly national" is a fool's errand.

I hope that the polyphonic conception can serve as a compelling alternative to these rearguard actions. Polyphonic federalism cannot provide definite answers to all issues of potential conflict between the states and the federal government. However, the polyphonic vision can provide a framework of analysis. The polyphonic perspective seeks to identify the key organizational principles that will promote the traditional federalism values of responsiveness, self-governance, and liberty. In the contemporary United States, dualist conceptions of federalism cannot reliably achieve these goals. Guided by a polyphonic understanding of federalism, legislatures and courts can facilitate the valuable interaction of the states and the federal government. Drawing on its unique history, a history of change and transformation, the United States can join the global effort to reap the rich rewards that federalism can bring.

NOTES

INTRODUCTION

1. *See* Garcia v. San Antonio Metro. Transit Auth., 469 U.S. 528, 556 (1985).
2. *See* Pennsylvania v. Union Gas, 491 U.S. 1 (1989).
3. EEOC v. Wyoming, 460 U.S. 226, 264 (1983) (Burger, C.J., dissenting).
4. United States v. Morrison, 529 U.S. 598, 617–18 (2000).
5. *See* Robert Post, *Federalism in the Taft Court Era: Can It Be Revived?*, 51 DUKE L.J. 1513, 1569–71 (2002).
6. Edward L. Rubin, *The Fundamentality and Irrelevance of Federalism*, 13 GA. ST. U. L. REV. 1009, 1056 (1997) (footnote omitted).
7. Lynn A. Baker & Ernest A. Young, *Federalism and the Double Standard of Judicial Review*, 51 DUKE L.J. 75, 150 n.335 (2001). Professor Young has since retreated somewhat from the argument that state identities are strongly distinctive: "Even in a place like Texas . . . national identity predominates. Without denying that considerable cultural distinctiveness remains, it is hard to deny that at the end of the day we are all Americans—not Texans, Okies, Hoosiers, and the like." Ernest A. Young, *Protecting Member State Autonomy in the European Union: Some Cautionary Tales from American Federalism*, 77 N.Y.U. L. REV. 1612, 1725 (2002).
8. James A. Gardner, *The Failed Discourse of State Constitutionalism*, 90 MICH. L. REV. 761, 818 (1992).
9. Davenport v. Garcia, 834 S.W.2d 4, 16 n.33 (Tex. 1992).
10. *See, e.g.*, YOCHAI BENKLER, THE WEALTH OF NETWORKS: HOW SOCIAL PRODUCTION TRANSFORMS MARKETS AND FREEDOM (2006).
11. *See* Edward L. Rubin & Malcolm Feeley, *Federalism: Some Notes on a National Neurosis*, 41 UCLA L. REV. 903 (1994).
12. *See* United States v. Lopez, 514 U.S. 549 (1995).
13. *See* United States v. Morrison, 529 U.S. 598 (2000).
14. *See* Fla. Prepaid Postsecondary Educ. Expense Bd. v. Coll. Sav. Bank, 527 U.S. 627 (1999).
15. *See* Kimel v. Fla. Bd. of Regents, 528 U.S. 62 (2000).
16. *See* Bd. of Trs. of the Univ. of Ala. v. Garrett, 531 U.S. 356 (2001).
17. *See* Alden v. Maine, 527 U.S. 706 (1999).
18. *See, e.g.*, Geier v. Am. Honda Motor Co., 529 U.S. 861 (2000) (preempting state

law concerning seat belts in cars); Cipollone v. Liggett Group, 505 U.S. 504 (1992) (preempting some state laws concerning cigarettes).

19. *See* Daniel J. Elazar, Federal Systems of the World: A Handbook of Federal, Confederal and Autonomy Arrangements xi–xv (2d ed. 1994) (asserting that more than fifty countries rely on federal principles to some extent and that more than 80 percent of the world's population lives in countries using some kind of federal arrangement); Ronald L. Watts, Comparing Federal Systems 4 (2d ed. 1999) (noting that there are currently twenty-four federations containing about 2 billion people or 40 percent of the world population).

CHAPTER ONE

1. *See* William H. Riker, Federalism: Origin, Operation, Significance 155 (1964).

2. *See* Robert F. Worth, *Sunni Arabs Rally to Protest Proposed Iraqi Constitution*, N.Y. Times, Aug. 27, 2005, at A6.

3. *See* Alison Mitchell, *Clinton Offers Challenge to Nation, Declaring "Era of Big Government Is Over,"* N.Y. Times, Jan. 24, 1996, at A1 (quoting President Clinton's State of the Union Address).

4. Pub. L. No. 104-4, 109 Stat. 48 (codified as amended in scattered sections of 2 U.S.C.).

5. UMRA has numerous exceptions to both its substantive scope and to its procedural requirements. For these reasons, UMRA may be of largely symbolic importance, *see* David A. Super, *Rethinking Fiscal Federalism*, 118 Harv. L. Rev. 2544, 2581 (2005) ("UMRA is subject to both procedural and definitional limitations that render it largely symbolic."), but it may still be taken as an important symbol.

6. 514 U.S. 549 (1995).

7. Seminole Tribe v. Florida, 517 U.S. 44 (1996).

8. *See* Alden v. Maine, 527 U.S. 706, 715 (1999).

9. Exec. Order No. 12,612, 52 Fed. Reg. 41,685 (Oct. 26, 1987).

10. U.S. Const. amend. X ("The powers not delegated to the United States by the Constitution, nor prohibited by it to the States, are reserved to the States respectively, or to the people.").

11. Memorandum on Federalism, 26 Weekly Comp. Pres. Doc. 264 (Feb. 16, 1990).

12. Exec. Order No. 12,875, 58 Fed. Reg. 58,093 (Oct. 26, 1993).

13. Exec. Order No. 13,083, 63 Fed. Reg. 27,651 (May 14, 1998).

14. *See, e.g.,* David S. Broder, *Executive Order Urged Consulting, but Didn't; State, Local Officials Want Federalism Say*, Wash. Post, July 16, 1998, at A15; Frank Shafroth, *Clinton Edict on Federalism Stirs Up State, Local Leaders*, Nation's Cities Wkly., July 13, 1998, at 1; Fred Thompson, Op-Ed., *Big-Government Power Grab*, Wash. Post, Aug. 7, 1998, at A25.

15. Exec. Order No. 13,132, 3 C.F.R. 206 (1999), *reprinted in* 5 U.S.C. 601 (2000).

16. *See* David S. Broder, *Federalism's New Framework; Revised Order Satisfies State and Local Officials*, Wash. Post, Aug. 5, 1999, at A21; National Conference of State Legislatures, Summary of Executive Order 13132 on Federalism Issued by Clinton Administration (Aug. 31, 1999), http://www.ncsl.org/statefed/federalism/exec13132.htm.

17. *See, e.g.,* Roderick H. Hills Jr., *The Eleventh Amendment as Curb on Bureaucratic Power*, 53 Stan. L. Rev. 1225, 1244 (2001) ("Most legislative or administrative devices for the avoidance of federal mandates have been widely acknowledged to be toothless failures."); U.S. Advisory Commission on Intergovernmental Relations, *Executive Order 12612 on Federalism: Performance, Problems, and Potential, in* Federal Regu-

LATION OF STATE AND LOCAL GOVERNMENTS: THE MIXED RECORD OF THE 1980S, at 38 (1993).

18. United States v. Fry, 421 U.S. 542 (1975) (Rehnquist, J., dissenting).

19. *See, e.g.,* McCleskey v. Zant, 499 U.S. 467 (1991); Teague v. Lane, 489 U.S. 288 (1989); Stone v. Powell, 428 U.S. 465 (1976).

20. Pub. L. No. 104-132, 110 Stat. 1214 (codified in scattered titles of U.S.C.).

21. 411 U.S. 1 (1973).

22. *See* John Dayton & Anne Dupre, *School Funding Litigation: Who's Winning the War?,* 57 VAND. L. REV. 2351, 2353 (2004).

23. Goodridge v. Dep't of Pub. Health, 798 N.E.2d 941 (Mass. 2003).

24. In re Marriage Cases, 183 P.3d 384 (Cal. 2008).

25. *See, e.g.,* Judith Burns, *Mutual Funds Under Fire,* WALL ST. J., Sept. 10, 2003, at C14; Jonathan Mathiesen, *Dr. Spitzlove or: How I Learned to Stop Worrying and Love "Balkanization,"* 2006 COLUM. BUS. L. REV. 311.

26. *See* Diana Jean Schemo, *Cuomo Plans to Broaden Student-Lending Inquiry,* N.Y. TIMES, June 7, 2007, at A20.

27. *All Things Considered: Job Not Finished in Student Loans Inquiry* (NPR broadcast June 9, 2007) (interview with Andrew Cuomo).

28. *See* Paul Basken, *Attorneys General and Senate Panel Cite More Evidence of Lender Corruption,* CHRON. HIGHER EDUC. (Wash., D.C.), June 29, 2007, at A18 (quoting letter of attorneys general).

29. *See, e.g.,* BARRY G. RABE, STATEHOUSE AND GREENHOUSE: THE EMERGING POLITICS OF AMERICAN CLIMATE CHANGE POLICY (2004); Felicity Barringer, *Officials Reach California Deal to Cut Emissions,* N.Y. TIMES, Aug. 31, 2006, at A1; Andrew C. Revkin & Jennifer 8. Lee, *White House Attacked for Letting States Lead on Climate,* N.Y. TIMES, Dec. 11, 2003, at A32.

30. *See* Gar Alperovitz, Op-Ed., *California Split,* N.Y. TIMES, Feb. 10, 2007, at A15.

31. John O. McGinnis, *Reviving Tocqueville's America: The Rehnquist Court's Jurisprudence of Social Discovery,* 90 CAL. L. REV. 485, 525 (2002). Wilfred McClay made a similar point: "There must be some point of emotional entry, some point of congruency between the shape of the polity and the shape of the human heart, if that polity is to draw out the participation of citizens and command their unfeigned loyalty and affection." Wilfred M. McClay, *A More Perfect Union? Toward a New Federalism,* COMMENTARY, Sept. 1995, at 28, 32–33.

32. *See* JOHN F. BIBBY & BRIAN F. SCHAFFNER, POLITICS, PARTIES, AND ELECTIONS IN AMERICA 70–71 (6th ed. 2008); WILLIAM M. LUNCH, THE NATIONALIZATION OF AMERICAN POLITICS 224–45 (1987).

33. *See* Sidney M. Milkis & Jesse H. Rhodes, *George W. Bush, the Party System, and American Federalism,* 37 PUBLIUS 1, 14 (2007).

34. *See* James G. Gimpel & Frances E. Lee, The Check Is in the Mail: Interdistrict Funding Flows in Congressional Elections 12 (Paper Presented at the University of Chicago's American Politics Workshop, April 2, 2007), http://harrisschool.uchicago.edu/Academic/workshops/ampolpapers/Gimpel_Funding%20Flows_Chicago.pdf ("Congressional campaigns are becoming progressively more dependent on flows of capital that are national in scope."); *see also* William Marshall, *American Political Culture and the Failures of Process Federalism,* 22 HARV. J.L. & PUB. POL'Y 139, 150 & n.56 (1998).

35. *See* Michael S. Gerber, *In the Neighborhood: Some With Certain ZIP Codes Are Particularly Generous Political Givers,* CAMPAIGNS & ELECTIONS, May 2005, at 28.

36. *See* Matthew Murray, *2006 Fundraising: A National Affair*, ROLL CALL, Sept. 21, 2006.

37. *See* Paul Frymer & Albert Yoon, *Political Parties, Representation, and Federal Safeguards*, 96 NW. U. L. REV. 977, 1007 (2002).

38. *See* U.S. PUBLIC INTEREST RESEARCH GROUP, THE WEALTH PRIMARY: THE ROLE OF BIG MONEY IN THE 2004 CONGRESSIONAL PRIMARIES 4 (2004), http://www.uspirg.org/home/reports/report-archives/campaign-finance-reform (select title from list; then follow "Download the full report" hyperlink).

39. *See* Darrell Preston, *National Parties Pour Money into Battles for State Legislatures*, BLOOMBERG.COM, Nov. 6, 2006, *available at* http://www.dlcc.org/news/news_bloomberg_11-6-06.html; David Schultz, *Laboratories of Democracy: Campaign Finance Reform in the States*, PUB. INTEGRITY, Spring 2004, at 115, 120.

40. *See 30th Anniversary Issue /Al D'Amato: Senator Pothole, Proudly*, NEW YORK, Apr. 6, 1998 (interview with Craig Horowitz); Esther B. Fein, *D'Amato Seeks Wide-Based Support*, N.Y. TIMES, Nov. 3, 1986, at B5.

41. *See* JACK BASS & MARILYN W. THOMPSON, STROM: THE COMPLICATED PERSONAL AND POLITICAL LIFE OF STROM THURMOND 156 (2005).

42. *See* Jeffrey Toobin, *The Great Election Grab*, NEW YORKER, Dec. 8, 2003, at 63.

43. Gary C. Jacobson, *The 1994 House Elections in Perspective*, POL. SCI. Q., Summer 1996, at 203, 205.

44. *See* Milkis & Rhodes, *supra* note 33, at 9–11.

45. *See* MARIAN C. MCKENNA, FRANKLIN ROOSEVELT AND THE GREAT CONSTITUTIONAL WAR 546–52 (2002).

46. *See* Alexander Bolton, *Roosevelt Splits Democratic Party President Campaigns for Liberals, against Conservatives in Primaries 1938*, ROLL CALL, May 13, 1999.

47. *See* Manuel Roig-Franzia & David S. Broder, *Ga. Effort Shows GOP Strengths*, WASH. POST, Nov. 7, 2002, at A1.

48. Milkis & Rhodes, *supra* note 33, at 12.

49. *See* Michael Grunwald, *Opposition to War Buoys Democrats*, WASH. POST, Nov. 8, 2006, at A31.

50. *See* Jeffrey Toobin, *Will Tom DeLay's Redistricting in Texas Cost Him His Seat?*, NEW YORKER, May 6, 2006, at 32.

51. *See* George Kuempel, *Debate Grows over Police Role in AWOL Senators' Flight; Philosophical, Practical Concerns Cited by Both Sides in Dispute*, DALLAS MORN. NEWS, Aug. 1, 2003, at 7A.

52. *See* Seth C. McKee & Daron R. Shaw, *Redistricting in Texas: Institutionalizing Republican Ascendancy, in* REDISTRICTING IN THE NEW MILLENNIUM 275, 293–94 (Peter F. Galderisi ed., 2005).

53. Cruzan v. Director, Mo. Dep't of Health, 497 U.S. 261 (1990).

54. *See* Arian Campo-Flores, *The Legacy of Terri Schiavo*, NEWSWEEK, Apr. 4, 2005, at 22; Daniel Eisenberg, *Lessons of the Schiavo Battle; What the Bitter Fight over a Woman's Right to Live or Die Tells Us About Politics, Religion, the Courts and Life Itself*, TIME, Apr. 4, 2005, at 22; Richard B. Schmitt, *The Terri Schiavo Case; Judicial Effect; For Schiavo, Republicans Invite Federal Activism; Congress, Unsatisfied with Florida Rulings, Encourages Higher Courts to Wield Power That It Usually Seeks to Limit*, L.A. TIMES, Mar. 24, 2005, at A22.

55. *See* Alan Cooperman, *Gay Marriage Ban in Mo. May Resonate Nationwide*, WASH. POST, Aug. 5, 2004, at A2; Elizabeth Mehren, *State Bans on Gay Marriage Galvanize Sides*, L.A. TIMES, Nov. 4, 2004, at A11.

56. *See* Janet D. McDonald, Mary F. Hughes & Gary W. Ritter, *School Finance Litigation*

and Adequacy Studies, 27 U. Ark. Little Rock L. Rev. 69 (2004); R. Craig Wood & Bruce D. Baker, *An Examination and Analysis of the Equity and Adequacy Concepts of Constitutional Challenges to State Education Finance Distribution Formulas*, 27 U. Ark. Little Rock L. Rev. 125 (2004).

57. *See Rodriguez*, 411 U.S. at 49–50; Milliken v. Bradley, 418 U.S. 717, 741 (1974) ("No single tradition in public education is more deeply rooted than local control over the operation of schools. . . ."); Molly S. McUsic, *The Future of* Brown v. Board of Education: *Economic Integration of the Public Schools*, 117 Harv. L. Rev. 1334, 1345 & n.69 (2004).

58. *See* Ankenbrandt v. Richards, 504 U.S. 689 (1992).

59. *See, e.g.*, 18 U.S.C. § 371 (2007) (criminal conspiracy); *id.* § 472 (counterfeiting); *id.* § 924(c)(1)(A) (drug trafficking); *id.* § 1341 (mail fraud); *id.* § 1343 (wire fraud); *id.* § 1348 (securities fraud); *id.* §§ 1956–57 (money laundering); *id.* §§ 1961–68 (racketeering); *id.* § 2113 (bank robbery); *id.* § 2119 (carjacking); *id.* § 2242 (sexual abuse).

60. *See* Violent Crime Control and Law Enforcement Act of 1994, Pub. L. No. 103-322, §§ 20102–03, 108 Stat. 1796, 1816–17 (codified at 42 U.S.C. § 13704 (2000)) (conditioning federal prison grant money on state compliance with truth-in-sentencing guidelines); Marc L. Miller, *A Map of Sentencing and a Compass for Judges: Sentencing Information Systems, Transparency, and the Next Generation of Reform*, 105 Colum. L. Rev. 1351, 1393 (2005).

61. Pub. L. No. 107-110, 115 Stat. 1425 (2002) (codified at 20 U.S.C. §§ 6301–6578).

62. *See* James E. Ryan, *The Perverse Incentives of the No Child Left Behind Act*, 79 N.Y.U. L. Rev. 932, 939–44 (2004).

63. *See id.* at 942–43.

64. The vote on the final bill in the House of Representatives was 381–41. *See* Adam Clymer, *National Briefing: House Passes Education Bill*, N.Y. Times, Dec. 14, 2001, at A36. The vote in the Senate was 87–10. *See* Diana Jean Schemo, *Senate Approves a Bill to Expand the Federal Role in Public Education*, N.Y. Times, Dec. 19, 2001, at A32.

65. *See* Gail L. Sunderman et al., NCLB Meets School Realities: Lessons from the Field xxxv (2005); *see also* Diane Ravitch, Op-Ed., *Every State Left Behind*, N.Y. Times, Nov. 7, 2004, at A23.

66. U.S. Const. amend V.

67. *See* Dolan v. City of Tigard, 512 U.S. 374 (1994) (holding unconstitutional a requirement that a landowner dedicate a portion of property to a bicycle/pedestrian pathway); *Lucas v. S.C. Coastal Council*, 505 U.S. 1003 (1992) (holding that a South Carolina law prohibiting beachfront construction was a taking under the United States Constitution).

68. Kelo v. City of New London, 545 U.S. 469 (2005).

69. *See* Strengthening the Ownership of Private Property Act of 2005, H.R. 3405, 109th Cong. (2005).

70. 18 U.S.C. § 228 (1994), *amended by* Deadbeat Parents Punishment Act of 1998, 18 U.S.C. § 228 (2000).

71. 28 U.S.C. § 1738A (2000).

72. *See* Michael J. Perry, Under God? Religious Faith and Liberal Democracy 20–34 (2003); Sue Hyde, *What Now for Marriage Equality*, Gay & Lesbian Rev., Mar.–Apr. 2005, at 22, 22–24; Jonathan Rauch, *A More Perfect Union: How the Founding Fathers Would Have Handled Gay Marriage*, Atlantic Monthly, Apr. 2004, at 88, 88–92.

73. *See* Rauch, *supra* note 72, at 88.

74. Daniel Sutter, *News Media Incentives, Coverage of Government, and the Growth of Government*, INDEP. REV., Spring 2004, at 562.

75. *See* ROPER STARCH WORLDWIDE, AMERICA'S WATCHING: PUBLIC ATTITUDES TOWARD TELEVISION 17 (1995).

76. *See* DAVID H. McKAY, AMERICAN POLITICS AND SOCIETY 139 (6th ed. 2005).

77. MEDIA ACCESS PROJECT & BENTON FOUND., WHAT'S LOCAL ABOUT LOCAL BROADCASTING? (1998), *available at* http://www.radiodiversity.com/localbroadcasting.html.

78. Samuel Krislov, *American Federalism as American Exceptionalism*, PUBLIUS, Winter 2001, at 1, 20.

79. *See* Felicia R. Lee, *Country Music in the City? 2005 Nashville Awards Go to New York*, N.Y TIMES, Oct. 6, 2004, at E1; Eric Wilson, *You're Looking at Country*, N.Y. TIMES, Nov. 10, 2005, at G1.

80. *See* Keith Dunnavant, *Middle America at 170 MPH*, MEDIAWEEK, Feb. 12, 2001, at 20; Jeff MacGregor, *Dale Earnhardt Jr. and NASCAR Nation*, SPORTS ILLUS., July 1, 2002, at 60 ("NASCAR has, for its fans, from Manhattan to Manhattan Beach, transcended its self-limiting Southern origins. Instead it has institutionalized Southern hospitality and charm.").

81. *See* Elizabeth Pleck, *The Making of the Domestic Occasion: The History of Thanksgiving in the United States*, J. SOC. HIST., Summer 1999, at 773, 775.

82. *See* Kevin Paul Dupont, *Warming Up to the Idea; Coyotes Are Making Phoenix Something of a Hotbed*, BOSTON GLOBE, Mar. 2, 1999, at C1; Helene Elliot, *Changing Face of the NHL; Overview: League Has Taken on a New Look in '90s with Influx of European Players and Franchises in the South*, L.A. TIMES, Jan. 23, 1999, at D1.

83. *See* Desa Philadelphia, *Crunk: Hip-Hop's Got a New Accent*, TIME, July 4, 2005, at 77, 77–78.

84. Rick Minter, *NASCAR Gains Glitz, Loses South*, ATLANTA J.-CONST., Mar. 19, 2006, at A1; *see also* Larry Woody, *NASCAR Now About Glamour, Not Grit*, TENNESSEAN, Mar. 12, 2006, at 12C.

85. Narrowcasting is becoming increasingly important in the political sphere as well. For a discussion of the significance of narrowcasting in politics, see Michael S. Kang, *From Broadcasting to Narrowcasting: The Emerging Challenge for Campaign Finance Law*, 73 GEO. WASH. L. REV. 1070 (2005).

86. *See* Lynn Spiegel, *Entertainment Wars: Television Culture after 9/11*, 56 AM. Q. 235, 256 (2004).

87. *See, e.g.*, Stephen Ansolabehere, Jonathan Roddern & James M. Snyder Jr., *Purple America*, J ECON. PERSP., Spring 2006, at 97.

88. *See* Douglas Laycock, *Protecting Liberty in a Federal System: The US Experience*, in PATTERNS OF REGIONALISM AND FEDERALISM: LESSONS FOR THE U.K. 120–21 (Jörg Fedtke & Basil S. Markesinis eds., 2006).

89. *See* Philip A. Klinkner, *Red and Blue Scare: The Continuing Diversity of the American Electoral Landscape*, FORUM, June 2004, http://www.bepress.com/cgi/viewcontent. cgi?article=1035&context=forum; Philip A. Klinkner & Ann Hapanowicz, *Red and Blue Déjà Vu: Measuring Political Polarization in the 2004 Election*, FORUM, July 2005, http://www.bepress.com/cgi/viewcontent.cgi?article=1079&context=forum.

90. *See* Klinkner, *supra* note 89; Klinkner & Hapanowicz, *supra* note 89.

91. E. J. Dionne Jr. & Michael Cromartie, *Introduction Modernist, Orthodox, or Flexidox? Why the Culture War Debate Endures*, in JAMES DAVISON HUNTER & ALAN WOLFE, IS THERE A CULTURE WAR? A DIALOGUE ON VALUES AND AMERICAN PUBLIC LIFE 5 (2006) (quoting *Is There a Culture War?* (May 23, 2006), http://pewforum.org/events/?EventID=112).

92. MORRIS P. FIORINA ET AL., CULTURE WAR? THE MYTH OF A POLARIZED AMERICA (2d ed. 2006).

93. *See id.* at 44.

94. 505 U.S. 833 (1992).

95. *See* FIORINA ET AL., *supra* note 92, at 94.

96. *See id.* at 109–24.

97. *See id.* at 66.

98. *See* Shawn Treier & Sunshine Hillygus, *The Contours of Policy Attitudes in the Mass Public* (June 2006) (unpublished working paper, on file with author).

99. *See, e.g.*, Alan I. Abramowitz, *Disconnected, or Joined at the Hip?, in* RED AND BLUE NATION? CHARACTERISTICS AND CAUSES OF AMERICA'S POLARIZED POLITICS 79–84 (Pietro S. Nivola & David W. Brady eds., 2006).

100. *See* Nicole Herther-Spiro, *Can Ethnic Federalism Prevent "Recourse to Rebellion?" A Comparative Analysis of the Ethiopian and Iraqi Constitutional Structures*, 21 EMORY INT'L L. REV. 321 (2007).

CHAPTER TWO

1. For overviews of the Articles of Confederation and their drafting, see RICHARD B. MORRIS, THE FORGING OF THE UNION, 1781–1789, at 80–110 (1987); JACK N. RAKOVE, THE BEGINNINGS OF NATIONAL POLITICS: AN INTERPRETIVE HISTORY OF THE CONTINENTAL CONGRESS 135–91 (1979) [hereinafter RAKOVE, BEGINNINGS OF NATIONAL POLITICS].

2. For accounts of the perceived failures of the Articles of Confederation, see, for example, DANIEL A. FARBER & SUZANNA SHERRY, A HISTORY OF THE AMERICAN CONSTITUTION 23–25 (1990); THE FEDERALIST NO. 15, at 89–98 (Alexander Hamilton) (Jacob E. Cooke ed., 1961); RAKOVE, BEGINNINGS OF NATIONAL POLITICS, *supra* note 1, at 333–400; GORDON S. WOOD, THE CREATION OF THE AMERICAN REPUBLIC, 1776–1787, at 354–63 (1969).

3. Recent scholarship suggests that the summer temperatures in Philadelphia were cooler than average that year. In June, July, and August 1787, the average temperatures in Philadelphia were 70.7, 72.4, and 74.5, respectively. However these figures compare to the long-term averages, in an era without air conditioning, these temperatures seem "hot" to me. *See* SUPPLEMENT TO MAX FARRAND'S THE RECORDS OF THE FEDERAL CONVENTION OF 1787, at 325–26 (James H. Hutson ed., 1987).

4. For analysis of the perceived failure of the Articles concerning foreign policy, see FREDERICK W. MARKS III, INDEPENDENCE ON TRIAL: FOREIGN AFFAIRS AND THE MAKING OF THE CONSTITUTION (1973); RAKOVE, BEGINNING OF NATIONAL POLITICS, *supra* note 1, at 342–52, Jack N. Rakove, *Making Foreign Policy: The View from 1787, in* FOREIGN POLICY AND THE CONSTITUTION 1 (Robert A. Goldwin & Robert A. Licht eds., 1990).

5. *See* WOOD, *supra* note 2, at 525–26.

6. For the classic account of the dual federalism model, see Edward S. Corwin, *The Passing of Dual Federalism*, 36 VA. L. REV. 1 (1950).

7. 3 DEBATES ON THE ADOPTION OF THE FEDERAL CONSTITUTION 301 (Jonathan Elliot ed., 2d ed., Philadelphia, J.B. Lippincott 1888), *cited in* WOOD, *supra* note 2, at 529.

8. 17 U.S. (4 Wheat.) 316 (1819).

9. 2 U.S. (2 Dall.) 419 (1793).

10. *See, e.g.*, JOHN V. ORTH, THE JUDICIAL POWER OF THE UNITED STATES: THE ELEVENTH AMENDMENT IN AMERICAN HISTORY (1987) (tracing the history of the Eleventh Amendment).

11. 22 U.S. (9 Wheat.) 1 (1824).
12. *Id.* at 209.
13. For both a detailed history of the facts surrounding *Gibbons* and an analysis of Chief Justice Marshall's reluctance to accept Justice Johnson's dormant Commerce Clause approach, see Norman R. Williams, *Gibbons,* 79 N.Y.U. L. REV. 1398 (2004).
14. 53 U.S. (12 How.) 299 (1851).
15. *See* PAUL BREST ET AL., PROCESSES OF CONSTITUTIONAL DECISIONMAKING 162 (4th ed. 2000); Stephen Gardbaum, *New Deal Constitutionalism and the Unshackling of the States,* 64 U. CHI. L. REV. 483, 508 (1997).
16. Ableman v. Booth, 62 U.S. (21 How.) 506, 516 (1859).
17. Barron v. Mayor of Baltimore, 32 U.S. (7 Pet.) 243 (1833).
18. *See* Harry N. Scheiber, *American Federalism and the Diffusion of Power: Historical and Contemporary Perspectives,* 9 U. TOL. L. REV. 619, 632 (1978).
19. *See id.* at 633–34.
20. *See* Daniel J. Elazar, *Theory of Federalism, in* 3 ENCYCLOPEDIA OF THE AMERICAN CONSTITUTION 1006 (Leonard W. Levy & Kenneth L. Karst eds., 2000) (asserting that the American "pattern of federalism has been cooperative since its beginnings").
21. *See* Harry N. Scheiber, *The Condition of American Federalism: A Historian's View, in* AMERICAN INTERGOVERNMENTAL RELATIONS: FOUNDATIONS, PERSPECTIVES, AND ISSUES 67–69 (Laurence J. O'Toole Jr. ed., 3d ed. 2000).
22. U.S. CONST. amend. XIV ("All persons born or naturalized in the United States, and subject to the jurisdiction thereof, are citizens of the United States and of the State wherein they reside.").
23. *Id.* ("No State shall make or enforce any law which shall abridge the privileges or immunities of citizens of the United States; nor shall any State deprive any person of life, liberty, or property, without due process of law; nor deny to any person within its jurisdiction the equal protection of the laws.").
24. For examinations of the effects of the Civil War and Reconstruction on the constitutional balance, see, for example, BRUCE A. ACKERMAN, 2 WE THE PEOPLE: TRANSFORMATIONS 17–23 (1998); JAMES M. MCPHERSON, ABRAHAM LINCOLN AND THE SECOND AMERICAN REVOLUTION 131–52 (1991).
25. For a classic account of the Compromise of 1877, see C. VANN WOODWARD, REUNION AND REACTION: THE COMPROMISE OF 1877 AND THE END OF RECONSTRUCTION (rev. ed. 1991).
26. 109 U.S. 3 (1883).
27. 163 U.S. 537 (1896).
28. *See* Scheiber, *supra* note 18, at 640.
29. Pub. L. No. 49-104, 24 Stat. 379 (codified as amended in scattered sections of 49 U.S.C.).
30. 26 Stat. 209 (codified as amended at 15 U.S.C. §§ 1–7).
31. *See* Scheiber, *supra* note 18, at 640.
32. 42 Stat. 187 (superseded by The Grain Futures Act, Pub. L. No. 67-331, 42 Stat. 998 (1922)) (current version at Commodity Exchange Act, 7 U.S.C. § 1).
33. *See* Hill v. Wallace, 259 U.S. 44 (1922).
34. *See* Bd. of Trade of City of Chicago v. Olsen, 262 U.S. 1, 37–38 (1923). For a discussion of the role of the congressional response in the transition from *Hill* to *Olsen,* see BARRY CUSHMAN, RETHINKING THE NEW DEAL COURT: THE STRUCTURE OF A CONSTITUTIONAL REVOLUTION 149–50 (1998); A. Christopher Bryant & Timothy J. Simeone, *Remanding to Congress: The Supreme Court's New "On the Record" Constitutional Review*

of Federal Statutes, 86 CORNELL L. REV. 328, 356–58 (2001); Philip P. Frickey, *The Fool on the Hill: Congressional Findings, Constitutional Adjudication, and* United States v. Lopez, 46 CASE W. RES. L. REV. 695, 708–10 (1996); Neal Kumar Katyal, *Judges as Advicegivers,* 50 STAN. L. REV. 1709, 1796–97 (1998).

35. *See* Robert A. Schapiro & William W. Buzbee, *Unidimensional Federalism: Power and Perspective in Commerce Clause Adjudication,* 88 CORNELL L. REV. 1199, 1210 (2003).

36. *See* United States v. Butler, 297 U.S. 1 (1936); Carter v. Carter Coal Co., 298 U.S. 238 (1936); A. L. A. Schechter Poultry Corp. v. United States, 295 U.S. 495 (1935); United States v. E. C. Knight Co., 156 U.S. 1 (1895).

37. *See* Robert Post, *Federalism in the Taft Court Era: Can It Be Revived?,* 51 DUKE L.J. 1513, 1605–34 (2002).

38. 135 U.S. 100 (1890).

39. *See id.* at 109–10.

40. *See* Gardbaum, *supra* note 15, at 511.

41. *See id.*

42. 222 U.S. 424 (1912).

43. *Id.* at 436.

44. 198 U.S. 45 (1905).

45. *See* David E. Bernstein, *The Story of* Lochner v. New York: *Impediment to the Growth of the Regulatory State, in* CONSTITUTIONAL LAW STORIES 326 (Michael C. Dorf ed., 2004).

46. *See* Post, *supra* note 37, at 1580–1605.

47. For discussions of the "court packing" episode, see JOSEPH ALSOP & TURNER CATLEDGE, THE 168 DAYS (1938); WILLIAM E. LEUCHTENBURG, THE SUPREME COURT REBORN: THE CONSTITUTIONAL REVOLUTION IN THE AGE OF ROOSEVELT (1995).

48. 317 U.S. 111 (1942).

49. Pub. L. No. 75-430, 52 Stat. 31 (codified as amended in scattered sections of 7 U.S.C.).

50. It is clear that the Filburn family would not have been able to consume the 239 excess bushels of wheat as bread, as that would have required the consumption of nearly 44 loaves of bread per day for the whole year. Rather, Roscoe Filburn's home consumption included the use of the excess wheat as feed for his chickens and dairy cows. *See* Jim Chen, *The Story of* Wickard v. Filburn: *Agriculture, Aggregation, and Congressional Power over Commerce, in* CONSTITUTIONAL LAW STORIES 69, 109 (Michael C. Dorf ed., 2004).

51. *Wickard,* 317 U.S. at 125.

52. *Id.* at 127–28.

53. *See* Barry Cushman, *Formalism and Realism in Commerce Clause Jurisprudence,* 67 U. CHI. L. REV. 1089, 1139 (2000).

54. *See id.* at 1138–40.

55. *See id.*

56. *Wickard,* 317 U.S. at 125.

57. *Id.* at 128–29 (emphasis added).

58. 328 U.S. 408 (1946).

59. *Id.* at 439 n.52 (quoting FREDERICK D. G. RIBBLE, STATE AND NATIONAL POWER OVER COMMERCE 211 (1937)) (internal quotation marks omitted). *But see* New York v. United States, 505 U.S. 144, 181–83 (1992) (expressing skepticism about such federal-state collusion).

60. Lester E. Mosher, *Mr. Justice Rutledge's Philosophy of the Commerce Clause,* 27 N.Y.U. L. REV. 218, 227–28 (1952); *see also id.* at 227 ("Justice Rutledge's opinion in the

Panhandle Eastern Pipe Line case gives full play for state power to work in coordination with federal authority, thereby indirectly giving new power to the states and supplementing that of Congress in the field of commerce.").

61. *See* Gardbaum, *supra* note 15, at 535–40.

62. 452 U.S. 264 (1981).

63. *Id.* at 281.

64. *Id.*

65. 347 U.S. 483 (1954).

66. *See* Gerald N. Rosenberg, The Hollow Hope: Can Courts Bring About Social Change? (1991); Paul Gewirtz, *Remedies and Resistance*, 92 Yale L.J. 585 (1983).

67. Pub. L. No. 88-352, 78 Stat. 241 (codified as amended in scattered sections of 28 U.S.C. and 42 U.S.C.).

68. *See* N.C. State Bd. of Educ. v. Swann, 402 U.S. 43 (1971) (striking down North Carolina Anti-busing Law); Swann v. Charlotte-Mecklenburg Bd. of Educ., 402 U.S. 1 (1971) (approving limited use of mathematical ratios for desegregation purposes).

69. *See* William H. Riker, Federalism: Origin, Operation, Significance 155 (1964).

70. Pub. L. No. 101-336, 104 Stat. 327 (1990) (codified as amended at 42 U.S.C. §§ 12,101–213).

71. Pub. L. No. 90-202, 81 Stat. 602 (1967) (codified as amended at 29 U.S.C. §§ 621–34).

72. *See* Hillary Rodham Clinton & Goodwin Liu, *Separation Anxiety: Congress, the Courts, and the Constitution*, 91 Geo L.J. 439, 446–47 (2003).

73. *See* Holly Doremus, *Shaping the Future: The Dialectic of Law and Environmental Values*, 37 U.C. Davis L. Rev. 233, 235 n.3 (2003).

74. *See* Edward Berkowitz, *Losing Ground? The Great Society in Historical Perspective, in* The Columbia Guide to America in the 1960s, at 98–108 (David R. Farber & Beth L. Bailey eds., 2001).

75. Timothy Conlan, From Federalism to Devolution: Twenty-five Years of Intergovernmental Reform 102 (1998).

76. Richard S. Williamson, *The 1982 New Federalism Negotiations*, Publius, Spring 1983, at 11, 12 (quoting Ronald Reagan, Acceptance Speech at the Republican National Convention, July 17, 1980).

77. *Id.*

78. Douglas Kneeland, *Reagan Campaigns at Mississippi Fair*, N.Y. Times, Aug. 3, 1980, at A11.

79. *See* David Brooks, *History and Calumny*, N.Y. Times, Nov. 9, 2007, at A27; Lou Cannon, *Reagan's Southern Stumble*, N.Y. Times, Nov. 18, 2007, at A15; Bob Herbert, *Righting Reagan's Wrongs?*, N.Y. Times, Nov. 13, 2007, at A29; Paul Krugman, *Republicans and Race*, N.Y. Times, Nov. 19, at A23; *see also* Joan Walsh, *Stop the New York Times Op-Ed Food Fight*, Salon.com, Nov. 19, 2007, http://www.salon.com/opinion/walsh/media/2007/11/19/reagan_race/.

80. U.S. Const. amend. X.

81. Williamson, *supra* note 76, at 12 (quoting Ronald Reagan, Inaugural Address, January 20, 1981).

82. Conlan, *supra* note 75, at 108 (quoting National Conference of State Legislatures: Remarks at the Annual Convention, July 31, 1981, in *Weekly Compilation of Presidential Documents*, August 3, 1981, at 834).

83. *See* Robert L. Cole & Delbert A. Taebel, *The New Federalism: Promises, Programs, and Performance*, Publius, Winter 1986, at 3, 6.

84. *See* Bob Herbert, *Racism and the G.O.P.*, N.Y Times, Dec. 12, 2002, at A39.
85. *Beyond the Pale*, Economist, Dec. 14, 2002, at 30.
86. Sheryl Gay Stolberg, *Under Fire, Lott Apologizes for His Comments at Thurmond's Party*, N.Y. Times, Dec. 10, 2002, at A28.
87. Carl Hulse, *Lott's Praise for Thurmond Echoed His Words of 1980*, N.Y. Times, Dec. 11, 2002, at A24.
88. *See* Herbert, *supra* note 79.
89. *See id.*
90. *See* Trent Lott, Herding Cats: A Life in Politics 274–76 (2005).
91. *See* Mark Leibovich, *In Senate Shift, Big Comeback for Trent Lott*, N.Y. Times, Nov. 16, 2006, at A1; Dana Milbank, *"Redemption" for the Pariah from Pascagoula*, Wash. Post, Nov. 16, 2006, at A2.
92. *See* John M. Coski, The Confederate Battle Flag: America's Most Embattled Emblem 104 (2005).
93. Governor Perdue's lack of ardor in fighting to restore the old flag led some "flaggers" to oppose his reelection bid in 2006. *See* Jim Tharpe, *Defenders of '56 Flag Set Out to Oust Perdue*, Atlanta J.-Const., Sept. 24, 2006, at B1.
94. *See* Coski, *supra* note 92, at 175.
95. *See* William H. Riker, The Development of American Federalism xiii (1987).

CHAPTER THREE
1. 317 U.S. 111 (1942).
2. Pub. L. No. 88-352, 78 Stat. 241 (1964) (codified as amended in scattered sections of 28 U.S.C. and 42 U.S.C.).
3. *See* Katzenbach v. McClung, 379 U.S. 294 (1964); Heart of Atlanta Motel v. United States, 379 U.S. 241 (1964).
4. *See, e.g.*, Rapanos v. United States, 547 U.S. 715 (2006).
5. *See, e.g.*, Child Support Recovery Act of 1992, Pub. L. No. 102-521, 106 Stat. 3403 (codified as amended at 18 U.S.C. § 228 (1994)).
6. *See* Am. Ins. Ass'n v. Garamendi, 539 U.S. 396 (2003); Ernest A. Young, *Dual Federalism, Concurrent Jurisdiction, and the Foreign Affairs Exception*, 69 Geo. Wash. L. Rev. 139, 167–85 (2001).
7. *See* United States v. Morrison, 529 U.S. 598 (2000) (holding unconstitutional the private cause of action created by the Violence against Women Act of 1994, 42 U.S.C. § 13,981(1994)); United States v. Lopez, 514 U.S. 549 (1995) (holding unconstitutional the Gun-Free School Zones Act of 1990, 18 U.S.C. § 922(q)(1)(A) (1994)).
8. *See Garamendi*, 539 U.S. 396 (finding state statute preempted by foreign policy of the United States).
9. *See, e.g.*, Erwin Chemerinsky, *Empowering States When It Matters: A Different Approach to Preemption*, 69 Brook. L. Rev. 1313, 1324 (2004) (finding preemption cases inconsistent with the Court's other federalism cases); Daniel J. Meltzer, *The Supreme Court's Judicial Passivity*, 2002 Sup. Ct. Rev. 343; James B. Staab, *Conservative Activism on the Rehnquist Court: Federal Preemption Is No Longer a Liberal Issue*, 9 Roger Williams U. L. Rev. 129, 183 (2003).
10. *See* Bd. of Trs. of the Univ. of Ala. v. Garrett, 531 U.S. 356 (2001); Kimel v. Fla. Bd. of Regents, 528 U.S. 62 (2000).
11. *See Rapanos*, 547 U.S. 715; Solid Waste Agency of N. Cook County (*SWANCC*) v. U.S. Army Corps of Eng'rs, 531 U.S. 159 (2001).
12. *See* Printz v. United States, 521 U.S. 898 (1997).

13. *See, e.g*, Geier v. Am. Honda Motor Co., 529 U.S. 861 (2000).

14. *See, e.g.*, C & A Carbone, Inc. v. Town of Clarkstown, 511 U.S. 383 (1994).

15. 426 U.S. 833, 852 (1976).

16. 469 U.S. 528 (1985).

17. *Id*. at 556.

18. 505 U.S. 144 (1992).

19. *See id*. at 149–50.

20. *See id*. at 195–99 (White, J., concurring in part and dissenting in part).

21. *See id*. at 181 (majority opinion) ("[T]he Constitution divides authority between federal and state governments for the protection of individuals.").

22. 521 U.S. 898 (1997).

23. Pub. L. No. 103-159, 107 Stat. 1536 (1993) (codified at 18 U.S.C. §§ 922 et seq.).

24. *See* Edelman v. Jordan, 415 U.S. 651 (1974).

25. *See Ex parte* Young, 209 U.S. 123 (1908).

26. *See* Fitzpatrick v. Bitzer, 427 U.S. 445 (1976).

27. *See id.;* U.S. CONST. amend. XIII, § 2 ("Congress shall have power to enforce this article by appropriate legislation."); *id*. amend. XIV, § 5 ("The Congress shall have power to enforce, by appropriate legislation, the provisions of this article."); *id*. amend. XV, § 2 ("The Congress shall have power to enforce this article by appropriate legislation.").

28. 491 U.S. 1 (1989).

29. 517 U.S. 44 (1996).

30. *See Garrett*, 531 U.S. at 362.

31. *See* 42 U.S.C. §§ 12,111–17 (2000) (Title I of the ADA).

32. See Katzenach v. McClung, 379 U.S. 294 (1964); Heart of Atlanta Motel v. United States, 379 U.S. 241 (1964).

33. *See* United States v. Morrison, 529 U.S. 598, 617–18 (2000) ("The Constitution requires a distinction between what is truly national and what is truly local."); *Lopez*, 514 U.S. at 567–68.

34. *See* Robert A. Schapiro & William W. Buzbee, *Unidimensional Federalism: Power and Perspective in Commerce Clause Adjudication*, 88 CORNELL L. REV. 1199, 1236–52 (2003).

35. *See SWANCC*, 531 U.S. 159.

36. 514 U.S. 549.

37. 529 U.S. 598.

38. 18 U.S.C. § 922(q).

39. The facts are recited in detail in a lower court opinion, Brzonkala v. Va. Polytechnic Inst. & State Univ., 132 F.3d 949, 953–56 (4th Cir. 1997), *vacated on reh'g en banc*, 169 F.3d 820 (1999), *aff'd sub nom. Morrison*, 529 U.S. 598.

40. *Morrison*, 529 U.S. at 618.

41. *Lopez*, 514 U.S. at 566 (quoting *id*. at 630 (Breyer, J., dissenting)).

42. *See, e.g.*, J. Randy Beck, *The New Jurisprudence of the Necessary and Proper Clause*, 2002 U. ILL. L. REV. 581, 625; Ernest A. Young, *The Rehnquist Court's Two Federalisms*, 83 TEX. L. REV. 1, 136 (2004).

43. *Wickard v. Filburn*, 317 U.S. 111, 125 (1942).

44. 531 U.S. 159.

45. 547 U.S. 715.

46. Pub. L. No. 92-500, 86 Stat. 816 (1992) (codified at 33 U.S.C. §§ 1251 et seq.).

47. *See Rapanos*, 547 U.S. at 737–38 (plurality opinion); *id.* at 776–77 (Kennedy, J., concurring in the judgment); *SWANCC*, 531 U.S. at 173–74.

48. *See* Jon Kusler, Association of State Wetlands Managers, The SWANCC Decision: State Regulation of Wetlands to Fill the Gap 6–7 (Mar. 4, 2004), http://www.aswm. org/fwp/swancc/aswm-int.pdf. Opinions on the impact of the *SWANCC* decision vary. In 2003, an official with the Environmental Protection Agency estimated that the *SWANCC* holding would likely reduce the amount of wetlands under federal protection by less than 20 percent. *See* Douglas Jehl, *Chief Protector of Wetlands Redefines Them and Retreats*, N.Y. TIMES, Feb. 11, 2003, at A1.

49. 323 F.3d 1062 (D.C. Cir. 2003).

50. Pub. L. No. 93-205, 87 Stat. 884 (1973).

51. *See* Rancho Viejo, LLC v. Norton, 334 F.3d 1158, 1160 (D.C. Cir. 2003) (Roberts, J., dissenting from denial of rehearing en banc).

52. *See* Rybar v. United States, 103 F.3d 273, 286 (3d Cir. 1996) (Alito, J., dissenting).

53. *See, e.g.*, GDF Realty Invs., Ltd. v. Norton, 362 F.3d 286 (5th Cir. 2004) (Jones, J., dissenting from the denial of rehearing en banc) (joined by Jolly, Smith, Demoss, Clement, & Pickering, JJ.) (questioning constitutionality of application of Endangered Species Act.); *Rancho Viejo*, 334 F.3d 1158 (Sentelle & Roberts, JJ.) (dissenting from the denial of rehearing en banc) (questioning constitutionality of application of Endangered Species Act); GDF Realty Invs., Ltd. v. Norton, 326 F.3d 622 (5th Cir. 2003) (upholding constitutionality of Endangered Species Act as applied to six species of subterranean invertebrates found only within two counties in Texas); Rancho Viejo, LLC v. Norton, 323 F.3d 1062 (D.C. Cir. 2003) (upholding Endangered Species Act as applied to development threatening arroyo southwestern toad).

54. 18 U.S.C. § 248 (2000).

55. *See* United States v. Gregg, 226 F.3d 253, 269–70 (3d Cir. 2000) (Weis, J., dissenting) (arguing that FACE exceeds congressional authority under the Commerce Clause); United States v. Bird, 124 F.3d 667, 684–92 (5th Cir. 1997) (DeMoss, J., dissenting) (same).

56. *See* Ernest A. Young, *Is the Sky Falling on the Federal Government? State Sovereign Immunity, the Section Five Power, and the Federal Balance*, 81 TEX. L. REV. 1551, 1607 (2003) (cautioning against exaggerating the limits on federal power).

57. *See* Jim Chen, Correspondence, *A Vision Softly Creeping: Congressional Acquiescence and the Dormant Commerce Clause*, 88 MINN. L. REV. 1764, 1793 (2004) (characterizing the dormant Commerce Clause as "the constitutional doctrine our students are likeliest to encounter in practice"); Stephen A. Gardbaum, *The Nature of Preemption*, 79 CORNELL L. REV. 767, 768 (1994) (characterizing preemption as "almost certainly the most frequently used doctrine of constitutional law in practice."); Lisa Heinzerling, *The Commercial Constitution*, 1995 SUP. CT. REV. 217, 217 (with regard to the antidiscrimination component of the dormant Commerce Clause, asserting that "few constitutional principles give the Court as regular . . . business").

58. It is clear that most state governments did not think that the federal regulation in *Morrison* infringed on state interests. Thirty-six states signed an amicus brief supporting the federal intervention. Only one state opposed it. *See* John O. McGinnis & Ilya Somin, *Federalism vs. States' Rights: A Defense of Judicial Review in a Federal System*, 99 NW. U. L. REV. 89, 114 (2004).

59. *See* Richard H. Fallon Jr., *The "Conservative" Paths of the Rehnquist Court's Federalism Decisions*, 69 U. CHI. L. REV. 429, 462–63 (2002); Alexander K. Haas, *Chipping Away*

at State Tort Remedies through Pre-emption Jurisprudence: Geier v. American Honda Motor Co., 89 CAL. L. REV. 1927, 1943–47 (2001); John O. McGinnis, *Reviving Tocqueville's America: The Rehnquist Court's Jurisprudence of Social Discovery,* 90 CAL. L. REV. 487, 526 n.203 (2002); Meltzer, *supra* note 9, at 365–71.

60. *See* Stephen Gardbaum, *New Deal Constitutionalism and the Unshackling of the States,* 64 U. CHI. L. REV. 483, 535–36 (1997).

61. For an excellent account of preemption and a defense of a presumption against preemption, see Roderick M. Hills Jr., *Against Preemption: How Federalism Can Improve the National Political Process,* 82 N.Y.U. L. REV. 1 (2007).

62. 529 U.S. 861 (2000).

63. *Geier,* 529 U.S. at 864–65.

64. 15 U.S.C. § 1397(k) (1988).

65. *See Geier,* 529 U.S. at 881–82.

66. *Id.* at 887 (quoting Coleman v. Thompson, 501 U.S. 722 (1991)) (internal quotation marks omitted).

67. *Compare* Cipollone v. Liggett Group, Inc., 505 U.S. 504, 517 (1992) (suggesting that implied preemption would not be found in statutes containing express preemption provisions), *with* Freightliner Corp. v. Myrick, 514 U.S. 280, 288 (1995) (noting that an express preemption provision did not foreclose the finding of implied preemption), *and Geier,* 529 U.S. at 869 (same). Other cases broadly construing preemption include Riegel v. Medtronic, 128 S. Ct. 999 (2008) (holding state products liability action preempted by federal regulatory scheme); *Garamendi,* 539 U.S. 396 (holding California statute requiring disclosure of information about Holocaust-era insurance policies preempted by foreign policy of the United States); Lorillard Tobacco Co. v. Reilly, 533 U.S. 525 (2001) (holding state statute regulating advertising of tobacco products preempted by federal law); Crosby v. Nat'l Foreign Trade Council, 530 U.S. 363 (2000) (holding state law restricting state transactions with companies doing business with Burma preempted by foreign policy of the United States); United States v. Locke, 529 U.S. 89 (2000) (holding state regulation of oil spills preempted by federal statute); Gade v. Nat'l Solid Waste Mgmt. Ass'n, 505 U.S. 88 (1992) (holding state law regulating workers at hazardous waste sites preempted by federal law); *see also* ALISON CASSADY, NAT'L ASS'N OF STATE PIRGS, TYING THE HANDS OF STATES: THE IMPACT OF FEDERAL PREEMPTION ON STATE PROBLEM-SOLVERS 2 (Nat'l Ass'n of State PIRGS, 2004), *available at* http://iowapirg.org/reports/TyingtheHandsofStates.pdf ("[F]ederal preemption has often tied the hands of state legislators and regulators eager to solve problems facing their constituents").

68. *See* Caleb Nelson, *Preemption,* 86 VA. L. REV. 225, 228–29 (2000); *see also* ERWIN CHEMERINSKY, CONSTITUTIONAL LAW: PRINCIPLES AND POLICIES § 5.2, at 394–98 (2d ed. 2002) (discussing preemption of state laws that impede federal objectives).

69. *See* Buckman Co. v. Plaintiff's Legal Comm., 531 U.S. 341 (2001); *see also* Meltzer, *supra* note 9, at 366 (discussing *Buckman*).

70. *See* Robert G. Natelson, *The Legal Meaning of "Commerce" in the Commerce Clause,* 80 ST. JOHN'S L. REV. 789, 847 (2006) (noting a "worldwide mega-trend" toward decentralization); *cf.* Judith Resnik, *Law's Migration: American Exceptionalism, Silent Dialogues, and Federalism's Multiple Ports of Entry,* 115 YALE L.J. 1564 (2006) (arguing that the boundaries between domestic and foreign legal norms are more porous than is frequently assumed).

71. *See* MICHAEL J. BAZYLER, HOLOCAUST JUSTICE: THE BATTLE FOR RESTITUTION IN AMERICA'S COURTS 110–11 (2003).

72. *See id.* at 113–14.
73. *See Garamendi,* 539 U.S. at 402.
74. *See id.* at 404–5; Burt Neuborne, *Preliminary Reflections on Aspects of Holocaust-Era Litigation in American Courts,* 80 Wash. U. L.Q. 795, 813 & n.62 (2002).
75. *See Garamendi,* 539 U.S. at 404–8.
76. *See id.* at 432–33 (Ginsburg, J., dissenting); Michael Maiello & Robert Lenzner, *The Last Victims,* Forbes, May 14, 2001, at 112; Joseph B. Treaster, *Holocaust List Is Unsealed by Insurers,* N.Y. Times, Apr. 29, 2003, at A26.
77. *See* Holocaust Victim Insurance Relief Act of 1999, Cal. Ins. Code §§ 13,800–13,807 (West Supp. 2003). One related statute, Cal. Civ. Proc. Code Ann. § 354.5. (West Supp. 2003), allowed California residents to bring claims for payment of Holocaust-era policies. Another related statute, Cal. Ins. Code § 790.15 (West Supp. 2003), allowed the state insurance commissioner to suspend the licenses of companies with unpaid valid claims. *See Garamendi,* 539 U.S. at 408–9.
78. *See Garamendi,* 539 U.S. at 401.
79. *Id.* at 427.
80. *See* Int'l Comm'n on Holocaust Era Ins. Claims, ICHEIC Claims Process 1 (Mar. 19, 2007), http://www.icheic.org/pdf/stats-19mar07.pdf.
81. Holocaust Insurance Accountability Act of 2007, H.R. 1746, 110th Cong. (2007).
82. *See* Jennifer Siegel, *Bill to Aid Survivors Could Undermine Settlements,* Jewish Daily Forward, May 4, 2007, *available at* http://www.forward.com/articles/10642.
83. *See, e.g.,* West Lynn Creamery, Inc. v. Healy, 512 U.S. 186 (1994) (holding state subsidy scheme unconstitutional); *see also* Fallon, *supra* note 59, at 460–61 (discussing the dormant Commerce Clause doctrine of the Rehnquist Court); Young, *supra* note 56, at 1591 ("Dormant Commerce Clause review has the effect of foreclosing or undermining a wide range of important state policies, such as responsible attempts at waste disposal, state safety regulation, and efforts to encourage important state industries.") (footnotes omitted).
84. *See, e.g.,* Julian N. Eule, *Laying the Dormant Commerce Clause to Rest,* 91 Yale L.J. 425 (1982); Martin H. Redish & Shane V. Nugent, *The Dormant Commerce Clause and the Constitutional Balance of Federalism,* 1987 Duke L.J. 569.
85. *See, e.g.,* United Haulers Ass'n v. Oneida-Herkimer Solid Waste Mgmt. Auth., 127 S. Ct. 1786, 1799 (2007) (Thomas, J., concurring in judgment) ("The negative Commerce Clause has no basis in the Constitution and has proved unworkable in practice."); Camps Newfound/Owatonna, Inc. v. Town of Harrison, 520 U.S. 564, 595 (1997) (Scalia, J., dissenting, joined by Rehnquist, C.J., and Thomas & Ginsburg, JJ.) ("The Court's negative Commerce Clause jurisprudence has drifted far from its moorings."); *id.* at 610 (Thomas, J., dissenting) (characterizing the Court's dormant Commerce Clause jurisprudence as "overbroad and unnecessary").
86. *See* Chen, *supra* note 57, at 1792.
87. Maxwell L. Stearns, *A Beautiful Mend: A Game Theoretical Analysis of the Dormant Commerce Clause Doctrine,* 45 Wm. & Mary L. Rev. 1, 10–11 (2003) (footnotes omitted).
88. As Professor Chen has noted:

> To the extent that contemporary doctrine has curbed Congress's ability to legislate under [the Commerce Clause], judicial review under the dormant Commerce Clause should correlatively shrink. None of the opponents of the dormant Commerce Clause on the contemporary Court, however, has expressed any interest in

wielding this latent limit on judicial review of state and local laws affecting the national economy. . . .

Chen, *supra* note 57, at 1783.

89. *See* Barry Cushman, *Formalism and Realism in Commerce Clause Jurisprudence*, 67 U. CHI. L. REV. 1089, 1121–25 (2000); *see also* Edward S. Corwin, *The Passing of Dual Federalism*, 36 VA. L. REV. 1, 22 (1950) (noting that Commerce Clause could inhibit state regulation).

90. *See* David S. Day, *The "Mature" Rehnquist Court and the Dormant Commerce Clause Doctrine: The Expanded Discrimination Tier*, 52 S.D. L. REV. 1, 3 (2007).

91. *See id.*

92. *See id.* at 47–51; Brad W. Joondeph, *Federalism, the Rehnquist Court, and the Modern Republican Party*, 87 OR. L. REV. (forthcoming 2009).

93. *See, e.g.,* DAVID SHAPIRO, FEDERALISM: A DIALOGUE (1995); Richard Briffault, *"What about the 'Ism'?" Normative and Formal Concerns in Contemporary Federalism*, 47 VAND. L. REV. 1303 (1994); Erwin Chemerinsky, *The Values of Federalism*, 47 FLA. L. REV. 499 (1995); Barry Friedman, *Valuing Federalism*, 82 MINN. L. REV. 317 (1997); Vicki C. Jackson, *Federalism and the Uses and Limits of Law:* Printz *and Principle?*, 111 HARV. L. REV. 2180, 2213–24 (1998); Larry Kramer, *Understanding Federalism*, 47 VAND. L. REV. 1485 (1994).

94. *See* Edward L. Rubin, *The Fundamentality and Irrelevance of Federalism*, 13 GA. ST. U. L. REV. 1009 (1997) [hereinafter Rubin, *Fundamentality and Irrelevance*]; Edward L. Rubin, *Puppy Federalism and the Blessings of America*, ANNALS AM. ACAD. POL. & SOC. SCI., Mar. 2001, at 37 [hereinafter Rubin, *Puppy Federalism*]; Edward L. Rubin & Malcolm Feeley, *Federalism: Some Notes on a National Neurosis*, 41 UCLA L. REV. 903 (1994).

Others who have expressed skepticism about the values of federalism are Frank Cross, *see* Frank Cross, *The Folly of Federalism*, 24 CARDOZO L. REV. 1 (2002), and Mark Tushnet, *see* Mark Tushnet, *Federalism as a Cure for Democracy's Discontent?*, *in* DEBATING DEMOCRACY'S DISCONTENT: ESSAYS ON AMERICAN POLITICS, LAW, AND PUBLIC PHILOSOPHY 310–13 (Anita L. Allen & Milton C. Regan Jr. eds., 1998).

95. *See* Rubin & Feeley, *supra* note 94, at 914–27; *see also* Cross, *supra* note 94, at 19–20 ("A federal structure is not necessary to acquire the multiple benefits of decentralization, and will in fact obstruct the achievement of those benefits.") (footnote omitted).

96. Classic treatments of the economic arguments for federalism include Friedrich A. Hayek, *The Economic Conditions of Interstate Federalism*, NEW COMMONWEALTH Q., Sept. 1939, at 131, *reprinted in* FRIEDRICH A. HAYEK, INDIVIDUALISM AND ECONOMIC ORDER 255 (1948), and Charles M. Tiebout, *A Pure Theory of Local Expenditure*, 64 J. POL. ECON. 416 (1956). For more recent discussions of market-based arguments for federalism, see, for example, SHAPIRO, *supra* note 93, at 77–85; William W. Bratton & Joseph A. McCahery, *The New Economics of Jurisdictional Competition: Devolutionary Federalism in a Second-Best World*, 86 GEO. L.J. 201 (1997) (critically reviewing the economic arguments for federalism); Jacques LeBoeuf, *The Economics of Federalism and the Proper Scope of the Federal Commerce Power*, 31 SAN DIEGO L. REV. 555 (1994); Michael McConnell, *Federalism: Evaluating the Founders' Design*, 54 U. CHI. L. REV. 1484, 1493–98 (1987); McGinnis, *supra* note 59, at 507–10; Barry Weingast, *The Economic Role of Political Institutions: Market-Preserving Federalism and Economic Development*, 11 J.L. ECON. & ORG. 1 (1995).

97. *See* McConnell, *supra* note 96, at 1494.

98. *See* New State Ice Co. v. Liebmann, 285 U.S. 262, 311 (1932) (Brandeis, J., dissenting) ("It is one of the happy incidents of the federal system that a single courageous state may, if its citizens choose, serve as a laboratory; and try novel social and economic experiments without risk to the rest of the country.").

99. In *Gregory v. Ashcroft*, the Court summarized these arguments as follows:

> This federalist structure of joint sovereigns preserves to the people numerous advantages. It assures a decentralized government that will be more sensitive to the diverse needs of a heterogenous society . . . ; it allows for more innovation and experimentation in government; and it makes government more responsive by putting the States in competition for a mobile citizenry.

501 U.S. 452, 458 (1991).

100. *See* Michael S. Greve, *Against Cooperative Federalism*, 70 Miss. L.J. 557, 573–75, 593–602 (2000).

101. *See id.* at 593–99; Weingast, *supra* note 96, at 6.

102. As the Court explained in *New York v. United States*,

> The Constitution does not protect the sovereignty of States for the benefit of the States or state governments as abstract political entities, or even for the benefit of the public officials governing the States. To the contrary, the Constitution divides authority between federal and state governments for the protection of individuals.

505 U.S. 144, 181 (1992); *see also* Greve, *supra* note 100, at 619–20 (discussing need for judicial intervention to prevent intergovernmental collusion).

103. *See* SHAPIRO, *supra* note 93, at 39 (discussing problem of externalities); Bratton & McCahery, *supra* note 96, at 231–33 (same); Friedman, *supra* note 94, at 407–8 (same); Kramer, *supra* note 93, at 1511 (same).

104. *See* Herbert Hovenkamp, *The Limits of Preference-Based Legal Policy*, 89 Nw. U. L. Rev. 4, 13–14 (1994).

105. *See, e.g.*, Kramer, *supra* note 93, at 1511 (noting the protection of individual rights as a reason to make decisions at a national level); McConnell, *supra* note 96, at 1494 (noting "compelling arguments from justice" as reason to oppose decentralization in certain areas).

106. *Cf.* Christopher L. Eisgruber, *Constitutional Self-government and Judicial Review: A Reply to Five Critics*, 37 U.S.F. L. Rev. 115, 116–17 (2001) (emphasizing distinction between "the people" and "the voters").

107. *See* Briffault, *supra* note 93, at 1320.

108. *See* 45 C.F.R. pt. 46 (2005); *see also* Susan M. Wolf, *Law & Bioethics: From Values to Violence*, 32 J.L. Med. & Ethics 293, 294–95 (2004) (discussing regulation of research using human subjects).

109. *See* Erwin Chemerinsky, *Federalism Not as Limits, But as Empowerment*, 45 U. Kan. L. Rev. 1219, 1236 (1997) ("[T]here is the basic question of who should decide when further experimentation is warranted or when there is enough knowledge to justify one approach."); G. Alan Tarr, *Laboratories of Democracy? Brandeis, Federalism, and Scientific Management*, Publius, Winter 2001, at 37, 40–41 (discussing need to limit the "experiments" that states perform).

110. Examples of important statutory prohibitions of discrimination include Title VII of the Civil Rights Act of 1964, 42 U.S.C. §§ 2000e to 2000e-17; the Age Discrimination in Employment Act, Pub. L. No. 90-202, 81 Stat. 602 (1967) (codified as amended at 29 U.S.C. §§ 621–634); and the Americans with Disabilities Act, Pub. L. No. 101-336, 104 Stat. 327 (1990) (codified as amended at 42 U.S.C. §§ 12,101–213).

Serious arguments were raised that the national government did not have the authority to preempt local decision making about the wisdom of allowing or prohibiting discrimination in the private sector. *See* Robert C. Post & Reva B. Siegel, *Equal Protection by Law: Federal Antidiscrimination Legislation after Morrison and Kimel*, 110 Yale L.J. 441, 492–94 (2002) (discussing opposition to the Civil Rights Act of 1964). The opposition, of course, is not merely historical. *See, e.g.,* Roger Pilon, *Discrimination, Affirmative Action, and Freedom: Sorting Out the Issues*, 45 Am. U. L. Rev. 775, 779 (1996) ("Clearly, the Civil Rights Act of 1964 and its progeny are inconsistent with all three implications of the principles of sovereignty and freedom of association.").

111. *See Lopez*, 514 U.S. 549 (1995) (holding unconstitutional the Gun-Free School Zones Act of 1990, 18 U.S.C. § 922(q)(1)(A) (1994)).

112. *See* United States v. Morrison, 529 U.S. 598 (2000) (holding unconstitutional the private cause of action created by the Violence against Women Act of 1994, 42 U.S.C. § 13,981 (1994)).

113. For discussions of federalism as promoting political participation, see, for example, Friedman, *supra* note 93, at 389–94; S. Candice Hoke, *Preemption Pathologies and Civic Republican Values*, 71 B.U. L. Rev. 685, 710–14 (1991); Deborah Jones Merritt, *The Guarantee Clause and State Autonomy: Federalism for a Third Century*, 88 Colum. L. Rev. 1, 7 (1988); Andrzej Rapaczynski, *From Sovereignty to Process: The Jurisprudence of Federalism after Garcia*, 1985 Sup. Ct. Rev. 341, 401–8.

114. For descriptions of republican political theory, see, for example, J. G. A. Pocock, The Machiavellian Moment: Florentine Political Thought and the Atlantic Republican Tradition (1975); Gordon S. Wood, The Creation of the American Republic, 1776–1787 (1969); Hoke, *supra* note 113, at 703–10; Cass R. Sunstein, *Beyond the Republican Revival*, 97 Yale L.J. 1539, 1547–58 (1988).

115. *See* Gregory v. Ashcroft, 501 U.S. 452, 458 (1991) (asserting that federalism "increases opportunity for citizen involvement in democratic processes"); Hoke, *supra* note 113, at 712 ("A vigorous republican federalism would repose substantial political authority in subnational governments because of their greater access to ordinary citizens and their participatory efforts."); Wilfred M. McClay, *A More Perfect Union? Toward a New Federalism*, Commentary, Sept. 2005, at 28, 32 [hereinafter, McClay, *More Perfect Union*] ("A federal regime properly constituted should offer a multitude of arenas for meaningful acts of citizenship—the kind of acts that elevate and deepen, while binding people more closely and affectionately to their locale and nation."); Wilfred M. McClay, *The Soul of Man under Federalism*, First Things, June-July 1996, at 21, 25 (discussing republican component of federalism).

116. *See* Rubin & Feeley, *supra* note 94, at 915–16.

117. *See* Lynn A. Baker, *Should Liberals Fear Federalism?*, 70 U. Cin. L. Rev. 433, 443 (2002) ("[F]ederalism seeks to create a space within which a local political community can make choices about how to govern itself without interference from the national government.").

118. *See* Roderick M. Hills Jr., *The Constitutional Rights of Private Governments*, 78 N.Y.U. L. Rev. 144, 183 (2003) (arguing that the ability actually to influence decisions is useful for gaining the full benefits of democratic deliberation).

119. *See* WOOD, *supra* note 114, at 499–506. In response, Madison deployed his theory of an "extended republic" as an antidote to faction. *See id.* at 504–6.

120. In 1787, the population of the United States was approximately 4 million. *See* 1 HISTORICAL STATISTICS OF THE UNITED STATES: COLONIAL TIMES TO 1970, at 8 (bicentennial ed. 1975). As of 2003, twenty-six states had a larger population. *See* COUNCIL OF STATE GOV'TS, THE BOOK OF STATES 582–83 (2003).

121. *See* Rubin & Feeley, *supra* note 94, at 915–16.

122. *See* Cross, *supra* note 94, at 2 ("While federalism is promoted as enhancing decentralization and associated benefits relating to the quality of government, federalism actually undermines those very values. Both theory and empirical data reveal that federal states will have less decentralized localism."); *see also* CHRISTOPHER L. EISGRUBER, CONSTITUTIONAL SELF-GOVERNMENT 191–94 (2001) (criticizing assumption that states are "closer to the people" than the national government); Rubin & Feeley, *supra* note 94, at 916 ("One might argue that the states, being 'closer to the people' than the federal government, are more likely to foster local participation. This is one of many unproven assumptions that fester in this field without either theoretical or empirical support.").

123. *See* Sunstein, *supra* note 114, at 1539.

124. *See* Linda C. McClain, *The Domain of Civic Virtue in a Good Society: Families, Schools, and Sex Equality*, 69 FORDHAM L. REV. 1617, 1653–57 (2001); Suzanna Sherry, *Responsible Republicanism: Educating for Citizenship*, 62 U. CHI. L. REV. 131, 156–82 (1995).

125. *See* Akhil Reed Amar, *Forty Acres and a Mule: A Republican Theory of Minimal Entitlements*, 13 HARV. J.L. & PUB. POL'Y 37, 37–39 (1990); Frank Michelman, *Law's Republic*, 97 YALE L.J. 1493, 1535 (1988).

126. *Cf.* U.S. CONST. art. IV, § 4 ("The United States shall guarantee to every State in this Union a Republican Form of Government. . . .").

127. *See* SHAPIRO, *supra* note 93, at 36; Friedman, *supra* note 93, at 402–5; Rapaczynski, *supra* note 113, at 380–89.

128. *See* Gregory v. Ashcroft, 501 U.S. 452, 458 (1991) ("Just as the separation and independence of the coordinate branches of the Federal Government serve to prevent the accumulation of excessive power in any one branch, a healthy balance of power between the States and the Federal Government will reduce the risk of tyranny and abuse from either front.").

129. *See* THE FEDERALIST NO. 28, at 180–81 (Alexander Hamilton) (Clinton Rossiter ed., 1961) ("Power being almost always the rival of power, the general government will at all times stand ready to check the usurpations of the state governments, and these will have the same disposition towards the general government."); THE FEDERALIST NO. 51, at 323 (James Madison) (Clinton Rossiter ed., 1961) ("Hence a double security arises to the rights of the people. The different governments will control each other, at the same time that each will be controlled by itself."); Fallon, *supra* note 59, at 441; Friedman, *supra* note 93, at 402–5.

130. *See* Rapaczynski, *supra* note 113, at 389–90.

131. *See* WILLIAM H. RIKER, FEDERALISM: ORIGIN, OPERATION, SIGNIFICANCE 145 (1964) ("[T]he abstract assertion that federalism is a guarantee of freedom is undoubtedly false."); SHAPIRO, *supra* note 93, at 56 ("[T]he historical record, viewed in its entirety, fails to support the existence of state autonomy as a critical means of protecting against the abuse of governmental power."); Chemerinsky, *supra* note 109, at 1220 (referring to "unsupported assumptions about which levels of government are most likely to act in a tyrannical fashion"); John Kincaid, *Foreword: The New Federalism*

Context of the New Judicial Federalism, 26 Rutgers L.J. 913, 935 (1995) ("By the twentieth century . . . states came to be associated more with coercive deprivations of rights than with protections of individual rights, while the federal government came to be seen as a potential liberator of persons from the tyranny of small places."). As discussed in chapters 1 and 2, William Riker, writing in 1964, went as far as to state, "if in the United States one disapproves of racism, one should disapprove of federalism." Riker, *supra*, at 155.

Moreover, part of the protection from governmental tyranny stems from federalism's ability to weaken governmental power by dividing it. If one understands tyranny to encompass abusive exercise of private power, then limiting government through federalism (or other means) does not necessarily impede tyranny. *See* Chemerinsky, *supra* note 109, at 1239 ("[M]y concern is not that there will be too much government action, but too little. Government must be empowered to deal with these difficult and entrenched social problems"); Seth F. Kreimer, *Federalism and Freedom*, Annals Am. Acad. Pol. & Soc. Sci., Mar. 2001, at 66, 68 ("A reasonable sense of liberty entails not simply the absence of government constraint, but the absence of unjust private constraints.").

132. Pub. L. No. 107-110, 115 Stat. 1425 (2002) (codified at 20 U.S.C. §§ 6301–6578).
133. NCLB mandates that states publish report cards on the performance of each school district. These reports must include graduation rates, disaggregated assessment data for each subgroup, and identification of schools undergoing interventions. *See* Kimberly Jenkins Robinson, *The Case for a Collaborative Enforcement Model for a Federal Right to Education*, 40 U.C. Davis L. Rev. 1653, 1678 (2007) (explaining 20 U.S.C. § 6311(c)(1), (h)).
134. *Cf.* Robert B. Ahdieh, *Making Markets: Network Effects and the Role of Law in the Creation of Strong Securities Markets*, 76 S. Cal. L. Rev. 277, 335–37 (2003) (discussing the role of law in helping to create markets).
135. *See, e.g.,* Robinson, *supra* note 133, at 1711–46 (proposing that Congress recognize a federal right to education via spending legislation that the federal and state governments would collaboratively enforce).
136. *See* Richard W. Riley, *Fulfilling the Promise of Brown*, 1 Geo. J. on Fighting Poverty 480, 483 (1994); *see also* William Safire, *Exegesis of Acceptance*, N.Y. Times, Aug. 7, 2001, at A19 (discussing President Clinton's use of the phrase "tyranny of low expectations").
137. *See* Kate Zernike, *Schools' Difficult Search For 'Just Right' Standards; Some Ask If It's Fair to Treat All Students Alike*, N.Y. Times, June 17, 2001, § 1, at 25.
138. Judges engage in related debates about state distinctiveness in the course of deciding whether to interpret a provision of the state constitution differently from a similarly worded clause of the federal Constitution. *See* Robert A. Schapiro, *Identity and Interpretation in State Constitutional Law*, 84 Va. L. Rev. 389, 404–14 (1998) (discussing examples from Texas and New York courts).
139. Dean Rubin explains his conclusion as follows:

> [C]ultural and political forces have rendered federalism irrelevant in contemporary America. Federalism is a political expedient to achieve partial unity when people are divided into territorial groups, with identifiable differences between them and a sense of loyalty to their particular group. In the United States, there are no longer any such territorial groupings; everyone lives in the same place, and that place is a vast, interacting, homogenized national culture.

Rubin, *Fundamentality and Irrelevance, supra* note 94, at 1056 (footnote omitted).

140. *See id.* at 1054–56; *see also* Rubin, *Puppy Federalism, supra* note 94, at 37 ("The main purpose of puppy federalism is to convince ourselves that . . . we are a geographically diverse nation, whose regions exhibit interesting differences, when, of course, we are a highly homogenized, commercial, media-driven culture smeared across the width of an entire continent."); Rubin & Feeley, *supra* note 94, at 949.

141. *See* Tushnet, *supra* note 94, at 313; *see also* Thomas W. Merrill, *A New Age of Federalism?*, 1 Green Bag 2d 153, 161 (1998) (asserting that distinctive communities of interest in the United States are increasingly less likely to correspond to geography).

142. *See* Daniel J. Elazar, American Federalism: A View from the States 11 (2d ed. 1972).

143. *See, e.g.*, Lynn A. Baker & Ernest A. Young, *Federalism and the Double Standard of Judicial Review*, 51 Duke L.J. 75, 150 n.335 (2001) (asserting, in response to Dean Rubin's claim of an absence of a meaningful distinction among states, that "[w]e do not have space to conclusively refute Professor Rubin's claim here; instead, we simply would invite him to come live in Texas for six months"); Jackson, *supra* note 93, at 2220–22; *see also* Briffault, *supra* note 93, at 1320 (noting that argument for federalism based on satisfying diverse preferences assumes the existence of "diverse state communities"). Professor Young has since retreated somewhat from the argument that state identities are strongly distinctive: "Even in a place like Texas . . . national identity predominates. Without denying that considerable cultural distinctiveness remains, it is hard to deny that at the end of the day we are all Americans—not Texans, Okies, Hoosiers, and the like." Ernest A. Young, *Protecting Member State Autonomy in the European Union: Some Cautionary Tales from American Federalism*, 77 N.Y.U. L. Rev. 1612, 1725 (2002).

144. *See* McClay, *More Perfect Union, supra* note 115, at 30–33; McGinnis, *supra* note 59, at 527 ("Without a renewal of citizens' emotional attachments to their states, it is unclear to what extent federalism can be revived as a discovery machine generating superior regulations and social norms."); *see also* Rui J. P. Figueiredo Jr. & Barry R. Weingast, *Self-Enforcing Federalism*, 21 J.L. Econ. & Org. 103, 128 (2005) (discussing importance of a "federal culture" in sustaining a federal system of government); Ernest A. Young, *Two Cheers for Process Federalism*, 46 Vill. L. Rev. 1349, 1373 (2001) (discussing importance of popular loyalty to states).

145. See Barnes & Noble Booksellers, Frequently Asked Questions, http://www.barnesandnobleinc.com/misc/faq.html (last visited on June 2, 2008).

146. James Gardner has done a fine job at debunking such generalized claims. *See* James A. Gardner, Interpreting State Constitutions: A Jurisprudence of Function in a Federal System 53–79 (2005); James A. Gardner, *Southern Character, Confederate Nationalism, and the Interpretation of State Constitutions: A Case Study in Constitutional Argument*, 76 Tex. L. Rev. 1219 (1998); *see also* James A. Gardner, *The Failed Discourse of State Constitutionalism*, 90 Mich. L. Rev. 761, 828–30 (1992).

147. Alexander Bickel, The Least Dangerous Branch 103 (1962).

148. *See* Jesse Choper, Judicial Review and the National Political Process 175–84 (1980); Larry D. Kramer, *Putting the Politics Back into the Political Safeguards of Federalism*, 100 Colum. L. Rev. 215 (2000); Herbert Wechsler, *The Political Safeguards of Federalism: The Role of the States in the Composition and Selection of the National Government*, 54 Colum. L. Rev. 543 (1954); *see also* Garcia v. San Antonio Metro. Transit Auth., 469 U.S. 528, 556 (1985) ("[T]he principal and basic limit on the federal . . . power is that inherent in all congressional action—the built-in restraints that our system provides through state participation in federal government action.").

149. *See* Daniel J. Elazar, *Cooperative Federalism, in* COMPETITION AMONG STATES AND LO-
CAL GOVERNMENTS: EFFICIENCY AND EQUITY IN AMERICAN FEDERALISM 75 (Daphne A.
Kenyon & John Kincaid eds., 1991); Kramer, *supra* note 148, at 227.

150. *See* Martin H. Redish, *Constitutionalizing Federalism: A Foundational Analysis*, 23 OHIO
N.U. L. REV. 1237, 1260 (1997) (asserting that the political process thesis "has
been subjected to substantial attack, usually with sound basis" and that the model's
premises are unsupportable "on either logical, empirical or intuitive bases").

151. *See, e.g., Garcia*, 469 U.S. at 565 n.9 (Powell, J., dissenting); William T. Mayton,
"The Fate of Lesser Voices": Calhoun v. Wechsler on Federalism, 32 WAKE FOREST L. REV.
1083, 1103–4 (1997) (describing importance of "federal majority" as opposed to
state and local interests).

152. *See, e.g.*, New York v. United States, 505 U.S. 144, 181 (1992) ("[T]he Constitution
divides authority between federal and state governments for the protection of individuals.").

153. *See id.* at 181–83.

154. *See, e.g.*, Stephen Gardbaum, *Rethinking Constitutional Federalism*, 74 TEX. L. REV.
795, 799–800 (1996); Jackson, *supra* note 93, at 2240–41; Young, *supra* note 144, at
1364 ("Process federalism's central insight is that the federal-state balance is affected
not simply by what federal law is made, but by how that law is made.")

155. Jackson, *supra* note 93, at 2219–20 ("Even if no areas of substantive legislative jurisdiction were reserved exclusively for a subnational-level government, it is at least
in theory possible that having independently elected and accountable subnational
leadership would provide a structural check on the actions and policies of the national government.").

156. Professor Jackson explains the judicial review of federalism as follows:

> [T]his standard would not involve the Court in substituting its judgment of what
> is "truly federal" and what is "truly local" for that of Congress. The Court's task
> would be to make sure Congress takes a serious look when Congress acts to extend
> the existing exercise of its implied powers, and that it has a reasonable basis for
> concluding that a federal law is needed to address conduct substantially affecting
> interstate commerce. But this inquiry—on the reason and need for federal regula-
> tion—would proceed unencumbered by a need to distinguish, in a categorical and
> a priori way, activity Congress can reach from that which it cannot.

Id. at 2245–46.

157. *Id.* at 2233.

158. *Id.* at 2228.

159. *See, e.g.*, Gardbaum, *supra* note 154, at 799–800; Young, *supra* note 42, at 130 ("The
fundamental point is that process federalism is unlikely to work without some substantive backstop."); *see also* David E. Engdahl, *Casebooks and Constitutional Com-
petency*, 21 SEATTLE U. L. REV. 741, 782 (1998) ("[T]he Constitution entitles the
people to have their electorally answerable *political* organs *actually and openly* in-
quire, debate, compromise, and resolve whether and how far it is necessary to reach
matters otherwise beyond the national government's scope, *in order to* effectuate
enumerated federal powers.").

160. Jackson, *supra* note 93, at 2220–21 (footnote omitted) (emphasis omitted).

161. *See* Chemerinsky, *supra* note 109, at 1239 (advocating conceptualizing federalism

as "empowering all three levels of government to act"); Chemerinsky, *supra* note 93, at 539 ("[F]ederalism can be reconceived not as about limiting federal power or even as about limiting state or local power. Rather, it should be seen as based on the desirability of empowering multiple levels of government to deal with social problems.").

162. *See* Deborah J. Merritt, *Federalism as Empowerment*, 47 FLA. L. REV. 541, 553–54 (1995) ("[W]e cannot empower two levels of government without offering some rule for mediating differences between them. . . .").

163. Chemerinsky himself tries to carve out some protected sphere for states by insisting that courts should narrowly interpret the scope of federal preemption through the application of clear statement principles. *See* Chemerinsky, *supra* note 109, at 1238. It is not entirely clear how this principle fits into the overall framework of empowerment federalism.

164. Professor Scheiber has described dual federalism as ending with the Civil War, followed by a transitional period, with cooperative federalism beginning with the New Deal. *See* Harry N. Scheiber, *American Federalism and the Diffusion of Power: Historical and Contemporary Perspectives*, 9 U. TOL. L. REV. 619, 676 (1978); *see also* Harry N. Scheiber, *Federalism and Legal Process: Historical and Contemporary Analysis of the American System*, 14 LAW & SOC. REV. 663, 679–83 (1980) (discussing periods of federalism). Professor Elazar describes dual federalism as the "regnant" theory until the 1930s, *see* Elazar, *supra* note 149, at 67, though he asserts that the American "pattern of federalism has been cooperative since its beginnings," Daniel J. Elazar, *Theory of Federalism*, *in* 3 ENCYCLOPEDIA OF THE AMERICAN CONSTITUTION 1006 (Leonard W. Levy & Kenneth L. Karst eds., 2000). The Scheiber-Elazar debate is discussed in chapter 2.

165. For discussions of the general characteristics of cooperative federalism, see Elazar, *supra* note 149; Roderick M. Hills Jr., *Federalism in Constitutional Context*, 22 HARV. J.L. & PUB. POL'Y 181, 190 (1998); John Kincaid, *The Competitive Challenge to Cooperative Federalism: A Theory of Federal Democracy*, *in* COMPETITION AMONG STATES AND LOCAL GOVERNMENTS: EFFICIENCY AND EQUITY IN AMERICAN FEDERALISM 87 (Daphne A. Kenyon & John Kincaid eds., 1991); Philip J. Weiser, *Federal Common Law, Cooperative Federalism, and the Enforcement of the Telecom Act*, 76 N.Y.U. L. REV. 1692, 1697–1703 (2001) (discussing the critical features of cooperative federalism); Philip J. Weiser, *Towards a Constitutional Architecture for Cooperative Federalism*, 79 N.C. L. REV. 663, 665 (2001); Joseph F. Zimmerman, *National-State Relations: Cooperative Federalism in the Twentieth Century*, PUBLIUS, Spring 2001, at 15, 18 (setting out postulates for general definition of cooperative federalism).

166. *See* Elazar, *supra* note 149, at 80–83.

167. *Cf.* Michael C. Dorf, *After Bureaucracy*, 71 U. CHI. L. REV. 1245, 1268 (2004) (noting that cooperative federalism, understood simply as state implementation of federal regulations, need not include dynamic interaction necessary to constitute "democratic experimentalism").

168. *See* Kincaid, *supra* note 165, at 106–4 (discussing progression from dual to cooperative federalism and the need for a new vision of federalism).

169. *See* Greve, *supra* note 100, at 619–20; John Kincaid, *From Cooperative to Coercive Federalism*, 509 ANNALS AM. ACAD. POL. & SOC. SCI. 139, 149 (1990) ("[President Ronald] Reagan saw cooperative federalism as collusive federalism—a cartellike venture by liberal federal, state, and local policy activists to expand the public sector.").

CHAPTER FOUR

1. Pub. L. No. 107-110, 115 Stat. 1425 (2002) (codified at 20 U.S.C. §§ 6301–6578).

2. *See* Morton Grodzins, *The Federal System*, in AMERICAN INTERGOVERNMENTAL RELATIONS: FOUNDATIONS, PERSPECTIVES, AND ISSUES 55 (Laurence J. O'Toole Jr. ed., 2000) (discussing "cakes" of federalism).

3. *See id.* (discussing layer cake and marble cake). For a discussion of the taxonomies of federalism, including a listing of forty-four different "types" of federalism, see Harry N. Scheiber, *Federalism and Legal Process: Historical and Contemporary Analysis of the American System*, 14 LAW & SOC. REV. 663, 669 & n.2 (1980).

4. As discussed below, if some kind of spatial metaphor is to be used, Daniel Elazar's notion of a matrix comes much closer to the polyphonic conception than does Grodzins's cake.

5. *See* U.S. Term Limits, Inc. v. Thornton, 514 U.S. 779, 838 (1995) (Kennedy, J., concurring) ("The Framers split the atom of sovereignty.").

6. OXFORD ENGLISH DICTIONARY ONLINE (draft revision June 2007), http://www.oed.com/.

7. Bernard J. Hibbitts, *Making Sense of Metaphors: Visuality, Aurality, and the Reconfiguration of American Legal Discourse*, 16 CARDOZO L. REV. 229, 345 (1994) (quoting DIANE ACKERMAN, A NATURAL HISTORY OF THE SENSES 219–20 (1990)) (footnotes omitted) (ellipses in original); *see also* Carol Weisbrod, *Practical Polyphony: Theories of the State and Feminist Jurisprudence*, 24 GA. L. REV. 985, 985 (1990) (describing polyphony as the "'harmonious combination of two or more melodies, *i.e.* composition considered horizontally as distinct from Homophony, which is vertical in the principle of its structure'" (quoting 4 GROVE'S DICTIONARY OF MUSIC AND MUSICIANS 220 (3d ed. 1927)).

8. MIKHAIL BAKHTIN, PROBLEMS OF DOSTOEVSKY'S POETICS 17 (R. W. Rotsel trans., 1973); *see also* Brian Walker, *John Rawls, Mikhail Bakhtin, and the Praxis of Toleration*, 23 POL. THEORY 101, 109 (1995) (describing Bakhtin's sense of polyphony as one in which "the voices together make up a contrapuntal unity in which all parts retain their distinctiveness, never fusing together").

9. *See* Wolf Frobenius, *Polyphony*, in GROVE MUSIC ONLINE § 1 (L. Macy ed., 2007), http://www.grovemusic.com/shared/views/article.html?section=music.42927.

10. *See id.* § 7.

11. *See* JONATHAN D. KRAMER, THE TIME OF MUSIC 1 (1988) ("Music unfolds in time.").

12. HAROLD J. BERMAN, LAW AND REVOLUTION: THE FORMATION OF THE WESTERN LEGAL TRADITION 7 (1983).

13. *See id.* at 10 ("Perhaps the most distinctive characteristic of the Western legal tradition is the coexistence and competition within the same community of diverse jurisdictions and diverse legal systems. It is this plurality of jurisdictions and legal systems that makes the supremacy of law both necessary and possible."). For a more general discussion of the place of polyphony in modern culture, see JAMES M. CURTIS, CULTURE AS POLYPHONY: AN ESSAY ON THE NATURE OF PARADIGMS (1978).

14. *See* Amelie Oksenberg Rorty, *Varieties of Pluralism in a Polyphonic Society*, 44 REV. METAPHYSICS 3, 18–20 (1990); *see also* Milner S. Ball, *Stories of Origins and Constitutional Possibilities*, 87 MICH. L. REV. 2280, 2288–95 (1989) (discussing how polyphony is more democratic and less dictatorial than monologism).

15. *See* Daniel J. Elazar, *Cooperative Federalism*, in COMPETITION AMONG STATES AND LOCAL GOVERNMENTS: EFFICIENCY AND EQUITY IN AMERICAN FEDERALISM 70–72 (Daphne A. Kenyon & John Kincaid eds., 1991).

16. Texas v. White, 74 U.S. (7 Wall.) 700, 725 (1869).
17. 505 U.S. 144 (1992).
18. 521 U.S. 898 (1997).
19. That is not to say that those cases were necessarily decided correctly based on the facts presented. The statutes at issue in *New York v. United States* and *Printz* did not actually threaten the institutional integrity of states. Neither requiring states to dispose of radioactive waste nor requiring local officials to enforce federal gun laws threatens the institutional integrity of states. Of course, both may involve the expenditure of state funds and the participation of state officers. However, many federal laws impose such strictures on states. The Americans with Disabilities Act, 42 U.S.C. §§ 12,101–213 (2000), for example, certainly entails vastly greater expenditures of time and money by states than the schemes struck down in *New York* or *Printz*, yet the constitutionality of its application to the states is well established. Nevertheless, the anti-commandeering principle does represent a valid concern from the polyphonic perspective.
20. *See* Todd E. Pettys, *Competing for the People's Affection: Federalism's Forgotten Marketplace*, 56 VAND. L. REV. 329, 362 (2003); Ernest A. Young, *The Rehnquist Court's Two Federalisms*, 83 TEX. L. REV. 1, 129 (2005).
21. *See, e.g.*, Child Support Recovery Act of 1992, Pub. L. No. 102-521, 106 Stat. 3403 (codified as amended at 18 U.S.C. § 228 (2000)).
22. *See, e.g.*, No Child Left Behind Act of 2001, Pub. L. No. 107-110, 115 Stat. 1425 (codified at 20 U.S.C. §§ 6301–6578 (Supp. II 2002)).
23. *See* Michael A. Simons, *Prosecutorial Discretion and Prosecution Guidelines: A Case Study in Controlling Federalization*, 75 N.Y.U. L. REV. 893, 902–29 (2000) (discussing "federalization" of criminal law); *see also* Sara Sun Beale, *Too Many and Yet Too Few: New Principles to Define the Proper Limits for Federal Criminal Jurisdiction*, 46 HASTINGS L.J. 979, 993 (1995) ("The current increase in federal criminal jurisdiction is in fundamental tension with the values of decentralization promoted by federalism.").
24. *See* United States v. Lopez, 514 U.S. 549 (1995) (holding unconstitutional the Gun-Free School Zones Act of 1990, 18 U.S.C. § 922(q)(1)(A) (1994)).
25. *See* United States v. Morrison, 529 U.S. 598 (2000) (holding unconstitutional the private cause of action created by the Violence against Women Act of 1994, 42 U.S.C. § 13,981 (1994)).
26. *See* PAUL E. PETERSON, THE PRICE OF FEDERALISM 17–20 (1995) (discussing the "functional" theory of federalism and suggesting that the national government should undertake redistributive programs, while local governments focus on developmental policies).
27. *See* Michael C. Dorf & Charles F. Sabel, *A Constitution of Democratic Experimentalism*, 98 COLUM. L. REV. 267 (1998).
28. Kirsten H. Engel, *Harnessing the Benefits of Dynamic Federalism in Environmental Law*, 56 EMORY L.J. 159 (2006).
29. *See id.* at 168–69.
30. *See* David E. Adelman & Kirsten H. Engel, *Adaptive Environmental Federalism*, in PREEMPTIVE CHOICE: THE THEORY, LAW, AND REALITY OF FEDERALISM'S CORE QUESTION (William W. Buzbee ed., 2009).
31. *See* William W. Buzbee, *Asymmetrical Regulation: Risk, Preemption, and the Floor/Ceiling Distinction*, 82 N.Y.U. L. REV. 1547 (2007); Robert Rabin, *Reassessing Regulatory Compliance*, 88 GEO. L.J. 2049, 2068–70 (2004).

32. 478 U.S. 186 (1986), *overruled by* Lawrence v. Texas, 539 U.S. 558 (2003).

33. *See, e.g.,* Powell v. State, 510 S.E.2d 18 (Ga. 1998); Commonwealth v. Wasson, 842 S.W.2d 487 (Ky. 1992).

34. 539 U.S. 558 (2003).

35. *See id.* at 570–73 (citing state cases).

36. *See* Roper v. Simmons, 543 U.S. 551, 564–67 (2005).

37. *See* James A. Gardner, *State Constitutional Rights as Resistance to National Power: Toward a Functional Theory of State Constitutions,* 91 Geo. L.J. 1003, 1033–43 (2003).

38. *See id.* at 1032–54 (discussing, in the judicial context, the important role of dissenting state voices in influencing national policy).

39. Yochai Benkler, *Coase's Penguin, or, Linux and the Nature of the Firm,* 112 Yale L.J. 369, 423 (2002).

40. *See, e.g.,* Patsy v. Bd. of Regents of the State of Fla., 457 U.S. 496, 506 (1982); Monroe v. Pape, 365 U.S. 167, 183 (1961).

41. *See* Robert M. Cover, *The Uses of Jurisdictional Redundancy: Interest, Ideology, and Innovation,* 22 Wm. & Mary L. Rev. 639, 656–57 (1981) (discussing the values of redundancy); Robert M. Cover & Alexander Aleinikoff, *Dialectical Federalism: Habeas Corpus and the Court,* 86 Yale L.J. 1035, 1042–46 (1977) (discussing federalism as providing a redundant system for protecting rights); Martin Landau, *Federalism, Redundancy and System Reliability,* Publius, Spring 1973, at 173, 188–89 (emphasizing role of federalism in providing redundancy).

42. 42 U.S.C. § 13,981 (2000).

43. The initial decision of the United States Court of Appeals for Fourth Circuit contains an extensive recitation of the facts. *See* Brzonkala v. Va. Polytechnic Inst. & State Univ., 132 F.3d 949, 953–56 (4th Cir. 1997), *vacated on reh'g en banc,* 169 F.3d 820 (1999), *aff'd sub nom.* United States v. Morrison, 529 U.S. 598 (2000).

44. *Morrison,* 529 U.S. 598.

45. *See* Erwin Chemerinsky, *In Defense of Judicial Review: A Reply to Professor Kramer,* 92 Cal. L. Rev. 1013, 1018–22 (2004).

46. *See Lopez,* 514 U.S. at 576 (1995) (Kennedy, J., concurring) ("The theory that two governments accord more liberty than one requires for its realization two distinct and discernable lines of political accountability. . . ."); *see also Morrison,* 529 U.S. at 611 ("Were the Federal Government to take over the regulation of entire areas of traditional state concern, areas having nothing to do with the regulation of commercial activities, the boundaries between the spheres of federal and state authority would blur. . . . " (quoting *Lopez,* 514 U.S. at 577 (Kennedy, J., concurring))).

47. *See* New York v. United States, 505 U.S. 144, 168 (1992) ("[W]here the Federal Government compels States to regulate, the accountability of both state and federal officials is diminished.").

48. *See Lopez,* 514 U.S. at 564–65 (citing family law, education, and crime as areas traditionally regulated by states).

49. *See, e.g.,* Erwin Chemerinsky, *The Values of Federalism,* 47 Fla. L. Rev. 499, 517 (1995); Edward Rubin, *The Myth of Accountability and the Anti-administrative Impulse,* 103 Mich. L. Rev. 2073, 2083–91 (2005).

50. *See, e.g.,* Child Support Recovery Act of 1992, Pub. L. No. 102-521, 106 Stat. 3403 (codified as amended at 18 U.S.C. § 228 (2000)).

51. *See, e.g.,* No Child Left Behind Act of 2001, Pub. L. No. 107-110, 115 Stat. 1425 (codified at 20 U.S.C. §§ 6301–6578 (Supp. II 2002)).

52. *See* Simons, *supra* note 23, at 902–29; *see also* Beale, *supra* note 23, at 993.

53. 22 U.S. (9 Wheat.) 1 (1824).

54. *See id.* at 205.

55. *See, e.g.,* Buckman Co. v. Plaintiff's Legal Comm., 531 U.S. 341 (2001); Geier v. Am. Honda Motor Co., 529 U.S. 861 (2000).

56. *See Geier,* 529 U.S. at 894 (Stevens, J., dissenting) (characterizing, in the preemption context, tort suits for personal injury as "within the scope of the States' historic police powers").

57. *See* 20 U.S.C. § 7861 (Supp. II 2002).

58. *See* James S. Liebman & Charles F. Sabel, *The Federal No Child Left Behind Act and the Post-desegregation Civil Rights Agenda,* 81 N.C. L. Rev. 1703, 1708–20 (2003). For a collection of essays addressing the issue of the No Child Left Behind Act and accountability, see No Child Left Behind? The Politics and Practice of School Accountability (Paul E. Peterson & Martin R. West eds., 2003).

59. *See, e.g.,* Task Force on No Child Left Behind for the Nat'l Conference of State Legislatures, Final Report (2005), *available at* http://www.ncsl.org/programs/educ/ nclb_report.htm.

60. *See* Gail L. Sunderman et al., NCLB Meets School Realities: Lessons from the Field 11 (2005).

61. *See* Gonzalez v. Raich, 545 U.S. 1 (2005).

62. *See* Class Action Fairness Act of 2005, Pub. L. No. 109-2, 119 Stat. 4 (to be codified in scattered sections of 28 U.S.C.).

63. Professor Ernest Young argues:

> [T]wo readily observable facts—that there are just *more* preemption and dormant commerce cases and that they seem to involve issues more central to the regulatory project than the cases in which the States have prevailed—strongly contradict the claim that the Court has 'sided' with the States against national power.

> Ernest A. Young, *Is the Sky Falling on the Federal Government? State Sovereign Immunity, the Section Five Power, and the Federal Balance,* 81 Tex. L. Rev. 1551, 1594 (2003); *see also* Young, *supra* note 20, at 163 ("Although it would require . . . difficult analysis to verify the claim empirically, it is easy to make an intuitive claim that the cases that the states have lost in the last ten years or so have been more important, practically speaking, than the cases they have won.").

64. Pub. L. No. 88-352, 78 Stat. 241 (1964) (codified as amended in scattered sections of 28 U.S.C. and 42 U.S.C.).

65. Pub. L. No. 89-110, 79 Stat. 437 (1965) (codified as amended in scattered sections of 42 U.S.C.).

66. *See* Marbury v. Madison, 5 U.S. (1 Cranch) 137, 163 (1803) (citing Blackstone).

67. U.S. Const. preamble.

68. U.S. Const. art. I, § 8 ("The Congress shall have Power . . . To regulate Commerce . . . among the several States. . . .").

69. *Id.* ("The Congress shall have Power . . . To make all Laws which shall be necessary and proper for carrying into Execution the foregoing Powers, and all other Powers vested by this Constitution in the Government of the United States, or in any Department or Officer thereof.").

70. The key question is how one understands the constitutional text in light of the remarkable social transformations that have occurred over the past two centuries. *See* Lawrence Lessig, *Translating Federalism:* United States v. Lopez, 1995 Sup. Ct. Rev.

125 (discussing the problem of interpretation over time); *see also* Larry Kramer, *Understanding Federalism*, 47 Vand. L. Rev. 1485, 1502 (1994) (asserting that from the perspective of originalism, the "best interpretation" of federalism "faithfully transposes" the goals of federalism into modern circumstances).

71. U.S. Const. art. I, § 8.

72. *See Lopez*, 514 U.S. at 566.

73. *See id.* at 584–602 (Thomas, J., concurring).

74. Professors Grant Nelson and Robert Pushaw, for example, have been engaged in a debate with Professor Randy E. Barnett about the original meaning of the Commerce Clause. *See* Randy E. Barnett, *The Original Meaning of the Commerce Clause*, 68 U. Chi. L. Rev. 101 (2001); Randy E. Barnett, *New Evidence of the Original Meaning of the Commerce Clause*, 55 Ark. L. Rev. 847 (2003); Grant S. Nelson & Robert J. Pushaw Jr., *Rethinking the Clause: Applying First Principles to Uphold Federal Commercial Regulations but Preserve State Control over Social Issues*, 85 Iowa L. Rev. 1 (1999); Robert J. Pushaw Jr. & Grant S. Nelson, *A Critique of the Narrow Interpretation of the Commerce Clause*, 96 Nw. U. L. Rev. 695 (2002). Even Nelson and Pushaw, who take a much broader view of the original meaning of the Commerce Clause than Barnett, conclude that some of the Court's decisions allow too broad an exercise of congressional power. Pushaw, for example, has criticized the Supreme Court's decision in Gonzales v. Raich, as construing the Commerce Clause too broadly. *See* Robert J. Pushaw Jr., *The Medical Marijuana Case: A Commerce Clause Counter-revolution?*, 9 Lewis & Clark L. Rev. 879 (2005). Professors Akhil Amar and Jack Balkin have suggested a broader understanding of the original meaning of the Commerce Clause. *See* Akhil Reed Amar, America's Constitution: A Biography 107–8 (2005); Jack M. Balkin, *Original Meaning and Constitutional Redemption*, 24 Const. Comm. 427, 431–32 (2007).

75. *See* United States v. Morrison, 529 U.S. 598, 617–18 (2000); *Lopez*, 514 U.S. at 567–68.

76. *See* Jack M. Balkin, *Abortion and Original Meaning*, 24 Const. Comm. 291, 295–97 (2007); Balkin, *supra* note 74, at 442–54.

77. *See* Barry Cushman, Rethinking the New Deal Court: The Structure of a Constitutional Revolution 169–70, 214–22 (1998).

78. *See* Young, *supra* note 63, at 1594; Young, *supra* note 20, at 163.

79. *See* William N. Eskridge Jr. et al., Legislation and Statutory Interpretation 354–62 (2000) (discussing federalism canons).

80. *Cf. Geier*, 529 U.S. at 907 (Stevens, J., dissenting) ("Our presumption against preemption is rooted in the concept of federalism.").

81. *See* Pike v. Bruce Church, Inc., 397 U.S. 137, 142 (1970); 1 Laurence H. Tribe, American Constitutional Law § 6-13, at 1100–1102 (3d ed. 2000) (discussing the balancing test).

82. *See* Tribe, *supra* note 81, § 6-6, at 1059–68 (discussing the discrimination prong of the Court's dormant Commerce Clause analysis).

83. 331 U.S. 218, 230 (1947); *see also* Medtronic, Inc. v. Lohr, 518 U.S. 470, 485 (1996) ("[B]ecause the States are independent sovereigns in our federal system, we have long presumed that Congress does not cavalierly pre-empt state-law causes of action.").

84. *See, e.g.*, City of Columbus v. Ours Garage & Wrecking Service, 536 U.S. 424, 432–33 (2002); United States v. Locke, 529 U.S. 89, 108 (2000).

85. Scholars find mixed evidence of the importance of the *Rice* presumption. *See, e.g.*, Samuel Issacharoff & Catherine Sharkey, *Backdoor Federalization*, 53 UCLA L. Rev.

1353, 1383 n.109 (2006) ("The Court has seemed to adhere to a 'presumption against preemption,' especially prevalent in situations in which the federal government regulates in areas traditionally within the domain of the states. . . . The current viability of the presumption is, however, subject to debate.").

86. *See, e.g.*, Lorillard Tobacco Co. v. Reilly, 533 U.S. 525, 591 (2001) (Stevens, J., dissenting); *Geier*, 529 U.S. at 907 (Stevens, J., dissenting).

87. *See* Young, *supra* note 20, at 130 (quoting Robert M. Cover, *The Supreme Court, 1982 Term: Foreword—Nomos and Narrative*, 97 Harv. L. Rev. 4, 40 (1983)).

88. *See* Issacharoff & Sharkey, *supra* note 85, at 1386–89.

89. *See, e.g.*, Camps Newfound/Owatonna, Inc. v. Town of Harrison, 520 U.S. 564, 571 (1997) ("If there was any one object riding over every other in the adoption of the constitution, it was to keep the commercial intercourse among the States free from all invidious and partial restraints.") (quoting Gibbons v. Ogden, 22 U.S. (9 Wheat.) 1, 231 (1824) (Johnson, J., concurring in the judgment)) (internal quotation marks omitted).

90. For a broad discussion of the significance of the declining importance of borders, see Paul Schiff Berman, *The Globalization of Jurisdiction*, 151 U. Pa. L. Rev. 311 (2002).

91. *See, e.g.*, Roderick M. Hills Jr., *Against Preemption: How Federalism Can Improve the National Legislative Process*, 82 N.Y.U. L. Rev. 1, 7 (2007) ("Ideally, federal law ought to preempt state law when state governments are untrustworthy because of their partiality, disruptive effects on national markets, and incentives for cost exporting."); Issacharoff & Sharkey, *supra* note 85, at 1368 (proposing an account of preemption that focuses on "interests in promoting national uniformity and protecting against spillover effects"); Thomas W. Merrill, *Preemption in Environmental Law: Formalism, Federalism Theory, and Default Rules, in* Federal Preemption: States' Powers, National Interests 166 (Richard A. Epstein & Michael S. Greve eds., 2007); Alan Schwartz, *Statutory Interpretation, Capture, and Tort Law: The Regulatory Compliance Defense*, 2 Am. L. & Econ. Rev. 1, 20–22 (2000) (discussing the problem of state regulation that externalizes costs and disrupts national markets in uniform products).

92. The federal legislative process, of course, may be subject to other dangers of predation. *See* Hills, *supra* note 91, at 10–16.

93. *See* Buzbee, *supra* note 31.

94. *See* Eric Helland & Alexander Tabarrok, *The Effect of Electoral Institutions on Tort Awards*, 4 Am. L. & Econ. Rev. 341 (2002) [hereinafter Helland & Tabarrok, *Effect of Electoral Institutions*]; Alexander Tabarrok & Eric Helland, *Court Politics: The Political Economy of Tort Awards*, 42 J.L. & Econ. 157 (1999) [hereinafter Helland & Tabarrok, *Court Politics*].

95. *See* Helland & Tabarrok, *Effect of Electoral Institutions, supra* note 94, at 359 ("The coefficients on nonpartisan out and on nonpartisan in are almost identical, which suggests that there is little or no penalty against out-of-state businesses in nonpartisan states."). The findings of the earlier Helland and Tabarrok study, by contrast, do suggest that even in states without partisan elections, out-of-state businesses fare worse. However, the authors note the potential for confounding factors, such as the possibility that out-of-state firms are systematically larger and involved in more serious cases than in-state firms. *See* Helland & Tabarrok, *Court Politics, supra* note 94, at 163, 169.

96. *See* Helland & Tabarrok, *Effect of Electoral Institutions, supra* note 94, at 367 ("[A]wards in cases with out-of-state defendants are larger in partisan elected states when state judges are deciding cases, but not when nonelected federal judges with life tenure

are deciding cases."); *see also* Gary T. Schwartz, *Considering the Proper Federal Role in American Tort Law*, 38 ARIZ. L. REV. 917, 936 (1996) ("The presence of these federal judge liability-expanding landmarks makes it difficult to believe that state court judges, in expanding liability, have been influenced in any major way by mere in-state preferences.").

97. *See* Kavan Peterson, *Cost of Judicial Races Stirs Reformers*, STATELINE.ORG, Aug. 5, 2005, http://www.stateline.org/live/printable/story?contentId=47067 (reporting that in judicial elections, "[b]usiness groups, lead by the U.S. Chamber of Commerce, doubled contributions from $8.4 million in 2002 to $15.8 million nationwide in 2004, exceeding for the first time total contributions by trial lawyers").

98. *See* Robert A. Schapiro, *Justice Stevens' Theory of Interactive Federalism*, 74 FORDHAM L. REV. 2133, 2165–68 (2006).

99. *See* ASARCO, Inc. v. Idaho State Tax Comm'n, 458 U.S. 307, 315 (1982).

100. *See* Schwartz, *supra* note 91, at 17.

101. *See* JOSEPH F. ZIMMERMAN, CONGRESSIONAL PREEMPTION: REGULATORY FEDERALISM 159–75 (2005) (discussing various forms of partial federal preemption).

102. *See* Jules Coleman, *The Cost of* The Cost of Accidents, 64 MD. L. REV. 337, 341 (2005) (discussing development of the view that "tort law is an available technology of cost avoidance: a potential tool of social policy"); John C. P. Goldberg, *The Constitutional Status of Tort Law: Due Process and the Right to a Law for the Redress of Wrongs*, 115 YALE L.J. 524, 582 (2005) (describing development of the conception of tort law as "public, regulatory law").

103. *See* Goldberg, *supra* note 102, at 596–611 (arguing that tort law should be conceived as the law for the redress of private wrongs).

104. *See, e.g.*, JULES L. COLEMAN, RISKS AND WRONGS (1992).

105. *See* Buzbee, *supra* note 31, at 1552 (giving examples of nuclear power and vaccine regulations, which have preemptive force but provide alternative compensatory schemes).

106. *See* Issacharoff & Sharkey, *supra* note 85, at 1374–76.

107. *See, e.g.*, Am. Ins. Ass'n v. Garamendi, 539 U.S. 396 (2003) (holding California statute requiring disclosure of information about Holocaust-era insurance policies preempted by foreign policy of the United States); Crosby v. Nat'l Foreign Trade Council, 530 U.S. 363 (2000) (holding state law restricting state transactions with companies doing business with Burma preempted by foreign policy of the United States); United States v. Locke, 529 U.S. 89 (2000) (holding state regulation of oil spills preempted by federal statute).

108. For a discussion of the development of the Westphalian order, see Berman, *supra* note 90, at 453–59.

109. *See* Gar Alperovitz, Op-Ed., *California Split*, N.Y. TIMES, Feb. 10, 2007, at A15.

110. *See* Kirsten H. Engel & Scott R. Saleska, *Subglobal Regulation of the Global Commons: The Case of Climate Change*, 32 ECOLOGY L.Q. 183, 192–93 (2005).

111. *See* Felicity Barringer, *California, Taking Big Gamble, Tries to Curb Greenhouse Gases*, N.Y. TIMES, Sept. 15, 2006, at A1.

112. *See* Kirsten H. Engel, *Mitigating Global Climate Change in the United States: A Regional Approach*, 14 N.Y.U. ENVT'L L.J. 54, 65–68 (2005).

113. *See id.*

114. *See* Kirsten H. Engel, *Harmonizing Regulatory and Litigation Approaches to Climate Change Mitigation: Incorporating Tradable Emissions Offsets into Common Law Remedies*,

155 U. Pa. L. Rev. 1563 (2007); Kirsten H. Engel, *Harnessing the Benefits of Dynamic Federalism in Environmental Law*, 56 Emory L.J. 159 (2006); Engel, *supra* note 112; Kirsten H. Engel, *State and Local Climate Change Initiatives: What Is Motivating State and Local Governments to Address a Global Problem and What Does This Say about Federalism and Environmental Law?*, 38 Urb. Law. 1015 (2006); Engel & Saleska, *supra* note 110.

115. *See* Judith Resnik, *Law's Migration: American Exceptionalism, Silent Dialogues, and Federalism's Multiple Ports of Entry*, 115 Yale L.J. 1564 (2006); *see also* Catherine Powell, *Dialogic Federalism: Constitutional Possibilities for Incorporation of Human Rights Law in the United States*, 150 U. Pa. L. Rev. 245 (2001).

116. Resnik, *supra* note 115, at 1640.

117. *See id.* at 1641–42.

118. *Id.* at 1642–43 (quoting L.A., Cal., Ordinance 175735 (Dec. 24, 2003)) (internal quotation marks omitted).

119. Of course, the initial rise of the nation-state served to displace political systems in which power tended to be more decentralized. The existence of significant and interactive subnational and supranational bodies has a long history, including the Holy Roman Empire. *See* Berman, *supra* note 90, at 453–56.

CHAPTER FIVE

1. *See also* John Kincaid, *From Cooperative to Coercive Federalism*, 509 Annals Am. Acad. Pol. & Soc. Sci. 139, 140–44 (1990).

2. *See* James A. Gardner, Interpreting State Constitutions: A Jurisprudence of Function in a Federal System 189–98 (2005).

3. Professor Redish has noted the application of cooperative federalism principles to the interaction of state and federal courts. *See* Martin H. Redish, The Constitution as Political Structure 26–29 (1995); Martin H. Redish, *Supreme Court Review of State Court "Federal" Decisions: A Study in Interactive Federalism*, 19 Ga. L. Rev. 861 (1985).

4. The United States is unusual in having a fully developed dual court system. By contrast, most other federal systems generally rely on a single set of lower courts, which apply both national and subnational law. *See* Ronald L. Watts, Comparing Federal Systems 3 (2d ed. 1999); Ronald L. Watts, *Foreword: States, Provinces, Lander, and Cantons: International Variety among Subnational Constitutions*, 31 Rutgers L.J. 941, 955–56 (2000).

5. *See* Daniel J. Meador, *Transformation of the American Judiciary*, 46 Ala. L. Rev. 763, 765 (1995); Mark Tushnet, *Federalism and Liberalism*, 4 Cardozo J. Int'l & Comp. L. 329, 336 n.14 (1996); Watts, *supra* note 4, at 955–56.

6. *See* Meador, *supra* note 5, at 765 (discussing Germany); Watts, *supra* note 4, at 955–56 (describing Australia and Canada).

7. *See* Robert A. Schapiro, *Polyphonic Federalism: State Constitutions in the Federal Courts*, 87 Cal. L. Rev. 1409, 1453–54 (1999) (discussing studies assessing the influence of electoral politics on state courts); *see also* Michael E. Solimine, *The Future of Parity*, 46 Wm. & Mary L. Rev. 1457, 1491–94 (2005).

8. *See, e.g.*, Barry Friedman, *Under the Law of Federal Jurisdiction: Allocating Cases between Federal and State Courts*, 104 Colum. L. Rev. 1211, 1236 (2004) ("One is likely to find little disagreement with the proposition that ceteris paribus it is better for a sovereign's own courts to resolve novel or unsettled questions regarding that sovereign's laws."); *see also* Paul M. Bator, *The State Courts and Federal Constitutional Litigation*, 22

Wm. & Mary L. Rev. 605, 607 (1981) (attributing to Charles Alan Wright the statement that "federal courts should adjudicate issues of federal law; state courts should adjudicate issues of state law"); Philip B. Kurland, *Toward a Co-operative Judicial Federalism: The Federal Court Abstention Doctrine*, 24 F.R.D. 481, 487 (1960).

9. Marbury v. Madison, 5 U.S. (1 Cranch) 137, 163 (1803).

10. *See* Richard H. Fallon et al., The Federal Courts and the Federal System 6–9 (5th ed. 2003).

11. U.S. Const. art. III.

12. *See* Erwin Chemerinsky, Federal Jurisdiction § 1.2, at 9 (4th ed. 2003); Wilfred J. Ritz, Rewriting the History of the Judiciary Act of 1789: Exposing Myths, Challenging Premises, and Using New Evidence 15 (Wythe Holt & L. H. LaRue eds., 1990) ("Congress did choose to establish inferior courts, and by this choice it set the course for the national judicial system that has prevailed to this day; but the Congress could have chosen otherwise.").

13. *See* Charles Alan Wright & Mary Kay Kane, Law of Federal Courts § 1, at 3, § 23, at 143–44 (6th ed. 2002); Henry J. Bourguignon, *The Federal Key to the Judiciary Act of 1789*, 46 S.C. L. Rev. 647, 687 (1995). For discussions of the origin of diversity jurisdiction, in particular, see Ritz, *supra* note 12, at 66; Patrick J. Borchers, *The Origins of Diversity Jurisdiction, the Rise of Legal Positivism, and a Brave New World for Erie and Klaxon*, 72 Tex. L. Rev. 79, 132 (1993); John P. Frank, *Historical Bases of the Federal Judicial System*, 13 Law & Contemp. Probs. 3, 22–28 (1948); Henry J. Friendly, *The Historic Basis of Diversity Jurisdiction*, 41 Harv. L. Rev. 483, 495–97 (1928); Wythe Holt, *"To Establish Justice": Politics, the Judiciary Act of 1789, and the Invention of the Federal Courts*, 1989 Duke L.J. 1421, 1453–66; Robert J. Pushaw Jr., *Article III's Case/Controversy Distinction and the Dual Functions of the Federal Courts*, 69 Notre Dame L. Rev. 447, 507 (1994).

14. *See* Bourguignon, *supra* note 13, at 694 (characterizing the failure to grant jurisdiction over all cases arising under federal law as a "glaring omission" in the Judiciary Act of 1789).

15. *See* Fallon et al., *supra* note 10, at 34–36.

16. *See* K. C. Wheare, Federal Government 66–68 (4th ed. 1964); Richard C. Risk, *The Puzzle of Jurisdiction*, 46 S.C. L. Rev. 703, 711–15 (1995); *see also* Herbert A. Johnson, *A Brief History of Canadian Federal Court Jurisdiction*, 46 S.C. L. Rev. 761, 761 (1995).

17. *See* Martin v. Hunter's Lessee, 14 U.S. (1 Wheat.) 304 (1816).

18. *See* Murdock v. City of Memphis, 87 U.S. (20 Wall.) 590 (1875).

19. *See* Robert A. Schapiro, *Article II as Interpretive Theory: Bush v. Gore and the Retreat from Erie*, 34 Loy. U. Chi. L.J. 89, 97–107 (2002).

20. *See* Green v. Lessee of Neal, 31 U.S. (6 Pet.) 291 (1832). The United States Supreme Court sometimes did assert independent interpretive authority even in these areas. *See* Twp. of Pine Grove v. Talcott, 86 U.S. 666, 677 (1873) (refusing to follow the Michigan Supreme Court's ruling that a statute authorizing the issuance of bonds was unconstitutional); Gelpcke v. City of Dubuque, 68 U.S. (1 Wall.) 175 (1863) (refusing to follow highest state court's most recent construction of its constitution); Randall Bridwell & Ralph U. Whitten, The Constitution and the Common Law: The Decline of the Doctrines of Separation of Powers and Federalism 73–75 (1977) (noting examples of federal courts engaging in independent interpretation in statutory cases); Michael G. Collins, *Before Lochner—Diversity Jurisdiction and the Development of General Constitutional Law*, 74 Tul. L. Rev. 1263, 1281–82 (2000)

(same); James A. Gardner, *The Positivist Revolution That Wasn't: Constitutional Universalism in the States,* 4 ROGER WILLIAMS U. L. REV. 109, 118–22 (1998) (same).

21. 41 U.S. (16 Pet.) 1 (1842).

22. *Id.* at 19. Justice Story's call for a general common law was intended to reinforce uniformity in the law. His reference to Cicero included the following quote in Latin: "*Non erit alia lex Romae, alia Athenis; alia nunc, alia posthac, sed et apud omnes gentes, et omni tempore una eademque lex obtinebit.*" *Id.* This translates to: "There will not be a different law of Rome and a different one of Athens, a different one now and a different one later, but among all nations and at every time one and the same law shall prevail." Harold J. Berman, *The Alien Torts Claim Act and the Law of Nations,* 19 EMORY INT'L L. REV. 69, 71 (2005).

23. *See* TONY FREYER, HARMONY & DISSONANCE: THE SWIFT & ERIE CASES IN AMERICAN FEDERALISM 15–16 (1981).

24. For discussions of the problems of *Swift,* see, for example, Erie R.R. Co. v. Tompkins, 304 U.S. 64, 74–78 (1938); FREYER, *supra* note 23, at 85–86; EDWARD A. PURCELL JR., BRANDEIS AND THE PROGRESSIVE CONSTITUTION 66–67 (2000).

25. 304 U.S. 64 (1938).

26. The highest court in each state is the highest judicial authority on interpretation. In the federal context, a lively scholarly debate focuses on the extent to which the courts, as opposed to other branches of government, should be understood to be the authoritative interpreters of the Constitution. *See, e.g.,* Larry Alexander & Frederick Schauer, *Defending Judicial Supremacy: A Reply,* 17 CONST. COMMENT. 455 (2000); Larry Alexander & Frederick Schauer, *On Extrajudicial Constitutional Interpretation,* 110 HARV. L. REV. 1359 (1997) [hereinafter Alexander & Schauer, *Extrajudicial Interpretation*]; Neal Devins & Louis Fisher, *Judicial Exclusivity and Political Instability,* 84 VA. L. REV. 83 (1998); Robert A. Schapiro, *Judicial Deference and Interpretive Coordinacy in State and Federal Constitutional Law,* 85 CORNELL L. REV. 656 (2000).

27. *See* AUSTL. CONST. ch. III, § 73; W. M. C. Gummow, *Full Faith and Credit in Three Federations,* 46 S.C. L. REV. 979, 989 (1995); Herbert A. Johnson, *Introduction,* 46 S.C. L. REV. 641, 645 (1995); Brian R. Opeskin, *Federal Jurisdiction in Australian Courts: Policies and Prospects,* 46 S.C. L. REV. 765, 771 & n.28 (1995); Risk, *supra* note 16, at 711–15.

28. *See* Johnson, *supra* note 27, at 645 ("The presence of one High Court or Supreme Court empowered to review the decisions of federal and state courts would suggest that Australia and Canada are inclined toward unitary common law."); L. J. Priestley, *A Federal Common Law in Australia?,* 46 S.C. L. REV. 1043, 1065–73 (1995) (discussing the theory of a unified common law in Australia).

29. Australia experimented with a system of "cross-vesting" jurisdiction, allowing federal and state courts to exercise broad concurrent jurisdiction, thus increasing the chance that a single court could exercise jurisdiction over all parts of a dispute. *See* GARRIE J. MOLONEY & SUSAN MCMASTER, CROSS-VESTING OF JURISDICTION: A REVIEW OF THE OPERATION OF THE NATIONAL SCHEME (1992); *see also* Peter Nygh, *Choice-of-Law Rules and Forum Shopping in Australia,* 46 S.C. L. REV. 899, 905–6 (1995) (discussing reasons for the cross-vesting scheme). The cross-vesting scheme was subsequently held unconstitutional. *See* Dung Lam, Case Note, Wakim, 22 SYDNEY L. REV. 155, 155–56 (2000).

30. *See* 28 U.S.C. § 1441 (2000).

31. *See* 28 U.S.C. § 1367 (2000).

32. *See* JACK H. FRIEDENTHAL ET AL., CIVIL PROCEDURE 69–70 (3d ed. 1999) (discussing the purposes of supplemental jurisdiction).

33. *See, e.g.*, Van Harken v. City of Chicago, 103 F.3d 1346, 1354 (7th Cir. 1997) (Posner, C.J.) (citing constitutional character of state law claim as supporting decision to decline supplemental jurisdiction); *see also* Chicago Title Ins. Co. v. Vill. of Bolingbrook, No. 97 C 7055, 1999 WL 259952 (N.D. Ill., Apr. 6, 1999) (following *Van Harken*); Clajon Prod. Corp. v. Petera, 854 F. Supp. 843, 846 n.1 (D. Wyo. 1994) ("It is hard to imagine issues that are more within the province of state courts than issues requiring interpretation of the state's own constitution.").

34. 411 U.S. 1 (1973).

35. *See* Allen W. Hubsch, *The Emerging Right to Education under State Constitutional Law*, 65 TEMPLE L. REV. 1325, 1343–48 (1992) (stating education provisions); Molly McUsic, *The Use of Education Clauses in School Finance Reform Litigation*, 28 HARV. J. ON LEGIS. 307 (1991).

36. *See* John Dayton & Anne Dupre, *School Funding Litigation: Who's Winning the War?*, 57 VAND. L. REV. 2351, 2353 (2004).

37. *Compare* GA. CONST. art. I, § 1, para. 1, *with* U.S. CONST. amend. XIV, § 1.

38. 478 U.S. 186 (1986), *overruled by* Lawrence v. Texas, 539 U.S. 558 (2003).

39. 539 U.S. 558 (2003).

40. 510 S.E.2d 18 (Ga. 1998).

41. *See* 1 JENNIFER FRIESEN, STATE CONSTITUTIONAL LAW: LITIGATING INDIVIDUAL RIGHTS, CLAIMS, AND DEFENSES 35 (4th ed. 2006) (citing increasing frequency of state constitutional claims in federal court).

42. *See* Ashwander v. Tenn. Valley Auth., 297 U.S. 288, 346–47 (1936) (Brandeis, J., concurring); Siler v. Louisville & Nashville R.R. Co., 213 U.S. 175, 193 (1909); Lisa A. Kloppenberg, *Avoiding Constitutional Questions*, 35 B.C. L. REV. 1003 (1994); *see also* LISA A. KLOPPENBERG, PLAYING IT SAFE: HOW THE SUPREME COURT SIDESTEPS HARD CASES AND STUNTS THE DEVELOPMENT OF LAW (2001) (critically examining a variety of judicial techniques to avoid controversial issues).

43. *See* sources cited *supra* note 8.

44. *See, e.g.*, Act of Apr. 9, 1866, § 3, 14 Stat. 27.

45. Act of March 3, 1875, § 1, 18 Stat. 470.

46. *See* England v. La. State Bd. of Med. Exam'rs, 375 U.S. 411, 415–16 (1964) ("[R]ecognition of the role of the state courts as the final expositors of state law implies no disregard for the primacy of the federal judiciary in deciding questions of federal law."); FELIX FRANKFURTER & JAMES M. LANDIS, THE BUSINESS OF THE SUPREME COURT 65 (1928); Martha A. Field, *Abstention in Constitutional Cases: The Scope of the Pullman Abstention Doctrine*, 122 U. PA. L. REV. 1071, 1084–85 (1974); Rex E. Lee & Richard G. Wilkens, *An Analysis of Supplemental Jurisdiction and Abstention with Recommendations for Legislative Action*, 1990 B.Y.U. L. REV. 321, 334 (the "highest and best use" of federal courts is deciding federal questions); *cf.* Bator, *supra* note 8 (attributing to Charles Alan Wright the statement that "federal courts should adjudicate issues of federal law; state courts should adjudicate issues of state law").

47. *See* R.R. Comm'n v. Pullman Co., 312 U.S. 496, 501 (1941).

48. For discussions of the operation of *Pullman* abstention and certification, see CHEMERINSKY, *supra* note 12, § 12.2, at 763–75, § 12.3, at 789–91; Jonathan Remy Nash, *Examining the Power of Federal Courts to Certify Questions of State Law*, 88 CORNELL L. REV. 1672 (2003).

49. *See* Robert J. Pushaw Jr., *Bridging the Enforcement Gap in Constitutional Law: A Critique*

of the Supreme Court's Theory That Self-Restraint Promotes Federalism, 46 W\m. & Mary L. Rev. 1289, 1304 (2005).

50. 213 U.S. 175 (1909).

51. 28 U.S.C. § 1367(c)(1) (2000). As I have discussed elsewhere, this ground appears to overlap with the bases for *Pullman* abstention. See Schapiro, *supra* note 7, at 1420.

52. See James A. Gardner, *State Constitutional Rights as Resistance to National Power: Toward a Functional Theory of State Constitutions*, 91 Geo. L.J. 1003, 1037–43 (2003).

53. See Donald H. Zeigler, *Gazing into the Crystal Ball: Reflections on the Standards State Judges Should Use to Ascertain Federal Law*, 40 Wm. & Mary L. Rev. 1143, 1181 (1999) (discussing "cooperative federalism in which both state and federal judges participate in a mutual endeavor to interpret and apply federal law").

54. See, e.g., Evan H. Caminker, *Why Must Inferior Courts Obey Superior Court Precedents?*, 46 Stan. L. Rev. 817, 849–54 (1994) (discussing the value of uniform interpretation of law).

55. Sandra Day O'Connor, *Proceedings of the Middle Atlantic State-Federal Judicial Relationships Conference*, 162 F.R.D. 173, 181–82 (1994).

56. For a discussion of the debate over interpreting the state constitution independently of the federal Constitution, see Robert A. Schapiro, *Identity and Interpretation in State Constitutional Law*, 84 Va. L. Rev. 389, 441–42 (1998).

57. Paul W. Kahn, *Interpretation and Authority in State Constitutionalism*, 106 Harv. L. Rev. 1147, 1169 (1993).

58. See, e.g., Alexander & Schauer, *Extrajudicial Interpretation, supra* note 26.

59. Brown v. Allen, 344 U.S. 443, 540 (1953) (Jackson, J., concurring in result).

60. See Leavitt v. Jane L., 518 U.S. 137, 144 (1996) (per curiam) (in context of summary reversal based on federal appellate court's interpretation of state law, asserting "[t]o be sure, we do not normally grant petitions for certiorari solely to review what purports to be an application of state law"); *see also id.* at 146 (Stevens, J., dissenting, joined by Souter, Ginsburg, Breyer, JJ.) ("It is contrary to our settled practice to grant a petition for certiorari for the sole purpose of deciding a state-law question ruled upon by a federal court of appeals.").

61. Chapter 4 analyzes federalism as a redundant system. For additional discussions of the role of federalism in providing redundancy, see Daniel J. Elazar, Exploring Federalism 30 (1987); Erwin Chemerinsky, *Federalism Not as Limits, But as Empowerment*, 45 U. Kan. L. Rev. 1219, 1234 (1997); Robert M. Cover, *The Uses of Jurisdictional Redundancy: Interest, Ideology, and Innovation*, 22 Wm. & Mary L. Rev. 639 (1981); Robert M. Cover & Alexander Aleinikoff, *Dialectical Federalism: Habeas Corpus and the Court*, 86 Yale L.J. 1042 (1977); Martin Landau, *Federalism, Redundancy and System Reliability*, Publius, Spring 1973, at 173.

62. See Geoffrey C. Hazard Jr., *Reflections on the Substance of Finality*, 70 Cornell L. Rev. 642, 647 (1985) (listing institutional differences between state and federal courts and suggesting that such differences are "synergistically, systematically, and ubiquitously 'outcome determinative'").

63. See Schapiro, *supra* note 7, at 1453–54 (discussing studies assessing the influence of electoral politics on state courts); *see also* Solimine, *supra* note 7.

64. See, e.g., William B. Rubenstein, *The Myth of Superiority*, 16 Const. Comment. 599, 622 (1999) ("[I]f federal courts enjoy an institutional advantage with regard to civil liberties issues, perhaps state courts have some institutional advantages in safeguarding group rights when equality claims are involved.").

65. CAL. CONST. art. I, § 4 ("Free exercise and enjoyment of religion without discrimination or preference are guaranteed.").

66. *See* Hewitt v. Joyner, 940 F.2d 1561, 1566–67 (9th Cir. 1991) (citing Sands v. Morongo Unified Sch. Dist., 809 P.2d 809 (Cal. 1991) (Kennard, J.), and Okrand v. City of L.A., 254 Cal. Rptr. 913, 916 (Ct. App. 1989)).

67. *See* Ellis v. City of La Mesa, 990 F.2d 1518 (9th Cir. 1993) (consolidated appeal of three cross cases).

68. *See* Murphy v. Bilbray, 782 F. Supp. 1420, 1422–24 & nn. 2, 6 (S.D. Cal. 1991), *aff'd sub nom.* Ellis v. City of La Mesa, 990 F.2d 1518 (9th Cir. 1993).

69. *See id.* at 1438; Robert Kittle, *The Cross Controversy*, SAN DIEGO UNION-TRIB., Dec. 7, 1991, at B12.

70. *See* David Harpster, *Hundreds Brave Cold to Pray at Mount Helix Cross; Decision on Site Remains*, SAN DIEGO UNION-TRIB., Dec. 22, 1992, at B2; Letter to the Editor, *Removal of Crosses: Was Decision Proper?*, SAN DIEGO UNION-TRIB., Dec. 12, 1991, at B22; Bob Rowland, *Candles Light Way for Protesters on March to Save Cross Atop Helix*, SAN DIEGO UNION-TRIB., Dec. 24, 1991, at B1; Lionel Van Deerlin, *Law Protects Judge from Being Crucified*, SAN DIEGO UNION-TRIB., Dec. 10, 1991, at B9.

71. The district court found scant evidence that the cross actually served as a war memorial. *See* Murphy v. Bilbray, 782 F. Supp. 1420, 1438 (S.D. Cal. 1991) ("Faced with this battery of evidence, it is difficult to conclude that the commemorative objective advanced by the City is anything other than pretext.").

72. *See* John Witt, *Cross Historically Used to Commemorate Veterans*, SAN DIEGO UNION-TRIB., Dec. 13, 1991, at B15.

73. Harold Roll & Donna Roll, *The Cross Debate*, SAN DIEGO UNION-TRIB., Dec. 6, 1991, at B11.

74. Neil Hokanson, *Cross Controversy*, SAN DIEGO UNION-TRIB., Dec. 8, 1991, at B2.

75. Van Deerlin, *supra* note 70, at B9. Appointed by President Nixon, Judge Thompson was described by one writer as a "conservative Republican." Lionel Van Deerlin, *Cross Fire Legal Challenge Is Demagoguery*, SAN DIEGO UNION-TRIB., Apr. 1, 1994, at B5.

76. *See* 39 COUNCIL OF STATE GOV'TS, BOOK OF THE STATES 266 (2007).

77. *See also* Carpenter v. City & County of San Francisco, 93 F.3d 627 (9th Cir. 1996) (finding that a cross in San Francisco park violated the No Preference Clause of the California Constitution). As is often the case in controversial settings, the public officials have continued to try to avoid the judicial mandate. The City of San Diego attempted to retain the Mt. Soledad cross by selling a small plot of land under the cross to a private party. Again relying on the California Constitution, Judge Thompson found that the sale failed to cure the constitutional violation. *See* Murphy v. Bilbray, No. 90-134 GT, 89-820 GT, 1997 WL 754604, at *9–*11 (S.D. Cal. Sept. 18, 1997).

78. *But cf.* Lori A. Adasiewicz, *Quetzalcóatl, Crosses and the New Constitutional Value of Multiculturalism*, 25 HASTINGS CONST. L.Q. 159 (1997) (criticizing Ninth Circuit's analysis of state and federal law in religious symbol cases).

79. *See* Savage v. Trammell Crow Co., 273 Cal. Rptr. 302, 310–11 (Ct. App. 1990) (citing Carreras v. City of Anaheim, 768 F.2d 1039 (9th Cir. 1985), as a guide in interpreting the liberty of speech clause of California Constitution).

80. The California Constitution has been amended over five hundred times since 1879. *See* BRIAN P. JANISKEE & KEN MASUGI, DEMOCRACY IN CALIFORNIA: POLITICS AND GOVERNMENT IN THE GOLDEN STATE 21 (2004).

81. In 1995, Donald Lutz estimated that the Constitution of the United States was the second most difficult to amend out of a sample of thirty national constitutions. In his survey, only the Constitution of Yugoslavia was more difficult to amend. *See* Donald S. Lutz, *Toward a Theory of Constitutional Amendment, in,* RESPONDING TO IMPERFECTION: THE THEORY AND PRACTICE OF CONSTITUTIONAL AMENDMENT 237, 260–61 (Sanford Levinson ed., 1995).

82. *See* Steven P. Croley, *The Majoritarian Difficulty: Elective Judiciaries and the Rule of Law,* 62 U. CHI. L. REV. 689, 690–91 & n.3 (1995).

83. *See San Diego Transfers Cross Land,* CONTRA COSTA TIMES, Sept. 4, 1999, at A14.

84. Mt. Soledad Veterans Memorial Acquisition, Pub. L. No. 109-272, 120 Stat. 770 (2006).

85. *See* Greg Moran, *Three Congressmen Subpoenaed in Battle over Mount Soledad Cross,* SAN DIEGO UNION-TRIB., Apr. 21, 2007, at B3. As of April 2008, the litigation showed no signs of nearing a conclusion. *See* Greg Moran, *Mount Soledad Cross Facing Second Round in Legal Fight,* SAN DIEGO UNION-TRIB., Apr. 15, 2008, at B1.

86. 397 U.S. 82 (1970).

87. *Id.* at 84 (quoting ALASKA CONST. art. VIII, § 3) (internal quotation marks omitted).

88. *Id.* (quoting ALASKA CONST. art. VIII, § 15) (internal quotation marks omitted).

89. *Cf.* Brown v. Allen, 344 U.S. 443, 540 (1953) (Jackson, J., concurring in result) ("We are not final because we are infallible, but we are infallible only because we are final.").

90. *See* G. Alan Tarr, *The New Judicial Federalism in Perspective,* 72 NOTRE DAME L. REV. 1097, 1112–13 (1997).

91. *See* Schapiro, *supra* note 7, at 1449 & n.182 (1999) (citing sources).

92. The relative significance of positivism, realism, and federalism for the *Erie* decision remains a subject of dispute. *See, e.g.,* Bradford R. Clark, *Ascertaining the Laws of the Several States: Positivism and Judicial Federalism after* Erie, 145 U. PA. L. REV. 1459, 1479–84 (1997) (discussing *Erie*'s connection with positivism); Michael C. Dorf, *Prediction and the Rule of Law,* 42 UCLA L. REV. 651, 708 (1995) (asserting the federalism, not realism or positivism, constituted the principal basis for *Erie*); Jack Goldsmith & Steven Walt, Erie *and the Irrelevance of Legal Positivism,* 84 VA. L. REV. 673 (1998) (discussing critically arguments connecting *Erie* with positivism); George Rutherglen, *Reconstructing* Erie: *A Comment on the Perils of Legal Positivism,* 10 CONST. COMMENT. 285 (1993) (same). For a valuable discussion of *Erie* and its historical context, see PURCELL, *supra* note 24.

93. *See* Green v. Lessee of Neal, 31 U.S. (6 Pet.) 291 (1832).

94. *See* Collins, *supra* note 20, at 1281–82; Gardner, *supra* note 20, at 117–22.

95. 86 U.S. (19 Wall.) 666 (1874).

96. *Id.* at 677.

97. Gelpcke v. City of Dubuque, 68 U.S. (1 Wall.) 175, 206–7 (1863).

98. *See* Erie R.R. Co. v. Tompkins, 304 U.S. 64, 78 (1938) ("[W]hether the law of the state shall be declared by its Legislature in a statute or by its highest court in a decision is not a matter of federal concern.").

99. *See* PURCELL, *supra* note 24, at 181–85.

100. Robert Post argues that before the New Deal transformation, the United States Supreme Court viewed itself as transcending the division of power between the states and the national government. *See* Robert Post, *Federalism in the Taft Court Era: Can It Be "Revived"?,* 51 DUKE L.J. 1513, 1604 (2002).

101. *See* FREYER, *supra* note 23, at 90 ("The *Swift* doctrine and its extensions in *Dubuque*

and other cases were for the jurist clear subversions of state sovereignty and the Constitution.").

102. Clark, *supra* note 92, at 1495 (quoting Daily v. Parker, 152 F.2d 174, 177 (7th Cir. 1945)) (alteration in original); *cf.* Goldsmith & Walt, *supra* note 92, at 706–7 (asserting that Clark's view of the interpretive responsibilities of federal courts is not mandated by legal positivism).

103. *See, e.g.,* Friedman, *supra* note 8, at 1236; Kurland, *supra* note 8, at 487.

104. *See* Friedman, *supra* note 8.

105. *See id.* at 1239 n.72 (citing Schapiro, *supra* note 7, at 1443).

106. *Id.*

107. All state and federal officials take an oath to uphold the Constitution, which seems to imply some duty in addition to obeying a judicial order in a particular case. *See* U.S. CONST. art. VI, cl. 3. For a discussion of each branch's duty to interpret the Constitution, see, for example, CONGRESS AND THE CONSTITUTION (Neal Devins & Keith E. Whittington eds., 2005); Frank H. Easterbrook, *Presidential Review,* 40 CASE W. RES. L. REV. 905 (1990); Michael Stokes Paulsen, *The Most Dangerous Branch: Executive Power to Say What the Law Is,* 83 GEO. L.J. 217 (1994); Michael Stokes Paulsen, *Protestantism and Comparative Competence: A Reply to Professors Levinson and Eisgruber,* 83 GEO. L.J. 385 (1994); David S. Strauss, *Presidential Interpretation of the Constitution,* 15 CARDOZO L. REV. 113 (1993); Keith E. Whittington, *Extrajudicial Constitutional Interpretation: Three Objections and Responses,* 80 N.C. L. REV. 773 (2002).

108. *See, e.g.,* Christopher L. Eisgruber, *The Most Competent Branches: A Response to Professor Paulsen,* 83 GEO. L.J. 347 (1994).

109. *See* ROBERT F. WILLIAMS, STATE CONSTITUTIONAL LAW: CASES AND MATERIALS 632–47 (3d ed. 1999) (discussing state constitutional interpretation by attorneys general and other officials).

110. *Cf.* Arthur L. Corbin, *The Laws of the Several States,* 50 YALE L.J. 762, 773 (1941) (discussing the extent to which "a federal court is as much the 'organ' of a state that has adopted our Constitution, as it is of the federal union of states that was created by their adopting it").

111. This history is discussed extensively in chapter 2. *See also* PURCELL, *supra* note 24, at 134–36; Edward S. Corwin, *The Passing of Dual Federalism,* 36 VA. L. REV. 1, 17 (1950).

112. 317 U.S. 111 (1942).

113. *See* W. Coast Hotel Co. v. Parrish, 300 U.S. 379 (1937) (overruling Lochner v. New York, 198 U.S. 45 (1905)).

CHAPTER SIX

1. *See* Marbury v. Madison, 5 U.S. (1 Cranch) 137, 163 (1803).

2. *See, e.g.,* Valley Forge Christian Coll. v. Ams. United for Separation of Church & State, Inc., 454 U.S. 464, 472–73 (1982); David M. Driesen, *Standing for Nothing: The Paradox of Demanding Concrete Context for Formalist Adjudication,* 89 CORNELL L. REV. 808, 815–26 (2004).

3. *See* Lujan v. Defenders of Wildlife, 504 U.S. 555 (1992).

4. *See* U.S. CONST. art. II, § 3; *see also Lujan,* 504 U.S. at 576–78.

5. *See, e.g.,* William A. Fletcher, *The Structure of Standing,* 98 YALE L.J. 221 (1988); Gene R. Nichol Jr., *Justice Scalia, Standing and Public Law Litigation,* 42 DUKE L.J. 1141 (1993); Richard J. Pierce Jr., Lujan v. Defenders of Wildlife: *Standing as a Judicially Imposed Limit on Legislative Power,* 42 DUKE L.J. 1170 (1993); Cass R. Sunstein,

What's Standing after Lujan? *Of Citizen Suits, "Injuries," and Article III*, 91 MICH. L. REV. 161 (1992).

6. *See* Christopher S. Elmendorf, Note, *State Courts, Citizen Suits, and the Enforcement of Federal Environmental Law by Non-Article III Plaintiffs*, 110 YALE L.J. 1003, 1004 (2001).

7. State court enforcement of statutes against the federal government or federal agents would face substantial hurdles. State court actions likely would be available only against states or private parties. *See id.* at 1040–41.

8. Sympathetic accounts of state courts' hearing claims by non-Article III plaintiffs include William Grantham, *Restoring Citizen Suits after* Lujan v. Defenders of Wildlife*: The Use of Cooperative Federalism to Induce Non-Article III Standing in State Courts*, 21 VT. L. REV. 977 (1997); Robert J. Pushaw Jr., *Bridging the Enforcement Gap in Constitutional Law: A Critique of the Supreme Court's Theory That Self-Restraint Promotes Federalism*, 46 WM. & MARY L. REV. 1289, 1291–1300 (2005); Elmendorf, *supra* note 6; and Brian A. Stern, Note, *An Argument against Imposing the Federal Case or Controversy Requirement on State Courts*, 69 N.Y.U. L. REV. 77 (1994).

9. 490 U.S. 605 (1989).

10. *See id.* at 617–19.

11. *See* SUPREME COURT AND SUPREME LAW 35 (Edmond Cahn ed., 1954) (remarks of Professor Paul Freund); William A. Fletcher, *The "Case or Controversy" Requirement in State Court Adjudication of Federal Questions*, 78 CAL. L. REV. 263, 283–84 (1990); *see also* William P. Murphy, *Supreme Court Review of Abstract State Court Decisions on Federal Law: A Justiciability Analysis*, 25 ST. LOUIS. U. L.J. 483, 497–98 (1981) (emphasizing importance of uniform interpretation of federal law); Martin H. Redish & John E. Muench, *Adjudication of Federal Causes of Action in State Court*, 76 MICH. L. REV. 311, 332 (1976) (same); Jonathan D. Varat, *Variable Justiciability and the* Duke Power *Case*, 58 TEX. L. REV. 273, 311–12 (1980) (same).

12. *See* Martin v. Hunter's Lessee, 14 U.S. (1 Wheat.) 304 (1816).

13. *See* Fletcher, *supra* note 11, at 274–75, 285 (discussing the implications of Fidelity Nat'l Bank & Trust Co. v. Swope, 274 U.S. 123 (1927)). *But cf.* RICHARD H. FALLON ET AL., THE FEDERAL COURTS AND THE FEDERAL SYSTEM 1435 (5th ed. 2003) (suggesting that a broad reading of Matsushita Elec. Indus. Co. v. Epstein, 516 U.S. 367 (1996), might case doubt on *Swope*).

14. *See* Fletcher, *supra* note 11, at 283–84 (asserting that "the Supreme Court's most important institutional function is to serve as the final appellate tribunal on questions of federal law"); Murphy, *supra* note 11, at 497–98 (noting the "traditional object of complete federal judicial oversight in reviewing federal law"); Varat, *supra* note 11, at 312 (noting the "Supreme Court's task of assuring the supremacy and uniformity of federal law").

15. *See, e.g.*, Norton v. S. Utah Wilderness Alliance, 542 U.S. 55 (2004); *Lujan*, 504 U.S. 555; Lujan v. Nat'l Wildlife Fed'n, 497 U.S. 871 (1990).

16. *See* Richard S. Arnold, *The Power of State Courts to Enjoin Federal Officers*, 73 YALE L.J. 1385, 1386–88 (1964); James A. Gardner, *State Courts as Agents of Federalism: Power and Interpretation in State Constitutional Law*, 44 WM. & MARY L. REV. 1725, 1785–86 (2003).

17. *See* McClung v. Silliman, 19 U.S. (6 Wheat.) 598 (1821).

18. The Fugitive Slave Act of 1850, ch. 60, 9 Stat. 462.

19. 62 U.S. (21 How.) 506 (1859).

20. 80 U.S. (13 Wall.) 397 (1872).

21. *See* Gen. Atomic Co. v. Felter, 434 U.S. 12 (1977); Donovan v. City of Dallas, 377 U.S. 408 (1964).

22. For contrasting scholarly views, compare Martin H. Redish & Curtis E. Woods, *Congressional Power to Control the Jurisdiction of Lower Federal Courts: A Critical Review and a New Synthesis*, 124 U. Pa. L. Rev. 45 (1975), with Arnold, *supra* note 16.

23. *See, e.g.*, Samuels v. Mackell, 401 U.S. 66 (1971) (prohibiting federal courts from issuing declaratory judgments, as well as injunctions, in the context of pending state criminal prosecutions).

24. For general discussions of the practice of state courts issuing advisory opinions, see Mel A. Topf, *State Supreme Court Advisory Opinions as Illegitimate Judicial Review*, 2001 L. Rev. Mich. St. U. Detroit C.L. 10; Jonathan D. Persky, Note, *"Ghosts That Slay": A Contemporary Look at State Advisory Opinions*, 37 Conn. L. Rev. 1155 (2005).

25. Professor Fletcher's view of standing in federal court has much to commend it. *See* Fletcher, *supra* note 5 (developing merits-based view of standing).

26. 469 U.S. 528 (1985).

27. 527 U.S. 706 (1999).

28. 517 U.S. 44 (1996).

29. *See* Erwin Chemerinsky, Federal Jurisdiction §§ 7.4–7.7, at 409–62 (3d ed. 2003) (setting forth Eleventh Amendment doctrine).

30. *See* Bd. of Trs. of the Univ. of Ala. v. Garrett, 531 U.S. 356 (2001).

31. *See* Ex parte Young, 209 U.S. 123 (1908); *see also* Chemerinsky, *supra* note 29, § 7.5, at 418–39 (discussing availability of injunctive relief).

32. *Cf.* Bivens v. Six Unknown Named Agents, 403 U.S. 388, 410 (1971) (Harlan, J., concurring) ("For people in Bivens' shoes, it is damages or nothing.").

33. *See* Fitzpatrick v. Bitzer, 427 U.S. 445, 456 (1976) (holding that Congress may override the states' Eleventh Amendment immunity when acting pursuant to the enforcement provision of the Fourteenth Amendment).

34. 29 U.S.C. §§ 201–19 (2000).

35. 29 U.S.C. §§ 621–34 (2000).

36. 42 U.S.C. §§ 12,111–17 (2000) (employment provisions).

37. In a series of cases, the United States Supreme Court held that Congress did not have the authority to make states liable for private suits seeking money damages for violations of federal statutes. *See Garrett*, 531 U.S. 356 (Title I of Americans with Disabilities Act); Kimel v. Fla. Bd. of Regents, 528 U.S. 62 (2000) (Age Discrimination in Employment Act); Alden v. Maine, 527 U.S. 706 (1999) (Fair Labor Standards Act).

    The Court has permitted private damages remedies in cases in which it found that the statutory prohibition tracked the Fourteenth Amendment with sufficient precision. *See* Tennessee v. Lane, 541 U.S. 509 (2004) (Title II of Americans with Disabilities Act); Nev. Dep't of Human Res. v. Hibbs, 538 U.S. 721 (2003) (Family and Medical Leave Act).

38. *Alden*, 527 U.S. at 755.

39. *See* U.S. Const. art. VI ("[A]ll executive and judicial Officers, both of the United States and of the several States, shall be bound by Oath or Affirmation, to support this Constitution. . . .").

40. *See* Lauren K. Robel, *Sovereignty and Democracy: The States' Obligations to Their Citizens under Federal Statutory Law*, 78 Ind. L.J. 543, 548–58 (2003) (discussing state waivers of sovereign immunity); *see also* Jennifer Friesen, State Constitutional Law: Litigating Individual Rights, Claims and Defenses § 8.04, at 8-22 to 8-27 (4th ed. 2006) (discussing waiver of immunity in specific contexts).

41. *See, e.g.*, Corum v. Univ. of N.C., 413 S.E.2d 276 (N.C. 1992).
42. For discussions of remedies provisions in state constitutions, see Friesen, *supra* note 40, § 6; John H. Bauman, *Remedies Provisions in State Constitutions and the Proper Role of the State Courts*, 26 Wake Forest L. Rev. 237 (1991); Jonathan Hoffman, *By the Course of Law: The Origins of the Open Courts Clause of State Constitutions*, 75 Or. L. Rev. 1279 (1995); William C. Koch Jr., *Reopening Tennessee's Open Courts Clause: A Historical Reconsideration of Article I, Section 17 of the Tennessee Constitution*, 27 U. Mem. L. Rev. 333 (1997); Martin B. Margulies, *Connecticut's Misunderstood Remedy Clause*, 14 Quinnipac L. Rev. 217 (1994); Thomas R. Phillips, *The Constitutional Right to a Remedy*, 78 N.Y.U. L. Rev. 1309 (2003); David Schuman, *Oregon's Remedy Guarantee: Article I, Section 10 of the Oregon Constitution*, 65 Or. L. Rev. 35 (1986); David Schuman, *The Right to a Remedy*, 65 Temp. L. Rev. 1197 (1992); Donald B. Brenner, Note, *The Right of Access to Civil Courts under State Constitutional Law: An Impediment to Modern Reforms, or a Receptacle of Important Substantive and Procedural Rights?*, 13 Rutgers L.J. 399 (1982); David M. Gareau, Note, *Opening the Courthouse Doors: Allowing a Cause of Action to Arise Directly from a Violation of the Ohio Constitution*, 43 Clev. St. L. Rev. 459 (1995); Daniel W. Lewis, Note, *Utah's Emerging Constitutional Weapon—The Open Courts Provision:* Condemarin v. University Hospital, 1990 BYU L. Rev. 1107; Donna B. Haas Powers, Note, *State Constitutions' Remedy Guarantee Provisions Provide More Than Mere "Lip Service" to Rendering Justice*, 16 U. Tol. L. Rev. 585 (1985); Note, *Constitutional Guarantees of a Certain Remedy*, 49 Iowa L. Rev. 1202 (1964).
43. *See* Friesen, *supra* note 40, § 6.04, at 6-38 to 6-44 (discussing interaction of state remedy provisions and governmental immunity); Bauman, *supra* note 42, at 265–66, 282–83; Hoffman, *supra* note 42, at 1316–17 (arguing for limited remedial scope of "open courts" provision); Koch, *supra* note 42, at 419–26 (critically noting tendency of courts to find few restrictions on legislative modifications of remedies). Some commentators have argued that particular remedies provisions should be understood to override sovereign immunity. *See, e.g.*, Gareau, *supra* note 42, at 492–94; Powers, *supra* note 42, at 605.
44. *See* Arnett v. Kennedy, 416 U.S. 134, 154 (1974); *see also* Kawananakoa v. Polyblank, 205 U.S. 349, 353 (1907) ("A sovereign is exempt from suit . . . on the logical and practical ground that there can be no legal right as against the authority that makes the law on which the right depends.").
45. *See* Robel, *supra* note 40, at 557–59 (discussing the importance of a judicial remedy).
46. Critical analyses of the Court's sovereign immunity jurisprudence include Akhil Reed Amar, *Of Sovereignty and Federalism*, 96 Yale L.J. 1425 (1987); William A. Fletcher, *The Diversity Explanation of the Eleventh Amendment: A Reply to Critics*, 56 U. Chi. L. Rev. 1261 (1989); William A. Fletcher, *A Historical Interpretation of the Eleventh Amendment: A Narrow Construction of an Affirmative Grant of Jurisdiction Rather Than a Prohibition against Jurisdiction*, 35 Stan. L. Rev. 1033 (1983); Vicki C. Jackson, *Seminole Tribe, the Eleventh Amendment, and the Potential Evisceration of* Ex Parte Young, 72 N.Y.U. L. Rev. 495 (1997); *The Supreme Court, the Eleventh Amendment, and State Sovereign Immunity*, 98 Yale L.J. 1, 40, 45 (1988).
47. *See* Timothy Egan, *U.S. Case Looks Weaker in Idaho Siege*, N.Y. Times, June 23, 1993, at A14.
48. *See id.*
49. Officials later admitted in court that Weaver had been given the wrong day for his trial. *See id.*

50. *See id.*
51. The following description of events is drawn from the Ninth Circuit's panel and en banc opinions. *See* Idaho v. Horiuchi, 215 F.3d 986 (9th Cir. 2000), *rev'd en banc,* 253 F.3d 359 (9th Cir. 2001), *vacated as moot,* 266 F.3d 979 (9th Cir. 2001); *see also* Seth P. Waxman & Trevor W. Morrison, *What Kind of Immunity? Federal Officers, State Criminal Law, and the Supremacy Clause,* 112 YALE L.J. 2195, 2205 (2003); Egan, *supra* note 47, at A14.
52. *See* Patricia Brennan, *Overkill; The Bloody Debacle in Idaho,* WASH. POST, May 19, 1996, at Y8.
53. Associated Press, *Judge Orders Sniper to Stand Trial,* IDAHO FALLS POST REGISTER, Jan. 8, 1998, at A1. Several other legal actions followed in the wake of the Ruby Ridge incident. Both Weaver and Harris were charged with murder and other crimes stemming from the incident. They were acquitted of substantially all charges. Both Weaver and Harris also filed civil suits against the federal government. The federal government subsequently settled the suits for $3.1 million and $380,000, respectively. *See Horiuchi,* 253 F.3d at 364.
54. *See* 28 U.S.C. § 1442(a) (2000).
55. *See Horiuchi,* 215 F.3d 986.
56. *See* Waxman & Morrison, *supra* note 51, at 2205.
57. Betsy Z. Russell, *Horiuchi Resolution Rescinded; Boundary County Commissioners Clarify Their Position in Ruby Ridge Sniper Case,* SPOKESMAN REV. (Spokane, WA), July 27, 2001, at A1.
58. *See id.*
59. Seminole Tribe v. Florida, 517 U.S. 44 (1996).
60. Alden v. Maine, 527 U.S. 706 (1999).
61. *See* ROBERT A. DAHL, A PREFACE TO DEMOCRATIC THEORY 12 & n.21, 29 (1956) (referring to James Madison's idea of the consequences of tyranny as "the severe deprivation of natural rights" and describing tyranny inflicted by private individuals).

CHAPTER SEVEN
1. *See* Medellin v. Texas, 128 S. Ct. 1346, 1356 (2008) (discussing distinction between treaties that automatically have effect as domestic law and those that do not); RESTATEMENT (THIRD) OF THE FOREIGN RELATIONS LAW OF THE UNITED STATES § 111 (1987) [hereinafter RESTATEMENT] (discussing "self-executing" and "non-self-executing" agreements).
2. RESTATEMENT, *supra* note 1, § 102(2).
3. RICHARD H. FALLON JR. ET AL., HART AND WECHSLER'S THE FEDERAL COURTS AND THE FEDERAL SYSTEM 753–54 (5th ed. 2003).
4. *See, e.g.,* Harold Hongju Koh, *Is International Law Really State Law?,* 111 HARV. L. REV. 1824 (1998).
5. *See, e.g.,* Curtis A. Bradley & Jack L. Goldsmith, *Customary International Law as Federal Common Law: A Critique of the Modern Position,* 110 HARV. L. REV. 815 (1997).
6. Filartiga v. Pena-Irala, 630 F.2d 876 (2d Cir. 1980).
7. 28 U.S.C. § 1350 (2000).
8. *See Filartiga,* 630 F.2d at 879.
9. *See id.* at 884–85.
10. *See* Edward Wong, *Following Up; Still Seeking Justice in a Brother's Death,* N.Y. TIMES, Oct. 1, 2000, at 33.

11. *See* William A. Fletcher, *International Human Rights in American Courts*, 93 Va. L. Rev. 653, 657 & n.21 (2007) (citing sources).

12. 542 U.S. 692 (2004).

13. United States v. Alvarez-Machain, 504 U.S. 655 (1992).

14. *See Sosa*, 542 U.S. at 697–700.

15. *See* Ernest A. Young, *Sosa and the Retail Incorporation of International Law*, 120 Harv. L. Rev. F. 28 (2007) ("Since its release in 2004, Justice Souter's majority opinion in *Sosa v. Alvarez-Machain* has become something of a Rorschach blot, in which each of the contending sides in the debate over the domestic status of customary international law (CIL) sees what it was predisposed to see anyway.") (footnote omitted).

16. *See* Harold Hongju Koh, *The Ninth Annual John W. Hager Lecture, the 2004 Term: The Supreme Court Meets International Law*, 12 Tul. J. Comp. & Int'l L. 1, 12 (2004) ("I know of no court that has followed the Bradley/Goldsmith position, while all of the other circuits have gone the other way (and now the U.S. Supreme Court has as well, in the [*Sosa*] case).").

17. *See Sosa*, 542 U.S. at 712.

18. *See* Curtis A. Bradley et al., *Sosa, Customary International Law, and the Continuing Relevance of Erie*, 120 Harv. L. Rev. 869, 873 (2007) ("[T]he decision in *Sosa* cannot reasonably be read as embracing the modern position and, indeed, is best read as rejecting it.").

19. *See id.* at 903.

20. For a forceful rejoinder to this position from the modern perspective, see Koh, *supra* note 4.

21. Ernest A. Young, *Sorting Out the Debate over Customary International Law*, 42 Va. J. Int'l L. 365, 460 (2002).

22. *See id.* at 496–508.

23. *See* Hinderlider v. La Plata River & Cherry Creek Ditch Co., 304 U.S. 92, 110 (1938). The classic discussion of the survival of federal common law after *Erie* is Henry J. Friendly, *In Praise of Erie—and of the New Federal Common Law*, 39 N.Y.U. L. Rev. 383 (1964).

24. *See, e.g.*, T. Alexander Aleinikoff, *International Law, Sovereignty, and American Constitutionalism: Reflections on the Customary International Law Debate*, 98 Am. J. Int'l L. 91 (2004) [hereinafter Aleinikoff, *International Law*]; T. Alexander Aleinikoff, *Thinking Outside the Sovereignty Box: Transnational Law and the U.S. Constitution*, 82 Tex. L. Rev. 1989 (2004). Professor Young has advanced a similar proposal. *See* Young, *supra* note 21.

25. *See* Aleinikoff, *International Law*, *supra* note 24, at 101–2.

26. *Id.* at 106.

27. *Id.*

28. *See* Fletcher, *supra* note 11, at 667–71.

29. Lawrence v. Texas, 539 U.S. 558, 570–71 (2003) (citing state court decisions).

30. Roper v. Simmons, 543 U.S. 551, 564–67 (2005) (discussing state practices).

CONCLUSION

1. U.S. Const. preamble.

2. Missouri v. Holland, 252 U.S. 416 (1920). Justice Souter quoted this language in Alden v. Maine, 527 U.S. 706, 807 (1999).

3. Goodridge v. Dep't of Pub. Health, 798 N.E.2d 941 (Mass. 2003).

INDEX

AAA (Agricultural Adjustment Act), 41–43
Ableman, Stephen, 155
Ableman v. Booth, 155
abortion issues, 29, 64, 115
Abrams, Samuel, 28–29
abstention, 146. See also *Pullman* abstention doctrine
accountability. *See* hierarchical accountability
ADA (Americans with Disabilities Act), 47, 60, 157, 203n19
Adelman, David, 99
Age Discrimination in Employment Act, 2–3, 47, 157
Agricultural Adjustment Act (AAA), 41–43
Alabama: Confederate flag controversy in, 51; Garrett's discrimination case in, 60, 156–57
Alaska: fishing regulations in, 142
alcohol regulations, 38
Alden v. Maine, 156–57, 162
Aleinikoff, Alexander, 170–71
Alien Tort Statute, 166, 167
Alito, Samuel, 64
Alvarez-Machain, Humberto, 166–67, 171
American Insurance Ass'n v. Garamendi, 69–70, 87, 164, 178
Americans with Disabilities Act (ADA), 47, 60, 157, 203n19
Amnesty International, 120
anachronism: federalism as, 3–4
anti-commandeering doctrine, 58–59, 60, 96, 102

antinomies of federalism: as unavoidable, 81–82; use of term, 73. *See also* economic model; liberal political theory; republican political theory
Antiterrorism and Effective Death Penalty Act (1996), 14
antitrust, 37
antitrust principle, 75–76
Articles of Confederation, 31–32, 114, 174
ASARCO Inc. v. Kadish, 153
Australia: "cross-vesting" jurisdiction in, 211n29; federal high court authority in, 127
automobile safety regulations, 66–67
avoidance principle, 130–33, 136

Bakhtin, Mikhail, 94
Balkin, Jack, 109
Bank of United States, 33
Barnes, Roy, 51
Barnett, Randy E., 206n74
Barnett, Ross, 46, 52
Benkler, Yochai, 100–101, 178n10
Berman, Harold, 95
Bickel, Alexander, 85
Blackmun, Harry Andrew, 58
Booth, Sherman, 155
Bowers v. Hardwick, 100, 129–30
Bradley, Curtis, 165
Brady Handgun Violence Prevention Act, 59
Brandeis, Louis, 75
Brazile, Donna, 50
Brooks, Garth, 26

Internet: borders and territoriality absent on, 10, 114–15; as decentralization example, 105; as news source, 25; political parties' use of, 16

interstate commerce: under Articles of Confederation, 32; complexity of state and federal overlap in, 103; federal regulation of, 11–12, 34, 37, 55; original package doctrine in, 38; overlapping state and federal regulatory regimes in nineteenth century in, 34–35; prohibition in nineteenth century of state regulation of, 38; substantial effects question in, 42–43, 44–45; unavoidable effects across states and, 114. *See also* dormant Commerce Clause.

Interstate Commerce Act (1887), 37

Interstate Commerce Clause: accountability concerns in, 102; commercial/ noncommercial distinction in, 61–63, 64, 72, 97, 103, 109–111; scholarly debate on, 206n74; state and federal laws struck down by before New Deal, 37–40; state power restricted by, 64–65, 70–72; state sovereign immunity abrogated through, 59–60; structural approach to, 109. *See also* dormant Commerce Clause

intersystemic adjudication: advantages and disadvantages of, overview, 128–30; allocation of cases in, 123–24, 127–28; challenge to legitimacy of, 144–46; customary international law as example of 169–73; defense of, 147–50; dual constitutional claims as, 129–33, 138–41; early embrace of, 125; goals of federalism and, 142–44; individual rights protected through, 133–38; judicial federalism and, 124–28; as judicial implementation of polyphonic federalism, 121–24; jurisdictional policies in, 130–33; limits of, 141–42; specter of judicial usurpation and, 123, 147; state court enforcement of rights as, 151–59; state criminal prosecution of federal officials as, 159–61

Iraq: governance system of, 10, 30

Israel: Holocaust-era insurance policies and, 68

Jackson, Robert, 41–43, 63, 136

Jackson, Vicki, 87–89, 200n156

Jacobson, Gary, 18

Johnson, Lyndon B., 10, 47

Johnson, William, 34

judicial federalism: allocation of issues in, 123–24, 127–28; in dual court system, 124–28; implied in *Erie*, 146–50; redundancy as result of, 137–38; structure of, 122; in unitary court system, 127, 209n4

judicial jurisdiction: allocation of cases in, 123–24, 127–28; Constitution on, 124–25; federal court review of state law in, 125–27; implications of polyphony for, 121–22

judicial review: of dormant Commerce Clause cases, 112–13; of preemption cases, 112–13; theory of federalism distinguished from theory of, 87

Kahn, Paul, 135

Kelo v. City of New London, 24

Kennedy, Anthony, 157

Keyes, Alan, 16

Klinkner, Philip, 28

Koh, Harold, 165

Krakauer case (Germany), 68

Krislov, Samuel, 25

Ku Klux Klan, 51

Kyoto Protocol, 119

land use and zoning: overlapping state and federal responsibility for, 22–24

latent exclusivity theory, 38–39, 65–67

law: corporate, 14–15, 37; courts as making, 146; diverse interpretations of, 134–35; judicial interpretation distinguished from, 147–49; redundancy in, 100–101; uniformity in, 101–2. *See also* common law; courts; international law

law, federal: difficulties in implementing, 152, 156–57; duty of state to enforce, 157–58; minimum wage, 12, 60; possibility of plural interpretation of, 154; state court enforcement of, 151–63. *See also specific acts*

law, state: definition of, 126–27; on end-of-life decisions, 20–21; federal

Pope, Jeremy, 28–29
positivism, 144, 145–46, 149
Post, Robert, 39, 215n100
Powell v. State, 130
Powering the Plains (organization), 119
preemption doctrine: cases broadly
    construing, 192n67; development of,
    38–39, 44; dormant Commerce Clause
    and, 64–65; in empowerment federal-
    ism, 90; foreign policy and, 67–70,
    118–20; judicial review of cases of,
    112–13; as monophonic, 113; in poly-
    phonic system, 112–20; as restricting
    state laws, 65–70; of state court activity,
    103; as threat to policy experimenta-
    tion, 105–7
presidential executive orders, 12–13
presumption of concurrent state and fed-
    eral authority, 112–13, 121
Printz v. United States, 59, 96, 203n19
process federalism: components of, 85;
    contemporary version of, 87–89; politi-
    cal safeguards theory of, 86–87
Prudential Insurance Co. v. Benjamin, 44
public religious display, 131–32, 138–41
public schools: federal desegregation orders
    for, 45–46; financing of, 14; guns in,
    11–12, 55, 61; overlapping state and
    federal concern for, 22–23, 97; tradition
    of state and local control of, 22. *See also*
    education; No Child Left Behind Act
    (NCLB, 2001)
Pullman abstention doctrine, 132, 142,
    213n51
Pushaw, Robert, 132, 206n74

racial discrimination: as illustrating limita-
    tions of market model of federalism,
    77. *See also* civil rights claims; discrimi-
    nation prohibitions; rights
racial segregation: declared unconstitu-
    tional, 45–46; Dixiecrats' support for,
    49–50; upheld by Court, 36
racism: Confederate flag as symbol of,
    50–52; federalism linked to, 10, 46–52,
    54, 172; in federalist vs. nationalist
    context, 4–5, 10
railroad regulations, 37
Rancho Viejo, LLC v. Norton, 64

Rapanos v. United States, 63–64
rape, 3, 61–62, 101. See also *United States
    v. Morrison*
Reagan, Ronald, 12, 47–49
realism, legal, 144, 145–46, 149
Reconstruction, 36–37
Redish, Martin H., 209n3
redistricting, 17–18, 20
redundancy: in intersystemic adjudica-
    tion, 122, 137–38, 141; in polyphonic
    system, 100–101, 103–4, 172; remedial
    gap bridged by, 124; state court enforce-
    ment of federal rights and, 154
Reetz v. Bozanich, 142
regionalism: critiques of, 4–5; declining
    influence of, 25–26, 27–28, 52; federal-
    ism distinguished from, 5. *See also* local-
    ism; states as distinctive
regulatory regimes: cooperative federal-
    ism applied to, 90; dialectical process
    in, 99; dialogue and finality in, 102;
    extension of federal authority over safety
    and workplace, 37; independent state
    development of, 14–15; innovation in,
    99–100; interstate effects and safety in,
    117–18; multiple approaches to, 98–99;
    overlapping state and federal, 34–36,
    43–45; redundancy in, 101; role in com-
    pensating for harm, 118; state competi-
    tion in as benefit of federalism, 75–76
Rehnquist, William: categorical frame-
    work of, 111; dualist federalism under,
    62–63, 64; on limits of national author-
    ity, 13–14; on local vs. national, 3;
    state/federal boundaries under, 55
religious symbols, 138–41
republic, state as, 78
Republican Party: anti–big government
    stance of, 47–50; nationalization of local
    elections by, 18, 19; Schiavo case and, 21
republican political theory: as argument
    for federalism, 78–80; guaranteeing
    meaningful self-government in, 78;
    intersystemic adjudication in context
    of, 143; limits of, 79–80; line drawing
    in, 81; NCLB viewed in, 82; role of state
    constitution in, 143; state as republic in,
    78; state court enforcement of federal
    laws in, 162